Understanding Research with Children and Young People

This Reader forms part of The Open University module *Research with children and young people* (EK313). This is a 60 credit module and is part of the BA (Hons) in Childhood and Youth. Details of this and other Open University modules can be obtained from the Student Registration and Enquiry Service, The Open University, PO Box 197, Milton Keynes MK7 6BJ, United Kingdom (tel. +44 (0)845 300 60 90, email general-enquiries@open.ac.uk).

www.open.ac.uk

Understanding Research with Children and Young People

Edited by Alison Clark, Rosie Flewitt, Martyn Hammersley and Martin Robb

The Open University

⑤SAGE

Los Angeles | London | New Delhi
Singapore | Washington DC

Los Angeles | London | New Delhi
Singapore | Washington DC

SAGE Publications Ltd
1 Oliver's Yard
55 City Road
London EC1Y 1SP

SAGE Publications Inc.
2455 Teller Road
Thousand Oaks, California 91320

SAGE Publications India Pvt Ltd
B 1/I 1 Mohan Cooperative Industrial Area
Mathura Road
New Delhi 110 044

SAGE Publications Asia-Pacific Pte Ltd
3 Church Street
#10-04 Samsung Hub
Singapore 049483

Editor: Alison Poyner
Assistant editor: Emma Milman
Production editor: Katie Forsythe
Copyeditor: Rosemary Campbell
Proofreader: Bryan Campbell
Indexer: Bill Farrington
Marketing manager: Tamara Navaratnam
Cover design: Naomi Robinson
Typeset by: C&M Digitals (P) Ltd, Chennai, India
Printed in Great Britain by
CPI Group (UK) Ltd, Croydon, CR0 4YY

The Open University
Walton Hall
Milton Keynes
MK7 6AA
United Kingdom
www.open.ac.uk

First published 2014

Library of Congress Control Number: 2013939974

British Library Cataloguing in Publication data

A catalogue record for this book is available from
the British Library

ISBN 978-1-4462-7492-7
ISBN 978-1-4462-7493-4 (pbk)

Contents

Contents

Notes on the Editors and Contributors

Priscilla Alderson (Institute of Education, University of London)
Priscilla Alderson is a research sociologist at the Institute of Education, University of London. She has been involved in health care research ethics since 1981 and more recently in the ethics of social and educational research. Her publications include *Young Children's Rights* (2008 Jessica Kingsley), *The Ethics of Research with Children and Young People: A Practical Handbook* (with V. Morrow, 2011 Sage) and *Childhoods Real and Imagined: An Introduction to Critical Realism and Childhood Studies* (2013 Routledge).

Tony Bertram (CREC Centre for Research in Early Childhood, Birmingham)
Professor Dr Tony Bertram is Co-Director of CREC and Co-ordinating Editor of the SSCI-rated EECERA journal. He has worked extensively at national level with organisations including the UK government, QCA and Ofsted and he has a particular interest in cross national, European early childhood projects. He is currently working with Professor Chris Pascal to develop policy and assessment modules as part of the upcoming Early Childhood Education Study (ECES) which will offer comparative data of early childhood systems across the world.

Sue Bucknall (Independent Consultant)
Formerly a Research Associate attached to the Children's Research Centre at The Open University, UK, Sue Bucknall is now working as an independent researcher. She maintains a strong interest in the involvement of children and young people in the research process and acts as a consultant academic tutor supporting young researchers who undertake empirical research in their own schools and communities.

Alison Clark (The Open University)
Alison Clark is a Senior Lecturer in Childhood Studies at The Open University. Her research interests include children's experience of place, school design and the development of participatory research methods across the life course. She developed the Mosaic approach with Peter Moss, first published in 2001. Recent

studies have included involving young children and adults in the design and review of schools.

Victoria Cooper (The Open University)

Victoria Cooper is a Senior Lecturer in Childhood Studies at The Open University. She has a background in early years teaching and professional development. Her research interests broadly fall into two areas: professional practice in education and identity development. Victoria has published on professional development in higher and early years education and children's developing identity.

Rosie Flewitt (Institute of Education, University of London)

Rosie Flewitt is a Senior Lecturer in Early Years and Primary Education at the Institute of Education, University of London, and a member of the London Knowledge Lab. Her research interests include young children's language, communication and literacy development in contemporary society, with a focus on ethnographic approaches, multimodal methodologies and research ethics.

Sandy Fraser (The Open University)

Sandy Fraser is a Senior Lecturer in the Faculty of Health and Social Care at The Open University. He has previously worked as a children and families social worker in Wales and England, and in academic social work research in Scotland. His current research interests relate to children, and personalisation and self-directed support in health and social care.

Martyn Hammersley (The Open University)

Martyn Hammersley is Professor of Educational and Social Research at The Open University. His early research was in the sociology of education. Later work has been concerned with the methodological issues surrounding social and educational enquiry. These include objectivity, partisanship and bias, and the role of research in relation to policymaking and practice. More recently he has investigated ethical issues in social research and how the news media represent social science research findings.

Helen Hearn (University of Nottingham)

Helen Hearn is a final year PhD student in the School of Education at the University of Nottingham. She has studied early years education, psychology and research methods in education, and is a student editor for the Nottingham Jubilee Press. Her research focuses on primary and secondary-school-aged girls' views of bullying and coping strategies, and on pupil voice.

Sheila Henderson (Independent Consultant)
Sheila Henderson is a Freelance Researcher and Senior Visiting Fellow at London South Bank University with a background in the development and evaluation of both youth and public health policy and practice. As a core team member throughout the Inventing Adulthoods study, she has written extensively about different aspects of young people's lives, contributed to the development of an Open University course on Youth and a series of short films that drew on the study, authored the Inventing Adulthoods website, and led projects that resulted in an archive of the study.

Mary Kellett (The Open University)
Mary Kellett is Professor of Childhood and Youth at The Open University. Perhaps best known for her pioneering work to empower children as researchers, she founded the Children's Research Centre to train and support children and young people to undertake their own research. Mary has authored widely on a range of childhood and education issues, most notably on children's participation and voice and on child-led research.

Alex Mann and Joseph Liley
Alex Mann and Joseph Liley are two child researchers from a Middle School in Bedfordshire, UK. Aged 11, they trained with the Children's Research Centre at The Open University before undertaking their own chosen research about children's worries. Alex presented their findings at an International Children's Research Conference in Istanbul.

Heather Montgomery (The Open University)
Heather Montgomery is a Reader in the Anthropology of Childhood at The Open University, UK. She has carried out research with young sex workers in Thailand and written extensively on issues of children's rights, global childhoods and representations of childhood.

Chris Pascal (Centre for Research in Early Childhood, Birmingham)
Professor Chris Pascal OBE is Co-Director of CREC – the Centre for Research in Early Childhood – based in Birmingham, and President of the European Early Childhood Education Research Association (EECERA). She has worked extensively at government level to support the development of early years policy, sitting on a number of national committees and serving as a ministerial advisor and also as an Early Years Specialist Adviser to the House of Commons Select Committee on Education. She has written extensively on early childhood development and the quality of early education services and recently served as an Expert Advisor to Dame Tickell's review of the Early Years Foundation Stage in England.

Martin Robb (The Open University)

Martin Robb is a Senior Lecturer in the Faculty of Health and Social Care at The Open University, where he has carried out research on young masculinities, fatherhood and male childcare workers. He has contributed to a number of OU modules on work with children and young people and currently chairs a core module in the MA in Childhood and Youth. Before joining the OU he worked in a number of community education projects with young people and adults.

Caine Rolleston (University of Oxford)

Caine Rolleston is Education Research Officer for Young Lives at the University of Oxford. He previously worked as a researcher for CREATE (Consortium for Research on Educational Access, Transitions and Equity), University of Sussex and has experience in education research in many countries including Ghana, Sri Lanka, India, Vietnam and Ethiopia, focusing on access, educational effectiveness and the economic benefits of education. He received his PhD from the Institute of Education, University of London.

Sandy Ruxton (Independent Consultant)

Sandy Ruxton is an independent policy advisor and researcher. He has worked as a consultant to a range of international bodies, including the EU Presidency, European Commission, UNICR, Oxfam, Save the Children and Eurochild. His recent publications include: *Call for an EU Recommendation on Child Poverty and Child Well-Being* (2010), *Governance Fit for Children* (2011), *and The Involvement of Men in Gender Equality in the European Union* (2012). He is an Honorary Research Fellow with the European Children's Rights Unit at the University of Liverpool.

Nicola Smith (University College, Birmingham)

Nicola Smith spent ten years as a classroom teacher before becoming an early years lecturer at University College Birmingham, as well as becoming involved with the work of the Centre for Research in Early Childhood, Birmingham. Her PhD research was carried out in two of the settings where she had been engaged as a Nursery and Reception teacher. Nicola's research interests include working with parents and issues of social justice in education.

Pat Thomson (University of Nottingham)

Pat Thomson is Professor of Education in the School of Education, and Director of the Centre for Advanced Studies in Arts and Social Sciences, at the University of Nottingham. She is an editor of the journal *Educational Action Research*, and publishes widely on policy and leadership in education, the arts and creativity in school and community change, and doctoral education. Her most recent book (with Barbara Kamler) is *Writing for Peer Reviewed Journals: Strategies for getting published*, Routledge, 2012.

Rachel Thomson (University of Sussex)
Rachel Thomson is Professor of Childhood and Youth Studies at the University of Sussex. She has worked in academia and in non-governmental organisations. A sociologist by discipline, her research explores personal and social change across the life course. Recent publications include *Making Modern Mothers* (2011, Policy Press), *Unfolding Lives: Youth, Gender And Change* (2009, Policy Press) and *Researching Social Change: Qualitative Approaches* (2009, Sage).

Acknowledgements

Many colleagues have contributed to the production of this volume. We would like to thank each of the authors and those colleagues at The Open University who have reviewed many drafts including Grace Clifton and Naomi Holford. Our thanks to the students who took part in the review process and to Catherine McNulty, Elizabeth Camp, Jill Stanton-Huxton and Christianne Bailey for their help in completing this volume.

The editors

October 2013

Publisher's Acknowledgements

Figures 4.1 and 9.1 are from the authors' own research.

Figure 12.1 is from the author's own research and republished with permission of Taylor and Francis Books UK.

Figure 12.2 is from the author's own research and republished with permission of Taylor and Francis Books UK.

Figure 14.1 © Young Lives / Phan Viet Anh. Republished with permission of Young Lives.

Figure 14.4 © Young Lives / Aida Ashanafi. Republished with permission of Young Lives.

Figure 18.2, 18.3, 18.4 and 18.5 are from the author's own research as part of a Children's Research Study for the Open University, available at: http://www.open.ac.uk/researchprojects/childrens-research-centre/research-children-young-people/aged-11-12

Understanding Research with Children and Young People: Introduction

A considerable amount of research has been carried out into the lives of children and young people, and some of it has been very influential for policy and practice. It has provided new understanding and raised important questions about widely accepted assumptions across a range of fields, including health, education, social work, and crime. This research has taken many different forms, and there have been intense debates about some aspects of it. These are concerned with how knowledge can be produced and its proper character, the practical value of such knowledge, and the very nature of childhood and youth. This book is designed as a broad introduction to understanding this whole field, with a particular focus on research that has actively involved children and young people in the research process. We hope it will encourage readers to reflect critically on the issues raised.

It is specifically concerned with the methods and strategies that have been employed by researchers, what these involve, how the data and findings they produce should be evaluated, and what contribution they can make to theory, policy, practice, and the lives of children and young people. So, this book is focused on methodology, but our aim is not so much to provide concrete guidance about how to do research with children and young people – there are many other books that do this (see, for example, Heath et al. 2009; Tisdall et al. 2009). Rather, the task is to critically examine what research in this field involves, what it can achieve, and why it is important. This requires addressing issues that are not always given the attention that they deserve, such as:

- What sort of worthwhile contribution can research concerned with children and young people make? What purposes lie behind it?
- What role should children and young people play in research that is focused on their lives?
- What role should adults play in this research?
- What considerations need to be taken into account in designing psychological and social research?

- What are the strengths and weaknesses of the various methods available, and what problems arise in their use?
- How does research with children and young people interface with various kinds of policymaking and practice that are relevant to their lives?

In the rest of this Introduction we outline the development of the field of Childhood Studies, before discussing how the chapters that follow approach the treatment of research methodology. Towards the end, we will come back to the relationship of research to theory, policymaking and practice, and to the contribution that research can make to the lives of children and young people, and to the wider society.

The field of Childhood Studies

For the most part, the authors of this book see themselves as contributing to work in the field of Childhood Studies. This area of research only emerged as a well-defined field in the 1980s. It is not that there had been no research dealing with the lives of children and young people before then, far from it. In fact there had been a great deal, from the nineteenth into the twentieth century. This included: studies concerned with childhood poverty; parents' observational studies of their own children, such as that of Charles Darwin; experimental work concerned with the capacities and development of babies and young children, most famously that of Jean Piaget; studies of young people involved in gangs or delinquency; research concerned with youth subcultures, such as those of Punks or Goths, and how these have shaped young people's lives; surveys of the sexual behaviour of young people; and so on. What was distinctive about the emergence of Childhood Studies as a discrete field was that this was more or less the first time researchers concerned with different aspects of childhood began to treat their work as complementary, as concerned with the 'whole' lives of children and young people, rather than with addressing separate issues that contribute to particular disciplinary areas, whether educational studies, health research, psychology, or criminology.

Equally important, though, Childhood Studies was founded upon some key methodological and ethical ideas that were felt to distinguish it from much previous work (see Christensen and James 2008). One of these ideas was that the lives of children and young people are of intrinsic interest. They should be valued and understood for what they are, rather than studied solely in relation to adult concerns, for example as regards their development into adulthood, what contribution they make to society, or what problems they cause.

Another theme was an insistence that children and young people must be seen as an important source of knowledge about their experience and their world, rather than being regarded, as they sometimes were, as lacking the intellectual skills and/or knowledge needed to provide researchers with useful information. Researchers in the field of Childhood Studies argued that even very young children are capable of being valuable informants, and that it must not be assumed that their adult carers or teachers are always an adequate source for understanding their lives.

Closely related to this was an ethical principle demanding that the rights of children be respected within the research process, and the charge was made that this had frequently not been the case in previous research. This commitment was seen as underpinned by the United Nations Convention on the Rights of the Child, and on the basis of this it was argued that rather than children and young people being treated solely as the focus of research, they should be actively engaged in the research process, having a say about what is to be investigated, how this is to be done, and how the findings should be reported. Indeed, perhaps they should do the research themselves so that it is 'child-led'.

The emergence of Childhood Studies as a field was shaped by the growing influence of qualitative research in the second half of the twentieth century, across many of the social sciences. While by no means all of the new work done in Childhood Studies employed qualitative methods, a great deal of it did. For example, it often drew on the ethnographic methods that had long been central to anthropology and that came to be used in other fields as well (Hammersley and Atkinson 2007), and on the use of relatively unstructured and biographical interviews that had been developed in sociology and other disciplines (see e.g. Kvale and Brinkmann 2009; Roberts 2002). But, more than this, the methodological ideas that shaped the field and gave it its distinctive character were closely related to those that animated qualitative research more generally in the second half of the twentieth century and into this century.

One very important influence here was the development of feminist views about how research should be carried out and what its purposes should be (see Fonow and Cook 1991, 2005). Feminists themselves tended to emphasise the use of qualitative method, often seeing this as uniquely capable of tapping into the voices of women, to provide real understanding of their experiences and circumstances. And, as we have seen, within Childhood Studies there is a similar emphasis on the need to listen to the voices of children. Equally important, feminist approaches insisted that research cannot but be political: that it is unavoidably implicated in the operation of the wider society, and must align itself against the various ways in which women are oppressed within society. This political conception of the character and function of research was similarly influential in the field of Childhood Studies. A central concern has been to highlight the restrictions that operate on the lives of children – even in supposedly liberal, Western societies – and the consequences of these. And it is often insisted that research must be aimed at improving the lives of children and young people by challenging those restrictions, rather than simply documenting their lives.

This, then, is the background against which the chapters in this book should be viewed. Some of the themes just mentioned are taken further in Section 1. The chapters here are concerned with the nature and purposes of research involving children and young people. There is an emphasis on how prevalent images of childhood have shaped research in different ways at different times, on the distinctive features of research in this field, and also on some of the complex concepts and contentious issues that arise within it. For example, while, as we saw, there is often great emphasis within Childhood Studies on the importance of allowing the voices of children and young people to come through in research reports, there are difficult questions about whether those voices can be treated as autonomous and authentic. How far, and in what ways, is it necessary to recognise that they are socio-culturally generated, and to examine the processes involved in this? What are the implications of this for how research should be carried out? Equally important are the distinctive ethical issues that arise in research with children and young people. These are also discussed.

Following on from this, the central sections of the book are concerned with the range of decisions that researchers must make in carrying out their work, and the resources and strategies that are available to them. In the next section of this Introduction we will outline some of the key features of the approaches to research concerned with children and young people which are examined in Sections 2 and 3.

Research methodology

There are two features of the methodological stance taken in this book that we want to highlight. The first is that, rather than organising the discussion primarily in terms of the distinction between qualitative and quantitative approaches, as is frequently done in methodology texts, we have focused instead on the range of specific methods of data production and analysis available to researchers working with children and young people. At the same time, we insist that it is essential to recognise the variety of methodological ideas, often highly contentious, that underpin decisions about what methods to use. A second feature is that there is an emphasis throughout the book, and especially in Section 3, on the fact that research is a practical matter that must be adapted to the particular circumstances in which it is carried out. Methodology is not a set of rules or recipes that can be applied indiscriminately.

The range of methods

Research with children and young people can involve a variety of methods, and generate a range of methodological issues. Section 2 of this book is designed to provide an outline of these, examining the process of research design and the main strategies available for data production: observation, interviewing, and the use of documents and artefacts. Much of what is involved is common to other areas of investigation as well, but it is also necessary to address the distinctive issues that working with children and young people raises, and so the discussions presented in the chapters belonging to this section link back to the themes of Section 1.

As we have noted, in discussing the methods that researchers use we have sought to avoid presenting these in terms of a fundamental contrast between qualitative and quantitative approaches. This distinction clearly captures something important about how psychological and social research can vary. However, it can also blind us to important features of research methodology, or even lead us astray. For example, it may encourage us to overestimate the extent to which work placed on each side of the qualitative–quantitative divide shares the same assumptions and practices. In fact, on the qualitative side especially, there are some fundamental differences in orientation; and these are at least as significant as the contrast with quantitative methodology. Equally, emphasis on the qualitative–quantitative distinction may lead us to neglect what is shared by some kinds of research that lie on opposite sides of that divide.

Given these dangers, the discussions in this book are primarily concerned with the specific options that researchers face: whether to use observational, interview, or documentary/artefactual data, or what combination of these; what kind of observation, interviewing, or documents/artefacts to employ; what strategies to use in analysing the data; and so on. We also discuss and give examples of studies where both qualitative and quantitative approaches have been used, and how 'mixing' methods in this way can give important insights into the lives of children and young people (for further reading on mixed methods, see Tashakkori and Teddlie 2010).

However, decisions about these matters are not simply pragmatic, in other words they cannot be made solely in terms of which strategy would be the most effective in finding answers to whatever research questions are being addressed, even though fitness for purpose is a very important consideration.

This is because there are assumptions built into research questions, and into the use of particular types of data and modes of analysis, that will often need to be addressed, and about which there may be disagreement: these are concerned with the nature of the phenomena being studied, how their character can best be understood, how they should be treated, and what should be the purposes and products of research. Some of the important variations in ideas about these matters, which have significantly shaped research with children and young people, are spelled out in the final chapter of Section 2 ('Methodological Ideas').

The reality of research practice

As noted earlier, it is one of our central assumptions that methodology does not outline a set of rules that are to be simply applied, or a set of recipes that, if followed closely, will automatically produce the knowledge required. Methodology can certainly identify important principles that ought to be taken into account by researchers, and also provide a broad variety of strategies that might be employed, along with their general advantages and disadvantages. However, the question of what are the most important methodological issues that need to be addressed in any particular study, of how they should be treated, and what would be the most appropriate strategies to adopt, must be decided according to the purposes of particular studies and the particular circumstances in which they are being carried out. The chapters in Section 3 of the book therefore present specific examples of studies with children and young people. Through these, we explore key decisions that the researchers had to take when faced with the reality of carrying out research. These examples illustrate a range of rather different approaches: from practitioner and participatory research, through longitudinal qualitative investigation, to 'mixed methods' work. The researchers involved outline what they were aiming to achieve, how they set about it, what problems they faced, and how they dealt with them.

As we indicated at the start of this Introduction, we are concerned in this book not just with how research is carried out and its aims, but also with how it engages with various audiences and the impact it has on them. Therefore, the chapters in Section 3 also address questions about how the research findings in the studies discussed were disseminated, how the researchers engaged with the children and young people whose lives they were studying, and with other stakeholders, and what contribution their work has made to the field and to policymaking and practice. This topic is then developed further in Section 4.

Dissemination, engagement, and impact

Much research is concerned with contributing to ongoing conversations within academic communities whose work focuses upon the lives of children and young people. These discussions normally take place in conferences and within the pages of journals, though significant contributions may also be made in book-length reports. Such conversations shape future research, but also frame the teaching that takes place on professional and other courses concerned with children and young people. At the same time, there is also research that is aimed directly at meeting the information needs of policymakers or practitioners. And, of course, it is also important to ask how research in this field engages with and impacts on children and young people themselves. All these aspects of dissemination, engagement, and impact are given attention.

Directly or indirectly, most research concerned with children and young people has been intended to influence policymaking and practice. Indeed, for many researchers the whole point of doing research in this field is to improve children's lives. However, the relationship between research and this outcome is by no means immediate or certain. Recognising this, there are various ways in which this relationship has been conceptualised. In the past, it was sometimes presented in rather idealised, linear terms. According to this model, knowledge is first produced by research, it is then disseminated to policymakers and practitioners, and they then act on it to bring about improvements. However, it came to be widely recognised that what actually happens rarely follows this pattern. Researchers often complain that policymakers and practitioners show little interest in research findings, and/or misinterpret and misapply them; while policymakers and practitioners object that research does not address what is most important, and/or does not tell them much that they did not already know. Of course, there have been times when particular research findings have been taken up by some group of policymakers or practitioners, thereby having an obvious impact, but most research most of the time does not have a direct and clear outcome in this manner.

There have been several rather different reactions to the general failure of this 'linear model' of the relationship between research and policymaking/practice. Some have insisted that the production of knowledge about the world is valuable in itself, even when it does not shape that world in significant ways (e.g. Hammersley 2011). Others have emphasised that the rarity of research findings having an obvious major impact is deceptive; that, in fact, research findings shape policymaking and practice in subtle and diffuse ways that are difficult to document in any strong manner, but which are nevertheless very important (see Weiss 1980; Hammersley 2002). However, there have also been those who have taken the 'failure' of the linear model to indicate that researchers need to operate in a very different way if their work is to bring about improvement. They have argued that researchers must engage directly with those whom they wish to influence and/or with those whose lives they want to improve.

In one form, this might involve a close, interactive relationship with some set of policymakers or practitioners, designed to try to ensure that the research addresses what is important to them, and also to bring them on board in the research process so that they will use the research findings in their work (Caswill and Shove 2000; Elliott 1991). Often, too, what is hoped for here is an iterative process of mutual influence, with the aim of gradually improving the effectiveness and value of both research and policymaking/practice. A rather different version of this interactive model involves researchers engaging directly with the people whose lives they want to help improve, for example children and young people themselves, both seeking to learn from them and assisting them in gaining knowledge and devising strategies to improve their situation (see Kellett 2005).

This interactive model of the research–practice relationship is often closely connected to ethical issues: to ideas about how researchers should relate to the people they study, or from whom they obtain data. There has been resistance on the part of many researchers in the field of Childhood Studies to what they see as the oppressive and alienating form that much psychological and social research takes, in which children and young people are effectively treated simply as objects to be studied (Alderson and Morrow 2011). Instead, it has been insisted that children and young people must be treated as equals, so that their rights are fully respected, and that this requires their becoming involved in key research decisions. Moreover, the objection here is not just to the sort of relationships that operate within the research process itself. Also challenged are the assumptions built into the linear model about how research relates to the knowledge of ordinary people, and the fact that research may be connected with forms of policymaking and practice that are themselves unethical, in that they do not respect the dignity and autonomy of children and young people. These ideas clearly lead to very different views about how researchers should operate, by comparison with those built into the linear model, and they generate distinctive forms of engagement and impact.

Conclusion

Our aim in addressing the issues outlined in this Introduction is to highlight their importance, to explore some of the complexities involved, and to examine the different views that have been taken towards research with children and young people. It is important that researchers operate as reflective practitioners, and that they are aware of the assumptions on which they rely, and the debates around these. But it is equally important that those who read research accounts dealing with the lives of children and young people assess what is provided thoughtfully and are mindful of the issues involved: neither immediately accepting what is presented as authoritative knowledge, nor rejecting it out of hand if it conflicts with what they believe they already know. Such thoughtful reflection is the spirit behind this book.

References

Alderson, P. and Morrow, V. (2011) *The Ethics of Research with Children and Young People: A Practical Handbook*, 2nd edition. London: Sage.

Caswill, C. and Shove, E. (2000) 'Introducing interactive social science', *Science and Public Policy*, 27(3): 154–7.

Christensen, P. and James, A. (eds) (2008) *Research with Children: Perspectives and Practices*, 2nd edition. London: Routledge.

Elliott, J. (1991) *Action Research for Educational Change*. Buckingham: Open University Press.

Fonow, M. and Cook, J. (1991) *Beyond Methodology: Feminist Scholarship as Lived Research*. Bloomington: Indiana University Press.

Fonow, M. and Cook, J. (2005) 'Feminist methodology: New applications in the academy and public policy', *Signs: Journal of Women in Culture and Society*, 30(4): 2211–36.

Hammersley, M. (2002) *Educational Research, Policymaking and Practice*. London: Paul Chapman/Sage.

Hammersley, M. (2011) *Methodology, Who Needs It?* London: Sage.

Hammersley, M. and Atkinson, P. (2007) *Ethnography: Principles in Practice*, 3rd edition. London: Routledge.

Heath, S., Brooks, R., Cleaver, E. and Ireland, E. (2009) *Researching Young People's Lives*. London: Sage.

Kellett, M. (2005) *How To Develop Children as Researchers*. London: Paul Chapman.

Kvale, S. and Brinkmann, S. (2009) *Interviews: Learning the Craft of Qualitative Research Interviewing*. Thousand Oaks, CA: Sage.

Roberts, B. (2002) *Biographical Research*. Buckingham: Open University Press.

Tashakkori, A. and Teddlie, C. (eds) (2010) *Handbook of Mixed Methods in Social and Behavioral Research*, 2nd edition. Thousand Oaks, CA: Sage.

Tisdall, E.K.M., Davis, J.M. and Gallagher, M. (2009) *Researching with Children and Young People: Research Design, Methods and Analysis*. London: Sage.

Weiss, C. (1980) *Social Science Research and Decision-Making*. New York: Columbia University Press.

SECTION 1
CRITICAL ISSUES IN RESEARCH WITH CHILDREN AND YOUNG PEOPLE

Introduction

In this opening section, the chapters address five core themes that we perceive as the bedrock for *Understanding Research with Children and Young People*. These are key considerations to bear in mind as you read through subsequent sections of this book, and throughout the process of your engagement with research. They include:

1 How images of childhood and youth have changed over the years, and how research is always conducted in particular historical, cultural and philosophical contexts which shape how we do research and what we find out;
2 What we mean by 'research' and by 'research with children and young people';
3 The purposes and potential impacts of such research;
4 How research can give voice to the perspectives of younger members of society;
5 How researchers can work to identify and maintain ethical standards.

We have chosen to begin this edited collection with a chapter by Mary Kellett, who encourages readers to reflect on the concept of childhood, how images of childhood have changed over time and how these images have shaped the nature of research about and with children and young people. Kellett established the Children's Research Centre at The Open University, the first of its kind in the UK, which exists to support children to undertake their own research (see http://childrens-research-centre.open.ac.uk), so this is a topic that lies at the heart of all her work. In this chapter, Kellett explores diverse images of childhood within and across historical and disciplinary boundaries and examines how different social and cultural understandings of children and young people have influenced the growth of childhood research. She also discusses her particular vision of critical issues that children and young people face in contemporary society, such as their human rights and participation as researchers and experts in their own lives.

In Chapter 2 'What is Research with Children and Young People?' Sandy Fraser, Rosie Flewitt and Martyn Hammersley review the historical origins and significance of 'empirical research'. They discuss how sociological and psychological research has developed over time, initially influenced by models of research used in the physical and natural sciences, which involved methods that controlled 'variables' in order to identify and test phenomena. This approach often included following explicit procedures in experiments, which could be interpreted through quantitative analysis. Through these rigorous procedures, it was believed that research would be objective and reliable. However, applying a model of research that was designed to investigate physical phenomena was problematic when applied to the study of human beings, whose behaviour is infinitely variable. The authors discuss how modifications were made to the scientific model, and how, in time, it became apparent that radically new approaches were needed. These included qualitative methods of data collection and interpretation which permitted more sensitive insights into the complexity of human life as it unfolds in people's day-to-day lives. In the second part of this chapter, the authors discuss how this shift in research approaches led to a questioning of the relevance of conducting research *on* children and young people, and to the emergence of participatory research *with* them as active and expert co-creators of knowledge about their own lives.

For research to be meaningful it must have a purpose, and this is the focus presented in Chapter 3. Here, Victoria Cooper addresses the potentially wide-ranging impacts of research, and encourages readers to consider the different contributions that investigations can make not only to how we understand children and young people, but also to how such knowledge can be used to inform future research, policy and practice. These themes will be explored more fully in Section 4 of the book. Here, Cooper introduces readers to some core principles and issues through specific examples of contemporary research projects across the academic disciplines of education, health and social care. These examples reflect different social and cultural settings, different methodological approaches and different research purposes. Yet, as Cooper highlights, they share a common commitment to developing greater understanding of the lives and experiences of children, young people and their families, using innovative methodologies and new analytic approaches which bring genuinely fresh insights into the lives and experiences of children and young people around the globe.

In Chapter 4, Sue Bucknall discusses how shifting the focus of research to include the voices of children and young people has brought to the fore a number of profound and problematic issues which must be attended to. Adding to the views expressed in the previous chapters, Bucknall begins by considering how and why participatory research has evolved and become increasingly common. Basing her discussion on examples taken from participatory research, she then reflects on the complex notion of children's 'voices' and discusses the related issues of silence, and how researchers can accurately reflect children and young people's viewpoints in their findings and subsequent research reporting. Lastly, Bucknall considers the research relationships which adults build with children and young people as 'other' to themselves, and how researchers need constantly to reflect critically throughout their engagement with research, whether as critical readers of studies, or as active co-researchers with children and young people.

The final chapter in this section turns to the question of ethics in research, particularly in research involving children and young people. The author, Priscilla Alderson, has written extensively about research ethics, and has spent many years advising on ethical issues as a member of research ethics committees, particularly in the field of medical health care. Alderson begins this chapter by considering the development of research ethics and the formal regulation of ethics. She then proposes three main frameworks for thinking about ethics, based on principles, outcomes and rights, which relate to research in education, welfare, youth, criminal justice and many other services that affect children and young people. Throughout this chapter, Alderson keeps a sharp focus on why research ethics matters, and also discusses criticisms of ethical regulations. Sound advice is given on the processes of applying to ethics review committees, and key questions are raised about how ethical issues arise throughout the research process, including potential harm and benefit, along with issues of privacy and confidentiality, information and consent.

Through these five chapters, our aim is to encourage readers to identify and reflect on core principles related to research into the lives of children and young people, and to retain a constantly questioning, critical approach to their own and others' research work with younger members of society.

1 Images of Childhood and their Influence on Research

Mary Kellett

Introduction

Was there ever a time when the concept of childhood did not exist? Is there an exclusive identity linked to the stage of childhood or is this merely subsumed within adult apprenticeship? Can children ever just 'be' or are they always in a state of 'becoming' an adult? These are some of the questions that have shaped people's images of childhood over time, constructed from a variety of conceptualisations and assumptions about what it is to be a child. This chapter explores the diversity of such perspectives within and across historical and disciplinary boundaries and examines how they have influenced approaches to research about childhood. There is a degree of over-simplification in separating out perspectives into opposing schools of thought. Contemporary notions favour a blended approach which fuses hitherto polarised views such as those held by biologists and sociologists (childhood as a biological phenomenon versus childhood as a social construct). Space in this chapter only permits an overview of these issues and interested readers can engage more fully with the individual topics via the cited references.

The chapter begins with a brief historical overview which sets the context and shows how different social and cultural understandings of childhood have influenced the growth of childhood research. A review of different disciplinary perspectives explores how these have further developed childhood research contours, and have in turn been shaped by diverse cultures, theories and politics. Finally, the chapter draws on critical issues in contemporary society such as human rights and children's participation as major drivers in present-day representations of childhood and concomitant approaches to research with children and young people.

Historical overview

This first section provides a brief overview of the evolution of conceptions of childhood, mainly in the UK context, showing the close relationship between images of childhood in research and wider society. Childhood research began as theory generation by philosophers and gradually took on more experimental and interventionist characteristics in keeping with changing constructions of childhood leading to the richly diverse and multi-faceted nature of contemporary approaches to research with children and young people.

The question of whether and when childhood was accepted as a separate entity was raised by the French historian Ariès who claimed that in the Middle Ages there was no understanding of the child as anything other than an 'adult in waiting' and no sense of a transitory period between infancy and adulthood (1962). Using images of children from historical paintings as the basis of his work he argued that once weaned, children were in effect treated as adults. There was much criticism of Ariès (see e.g. Evans 1997) for not appreciating that parents dressed their children in small versions of adult clothing for the grandeur of portraiture and that this would not have been how they were dressed in normal daily life. Ariès' work was further undermined by those who pointed to medical treaties on the subject of childhood diseases (Cunningham 1991) as evidence of an interest in the life stage of childhood. The division of childhood into sub-periods was also evident in literature (Shahar 1990). Ariès has been further criticised for an over-emphasis on middle- and upper-class children, taking no account of social class and gender in determining the nature of childhood. Nevertheless, Ariès' work did challenge the notion of childhood as universal for all societies in all times in history. He showed how conceptions of childhood change and are rooted in their own times and cultures and, to an extent, the role of research mirrors this work since it seeks to confirm or challenge assumptions and images that have been constructed in different social and historical periods.

Early conceptualisations of childhood are attributed to the seventeenth century (Hendrick 1997) when images of childhood came to be dominated by Puritan dogma. This was epitomised in the belief that children were innately evil, born with 'original sin' that must be purged from them. The Puritans maintained that children could only be 'enlightened' or 'improved' through education, strict discipline and control. Sayings such as 'spare the rod and spoil the child' and 'only fire can straighten crooked wood' originate from this time and aptly illustrate the harsh images that prevailed. Later in the seventeenth century Locke (1632–1704) challenged the idea that children were innately evil, or innately anything for that matter, arguing they were merely a product of their environment. He posited the image of children as a *tabula rasa*, 'a blank slate' capable of being shaped by their environment and experiences. With the right environment and education this blank slate child could become a responsible adult, and developing logic and reasoning were seen as key elements of this process. While Locke recognised that children had specific needs of their own, the emphasis was still on the importance of 'becoming' rather than 'being' (Uprichard 2008).

By the eighteenth century secular discourse had, to a large extent, replaced religious dogma. Instead of 'evil', there was a dominant view of childhood as a time of innocence and of children as needing to be saved from corruption and moulded into responsible adults. At this time, children were perceived as being born pure and naturally good and any wrongdoing could be attributed to the corrupting influence of adult society. One of the principal proponents of this discourse was Rousseau. In his book, *Emile, or On Education* (1762) he expounded his theories on how he thought children should be educated. He argued that they needed a natural environment where they could develop at their own pace. Rousseau's construction of childhood fostered an idyllic image. Children were commonly portrayed in angelic garb surrounded by the beauties of Nature. Poets exalted their natural wisdom and spiritual vision. Becoming adult represented a process of steady decline from innocence to corruption.

A century later, this idealised, romantic construction of childhood had become solidly rooted amongst wealthy middle-class families who tended to advocate that childhood was something to be enjoyed and protected. It was a different situation for poorer, working-class families where children as young as 5 might be put to work. Harsh economic reality put paid to any notions of childhood innocence or the preservation of a special child identity. With industrialisation, women and children could now undertake work that had previously required the strength of an adult male (Humphries 2010). Indeed, some of the early spinning machines in cotton factories were designed to suit the smaller fingers – and cheaper wages – of children. In this social sphere children were an important economic commodity and the survival of many families depended on them. These conditions did not favour the spread of idealised images of childhood. 'Childhood', as we understand it in modern terms, was delayed for the poorer classes until social reforms in the late nineteenth century began to have a real impact on the lives of children. The 1842 Mines Act that banned the employment of those under 10 significantly reduced the number of young working children. The introduction of half-time working for school-age children in the 1844 Factory Act caused the number of working children to dwindle further and almost disappear when compulsory schooling became a reality in 1880, with the exception of some rural areas where schools were sparse and child labour an essential part of agricultural life.

Extensive social reform and subsequent child labour legislation brought significant changes in the construction of modern childhood. Children were no longer so important in the workplace. Zelizer (1985) argued that childhood assumed an 'economically worthless' but 'emotionally priceless' image. She claimed that by the second half of the nineteenth century most urban middle classes had accepted this view of childhood, although poorer families continued to rely on whatever wages children could earn until legislation and compulsory schooling finally put an end to this. In some societies, this prompted a 'sacralisa-tion' of childhood, for example some American reformers asserted that to profit from children's labour was a profanity (Heywood 2001). This led to a more sentimental attitude towards children being adopted.

The aftermath of World War 1 led to a re-appraisal of childhood and its importance. Children began to be seen as the 'future of the nation', as valuable commodities to be emotionally prized and preserved at all costs. They were viewed as having a singular identity with physical, mental and emotional needs. This era of preserving and protecting children brought about a major shift in the approach to research. Investigations centred on the areas of nutrition, health and preventative medicine such as childhood vaccinations, heralding a wave of 'applied research' where results were fed into practice to improve the health and welfare of children and enhance their mental prowess. Comparative studies of children's physical well-being and mortality rates exposed inequalities between different social classes, and this laid the seeds for emancipatory research approaches to develop.

The rise of the Welfare State brought with it an increasing political interfer-ence in child-rearing practices in Britain. Reformers tried to impose middle-class values on working-class families, eschewing many of their more flexible, tradi-tional practices in favour of rigid rules such as advice on breast feeding on demand that took no account of mothers who needed to work. The numbers of Child Guidance Clinics grew rapidly and with it a new impetus for childhood research:

> The significance of the clinics was that they took 'nervous', 'maladjusted' and delinquent children and 'treated' them, producing as they did a new perspective on the nature of childhood. (Hendrick 1997: 53)

Schools became an important focal point for this research when control of most children's education passed into the hands of the government through the intro-duction of state-funded education. Local authorities now decided what was taught, how it was taught and for how long. This significant phase of research was heavily influenced by politics and fuelled by educational reformers. Compul-sory schooling presented new opportunities for the study of childhood with ready-made, convenient samples of participants. Childhood research became more discipline-focused, and characterised by distinctive theories and practices. The first of these to emerge was developmental psychology. By 1923 the field of child development had acquired its own research council, which launched the first issue of *Child Development Abstracts and Bibliography*. Ten years later the learned Society for Research in Child Development had been established. The influence of different disciplines on the growth of childhood research is discussed later in this chapter.

In Western society, the early twenty-first century brought new representations of childhood influenced by advertising and the media. Perspectives became preoccupied with images of the toxicity of youth and childhood in crisis. The 2006 campaign in the UK 'Hold on to Childhood', led by the *Daily Telegraph* newspaper, bemoaned the loss of public play space, the obsessive engagement with digital social media and rising consumer culture which were blurring the boundaries between childhood and adulthood. Kehily (2010) considers this to be a reflection of adult anxiety and insecurity in reaction to the increased risks and uncertainties of late modernity as perceived in cultural shifts, which have led to the reconstruction of conceptualisations of the family and child rearing, including, for example, the way young people are frequently being pilloried in the media. A study by a group of young researchers (Clarke et al. 2009) investigated how young people were portrayed in the popular national UK press. They found that the vast majority of media coverage of young people was negative and focused on minority groups. Most of the stories published were about crime, gangs, education or social inclusion. The imbalance in the amount of positive coverage resulted in misleading portraits of young people as knife-wielding rogues, defined by their choice of clothes, roaming around in gangs:

> Adults do not trust you if you wear fleeces with hoods on or 'hoodies' – they presume you are in with a knife carrying gang and are on drugs. (Focus group comment by young person). (Clarke et al. 2009: 18)

Greater politicisation accompanied these representations of childhood along with new ways of thinking about research, largely influenced by the advance of children's rights. This will be addressed specifically in the final section of this chapter. Before that, we consider the influence of different disciplines on the changing nature of childhood research.

Influences of different disciplines

The perspectives of different disciplines have influenced the ways in which childhood research has evolved. Both the distinctive discipline characteristics and cross-fertilisation between disciplines have been important in shaping our approaches to research with children and young people. To date, influences on childhood research have come from three main areas: developmental psychology, anthropology and sociology, ultimately fusing into a new discipline of Childhood Studies.

The influence of developmental psychology

Developmental psychology fostered images of the child as an incomplete, malleable organism developing differently in response to different stimuli. 'The child is portrayed, like the laboratory rat, as being at the mercy of external stimuli: passive and conforming' (James and Prout 1997: 13). The notion of 'childhood' tended to be viewed in terms of a preparation for adulthood but now it was 'theorised' within the discipline of developmental psychology and divided into age-graded developmental stages. Schools and nurseries provided ideal opportunities to observe large numbers of children of the same age at the same time and under 'controlled' conditions. This made it possible to analyse average ability and arrive at standardised definitions of what constituted 'normal'. One of the tools for establishing 'normal' was the intelligence test, and psychologists produced a range of different tests for measuring mental processes. This led to the 'labelling' of children and segregation according to their IQ. Whilst research of this nature added to the body of knowledge about cognitive development, it also produced some negative outcomes, particularly for those children who were assigned to institutions for the 'mentally defective' on the basis of their IQ scores. Moreover, it opened the door to abusive practices of eugenic social control and to the promotion of the image of the white child as superior, as in the notion promoted by Terman and others (Terman 1925; Richardson 2011). It should be noted that there was a more progressive side to the development of intelligence tests in that they enabled intelligent working-class children to be recognised and thus dispelled some of the assumptions that the lower classes lacked intelligence. A beneficial consequence of this was the generation of education scholarships.

The influence of Jean Piaget (1896–1980) has been pivotal within developmental psychology. His work outlined clearly defined stages of cognitive growth from the *sensory-motor* stage of infancy through *pre-conceptual*, *intuitive* and *concrete* stages to the *formal operations* of adolescence and adulthood. Movement from one stage to the next was argued to be dependent on the achievement of a specific 'schema' of physical and mental actions and a gradual process of 'de-centring' from the self and orientation to others' perspectives. Piaget maintained that all 'normally' developing children pass through these stages, not at the same rate but certainly in the same sequence. Critics of Piaget's work point to the hierarchical assumptions that are implied in the incremental and linear nature of his version of child development (with infant sensory-motor intelligence at the lowest end and adult formal operative intelligence at the highest). Piaget was also critiqued for failing to take sufficient account of socio-cultural considerations, and the impact of the environment a child grew up in. Paradoxically, as interest in the phenomenon of childhood grew, research focused increasingly on cognitive development and the process of becoming adult.

An alternative perspective to Piaget's staged interpretation of development came from the Russian psychologist Lev Vygotsky (1896–1934), who proposed a social constructivist model of child development, with an emphasis on the socially interactive nature of learning (Burman 1994; Woodhead 1999). Although he too was concerned with bringing about adult models of thought as exemplified in his 'zone of proximal development', which is the term he gave to the gap between what a child can achieve alone and what can be achieved with adult support. Wood, Bruner and Ross (1976) developed this into a notion of 'scaffolding' children to function at a higher level through adult assistance. In essence, within a socially constructed world there are no constraints and childhood is not viewed in any precise, identifiable form. A child's cultural background – such as language, cultural heritage, social context – provides the cognitive development tools which adults help them to acquire (for a more detailed exposition of the social constructivist position see James et al., 1998).

The influence of anthropology

The origins of modern anthropology date from a period when interest focused on discovering, and in some cases conquering, unfamiliar corners of the globe, particularly in what were regarded as 'primitive' societies. Malinowski (1884–1942) is regarded as one of the most influential founders of the discipline and the first researcher to establish 'ethnographic research'. Chapter 7 includes a more detailed consideration of ethnographic and anthropological methods, but for the purposes of this overview it can be said that anthropology is a global discipline studying human behaviour, cultural and social organisation, which draws on a range of methods, particularly ethnographic approaches. Ethnography is a specific methodological approach to studying human behaviour, where the researchers immerse themselves as participants in people's daily lives in order to observe, record and gain insights into naturally occurring events over an extended period of time.

Traditional anthropology has been criticised for rarely examining children in their own right. In the 1920s, Mead was among the first anthropologists to complete work on children. Her ethnographic studies titled *Coming of Age in Samoa* (1928) and *Growing up in New Guinea* (1930) gave insights into the lifestyles of Samoan and New Guinean children and young people. She had an abiding interest in the extent to which nature or nurture determined human behaviour and set out to discover whether biology or socialisation shaped adolescent behaviour. She has since been criticised for using Western developmental principles as her theoretical base. For example, although the pioneering nature of her work is still esteemed, Freeman (1983) challenged the accuracy of her fieldwork claiming she had been gullible in her use of the accounts provided by her informants.

Later anthropologists shifted away from using Western theoretical constructs about childhood as a starting point for interpreting the lives of children in other societies. In the 1950s, Briggs engaged in ethnographic research with the Inuit people of Qipsia. She found that children behaved and were treated differently because of environmental factors. For example, she describes a 3-year-old girl sobbing and being left without comfort once her younger sibling was born. In the Inuit people, the cultural practice was for older siblings to defer to the needs of the baby. As a result the young girl learnt not to cry, but to withdraw into herself silently when she became upset: in this way silence rather than crying was an indication of distress among children just out of infanthood (Briggs, 1970).

The work of anthropologists raised questions about the tendency to assume that Western patterns are universal, and in some respects it poses a challenge for universalist discourses, such as those focusing on children's rights.

The influence of sociology

The perceived inadequacy of universal models was a major influence in the rise of sociological thinking. Sociology has developed through a wide range of theoretical approaches from those that consider the economic and social structure of whole societies, to approaches which study the minutiae of day-to-day interactions between people (Giddens 1995). Sociologists question assumptions about how roles and relationships in society are understood, particularly regarding power relations, and this raises many ethical and political issues and affects the way we think about research. Frones et al. (1990) warned against viewing childhood as a homogenous entity, stressing the importance of accommodating diversities such as race, gender, class, disability and religion. However, despite a substantial focus on the 'family', and a foregrounding of feminist work on the roles of women, children in their own right remained largely invisible in the sociological discipline until the later decades of the twentieth century. The biggest influence on contemporary research understandings of childhood has emerged in the wake of the United Nations Convention on the Rights of the Child (1989) in what has come to be known as the 'new sociology of childhood'. James and Prout (1990, 1997) reconstructed childhood as a concept where children and young people have agency in their own lives and are accepted as valued members of society in their own right. This became firmly established in James et al's seminal theorisation of childhood (1998) which documented the changing perceptions of children's status in society, through four models of childhood representations: *developing child, tribal child, adult child* and *social child*. The first model, *developing child*, has already been described in the section about developmental psychology. The *tribal child* assumes children are socially competent and autonomous within their own cultural worlds, an assertion of the integrity of the child perspective:

> Children were no longer simply to be judged as non-adult by reference to idealized standards of adult rationality. They were not to be labeled as *'pre*-operational' or *'pre*-moral' or *pre*-anything else. Children were just different ... what children meant was what they said ... nor was it a problem that these meanings might not be congruent with those of the adult world. (James 1999: 239)

James et al's focus on children in the here and now has been superseded, to an extent, by Uprichard's (2008) construct of children as both beings *and* becomings. The third model *'adult child'* represents the child as a competent participant in a shared adult–child world. Here, although the emphasis is still on the adult, children and young people's perspectives are acknowledged and valued. James et al's fourth model, the *social child* signifies children as agents in their own lives, as what the authors refer to as 'social actors'. While accepting that children ultimately become adults, the new sociology of childhood emphasises the separate and unique identity of childhood in the here and now.

From this sociological perspective, childhood is viewed as a dynamic and transient life stage where children are social actors in ever-changing social and cultural contexts. Whilst not all theoreticians acknowledge these particular models of childhood, the widening of the scope of childhood to a societal level along with the shift towards human rights most closely characterise contemporary images of the status of children and young people.

So far we have considered how images of childhood in research have changed over time, how they have been shaped by the different theoretical approaches adopted by researchers working in the disciplines of psychology, anthropology and sociology, and how ideas about childhood have spread across these disciplines, particularly in the field of Childhood Studies. There are other factors that affect how approaches to childhood research have evolved. These are the critical issues that bubble up at certain times creating waves that impact on the global community more universally. In the contemporary era, one of the biggest waves was created by the United Nations Convention on the Rights of the Child (commonly referred to as the CRC, 1989) and its impact on the status of the child.

The influence of human rights

Power

The CRC is frequently referred to in terms of the three Ps – provision, protection and participation. John (2003) asserts we should include a fourth 'P' – power. Giddens' (1995: 54) rendition of power is:

> ... the ability of individuals or groups to make their own concerns count, even when others resist. Power sometimes involves the direct use of force, but is almost always accompanied by the development of ideas (ideologies) which justify the actions of the powerful.

Justifications for adults maintaining power over children are readily found in paternalistic and maternalistic assertions of acting in children's best interests, of protecting children from harm and in adults' claim to superior knowledge and better judgement. While most people, including many children, agree that some adult power is necessary and legitimate, there are others who question the degree of this. For example, Mayall (2000: 120) asserts that generational ordering is key to adult–child power dynamics: 'Adults have divided up the social order into two major groups – adults and children with specific conditions surrounding the lives of each group: provision, constraints and requirements, laws, rights, responsibilities and privileges'.

One of the ways that power is manifested is in how the term 'knowledge' is employed and, until recent times, knowledge-making was considered to be the domain of adults. However, with new considerations of human rights and recognition of children's agency, the prospect of children sharing power as co-creators of knowledge becomes more real. This is evident in knowledge that is generated through consultations with children and through the findings of their own research (Kellett 2011). Interested readers can learn more about concepts of power within sociological thinking in the *Sage Handbook of Sociology* (Calhoun et al. 2005), or for a more in-depth discussion see Foucault (1980) or Hoyle (2000).

Children's rights

As indicated in the introduction, it is overly simplistic to separate out perspectives on childhood into opposing schools of thought. A unifying theme of contemporary thinking in much research on children's lives is the importance of children's rights, which signals that a clear, discursive space has been delineated for children and young people. Within the field of Childhood Studies, for example, children are now considered as having an autonomy that exists outside family, school and institutions, and a voice conditioned neither by competence nor chronological age. Freeman's (2009) distinction between the politics *for* children and politics *with* children is relevant here. In the former, children's rights are subsumed within a concept of childhood as being an integral part of family and therefore of children as the possessions of parents. Hence many rights, such as choice of schooling, are vested in the parents not the child. In the latter, children's rights are positioned both within and beyond the family, with children's status recognised in society and their consequent access to the civil and human rights encompassed by modern welfare states.

Historically, children have been denied decision-making rights that affect their lives, such as decisions about the use of corporal punishment, on the basis of moral and cognitive incompetence, as epitomised in the paternalist stance of so-called 'child savers' (Archard 2004) who are primarily concerned with protecting children from a stance of adults' superior knowledge about children's best interests. This standpoint has been challenged by liberationists who argue that even young children can make rational decisions (Hyder, 2002; Lansdown, 2005). The concept of children and young people's rights is bound up in central principles of entitlement to be consulted, to be heard and to participate meaningfully in matters affecting their lives as constituted in the CRC, as articulated in articles 12 and 13:

Article 12
States parties shall assure to the child who is capable of forming his or her own views the right to express those views freely in all matters affecting the child, the views of the child being given due weight in accordance with the age and maturity of the child.

Article 13
The child shall have the right to freedom of expression; this right shall include freedom to seek, receive and impart information and ideas of all kinds, regardless of frontiers, either orally, in writing or in print, in the form of art, or through any other media of the child's choice. (UNCRC 1989)

Even within the Convention itself, there is room to open up or close down children's entitlements depending on the interpretation of the term 'is capable of' (see Article 12 above) and its mediation through the adult lens. In the aftermath of CRC, rights-based conceptualisations of childhood began to be embodied in contemporary participation and voice agendas in all societal arenas of childhood, but increasingly in political agendas. This was because the United Nations Committee on the Rights of the Child regularly reviewed signatory countries' progress against implementing the CRC articles and this catalysed political activity around consultation and participation with children.

Participation

The participation agenda evolved in three phases: listening, consulting and involving children in decision-making processes. Hart's (1992) 'Ladder of children's participation' was the first sustained attempt to theorise participation. Using the metaphor of a ladder, he classifies the first three rungs as non-participation (*manipulation, decoration* and *tokenism*). The next four rungs become increasingly empowering: *assigned but informed, consulted and informed, adult-initiated shared decisions with children* and *child initiated and directed*, while the highest rung is reserved for *child-initiated shared decisions with adults*. While some have found this to be a powerful evaluation tool, others (e.g. Reddy and Ratna 2002) criticise its hierarchical structure. John (1996) decries the implied power dynamic of the bestowing of participation rights on the powerless by the powerful adult, and Treseder (1997) critiques the failure to acknowledge cultural contexts, because children can participate to different degrees depending on the societal context.

By contrast, Shier's model (2001) of participation focuses more on the adult roles than the status of children within projects. From the lowest level ('children are listened to') to the highest ('children share power and responsibility for decision making'), Shier frames questions for adults to consider when planning or evaluating participatory projects around 'openings', 'opportunities' and 'obligations'. He places a lot of emphasis on the collaborative activity of adults and children to bring about the most effective participation.

Kirby and Gibbs (2006) criticise all of these models on the basis that an individual initiative or task cannot be assigned a single level of participation because levels of decision-making power constantly shift within projects and within tasks. There is a gap between the rhetoric and reality of meaningful participation that I would argue is best understood through young people's own lived experiences. One group for whom the gap resonates is children who are in the care of the state, sometimes referred to as 'Looked-After' children. Research has found that many of these children resent the statutory medical and 'adultist' reviews (Sayer 2008) that frequently dominate their service provision and deny them any choice regarding their placement. A group of looked-after young people (Bradwell et al. 2011) in North Tyneside carried out their own research about the care review system. They designed and distributed a questionnaire to all children and young people in care in North Tyneside and then collected evidence from focus groups with 36 children and young people about their review meetings. They found that while they were generally listened to in the actual review meeting, young people had no input into the timing, venue, membership or agenda of the reviews. Some young people reported resentment that adults talked about them amongst themselves, as if the young person was not there:

'I didn't want myself to be there to be honest. I don't like going to them but I can't not go to them because otherwise you don't get told what is happening'.

'I don't like going to meetings and sitting in front of loads of people'.

'The social worker just decides'.

(Quotes from young people in Bradwell et al. 2011: 227)

Others wanted professionals with specific roles – such as teachers – to be present only for the education elements and felt embarrassed when more personal issues were discussed in front of their teacher, yet their requests that the teacher withdraw were not respected. While decision making for children in care is a complex process determined by multi-agency review, this piecemeal implementation of how much voice and participation children can exercise within that review process is indicative of earlier discussion points about adults holding the central ground of 'what is in the child's best interest' (Archard 1962) and choosing the degree to which participation is facilitated according to context (Treseder 1997).

Voice
Participation is the act of doing and being involved, voice is the right to free expression of views that may, or may not emanate from participation and relates to Article 13 of CRC. Lundy (2007: 933) maintains that voice is only one component of children's right for their views to be given a valued platform, recognition and impact. She conceptualises voice in four parts:

Space: Children must be given the opportunity to express a view
Voice: Children must be facilitated to express their views
Audience: The view must be listened to
Influence: The view must be acted upon as appropriate.

This is a helpful orientation and highlights the inefficacy of voice operating in a vacuum. There have to be the right conditions in place before children can exercise voice and mechanisms to carry that voice to an audience in a way that can bring influence to bear at a local or societal level. As Lundy states, creating space for children to exercise voice is an essential part of this process. So, researchers, educationists and policymakers need to be proactive rather than passive in providing for, and encouraging, children to express their views in safe spaces without fear of reprisal.

From within the education domain, the rise of pupil voice typifies many of the contradictions and tensions of this concept. UK legislation requires that schools consult with their pupils and that inspectors report on how a school seeks and acts on the views of its pupils. However, there is an implicit contract pupils must enter into requiring them to 'speak responsibly, intelligently and usefully' (Bragg 2001: 73). Moreover, they are being invited to participate within a context where their attendance is compulsory rather than under their own control. Indeed, voice initiatives in schools can sometimes reinforce existing divisive practices rather than question them (Rudduck and Flutter 2004). This situation worsens if participating children are viewed as privileged, with a very real danger of creating or reinforcing hierarchical power structures within the pupil body.

In relation to pupil voice, Fielding (2001) observed that teaching and learning were largely forbidden areas of enquiry (Lodge 2005) and that softer topics such as school uniform or toilets were more commonly explored. However, the growth of school councils is beginning to change some of these perceptions and render more agency to pupil voice. In some schools students now sit on governing bodies and have a limited role in staff appointment processes. Other schools are empowering pupils as researchers to investigate issues that concern them, including pedagogy, leadership and management (e.g. see Priyasha 2010; Nijjar 2012). Moving through the second decade of the twenty-first century, an abiding, if at times aspirational, image of childhood is of the growing child and youth voice beginning to pervade policy and practice.

Agency

Children's agency is the fulfilment of participation and voice through actions that change or influence aspects of their lives. Children and young people as agents of change and knowledge-bearing experts are comparatively recent childhood images that have only recently begun to impact on childhood research. This can be traced back to the influence of theories such as Foucault's conceptualisations of power (1980). These have been explored through the lens of participation (Hart, 1992; Treseder 1997) before Lundy's (2007) visualisation of voice led to the recognition that agency had to follow to ensure participation and voice were not operating in a vacuum. Space is limited so we will explore the notion of children's agency through an illustration of young people with chronic health conditions.

The Getting Sorted project designs, delivers and evaluates self-care workshops to empower children and young people with type 1 diabetes (Webster 2007) and asthma (Webster and Newell 2008) to manage their own conditions and attain more life independence. Young people are involved in all aspects of the project as advisers, co-researchers and evaluators. Findings emerging from the project suggest that many of the children and young people involved have negative experiences of paediatric clinics such as those that children attend as part of their diabetic care plans. They feel disempowered by consultants who either do not listen to them or give them no opportunity to express a view. Critically, they feel that professionals do not understand what it is like trying to be a typical teenager and engage in typical teenage activities while trying to manage their conditions. They report that medical staff only appear to be interested in the clinical management of blood sugar levels and are oblivious to the emotional impacts of their condition. Children speak of feeling nagged, judged and criticised to a point where their self-esteem gets crushed. Many also feel suffocated by parental restrictions on their activities. 'It depends on my blood sugar levels whether I am allowed to go out or not' (young person quote from Webster 2007: 26).

Children and young people are also becoming more agentic in the area of mental health. For example, Young Minds VIK (Very Important Kids) is a group of children and young people aged between 5 and 25 in England who offer support to peers experiencing mental health problems. Their virtual panel Healthy Heads, which was set up in 2007, enables children and young people with various experiences of mental health services to feed into national agendas and policy formation regarding service provision.

Concluding thoughts

Tracing images of childhood over time, across disciplines and in the field of human rights has revealed a kaleidoscope of shifting concepts and theories that have shaped our understanding of this life stage. Different discourses arising from diverse theoretical disciplines along with constructs from different social and cultural value systems all contribute to the mix that informs our present-day images of childhood. There is no characteristic single image that we can latch on to. Children are at one and the same time portrayed as victims, consumers, social actors, innocents and criminals. They are perceived as threats to established order just as readily as keys to the future. So what might the next decades hold? Will the increasing focus on children as social actors foster more research by children themselves? Where is the next twisting contour of the saga heading? To unchartered waters in the guise of greater power-sharing with adults and partners in policy making? Or possibly a return to a more paternalistic and repressive era should a backlash against children's rights take hold and give way to collective panic? If 'childhood is the life-space which our culture limits it to be' (Qvortrup 1994: 3), then hopefully future images of childhood will continue to challenge the extent of those limits.

Bibliography

Archard (1962) *Children: Rights and Childhood*. London and New York: Routledge.

Archard, D. (2004) *Children: Rights and Childhood*. London: Routledge.

Ariès, P. (1962) *Centuries of Childhood*. London: Cape.

Bradwell, J., Crawford, D., Crawford, J., Dent, L., Finlinson, K., Gibson, R., Porter, E. and Kellett, M. (2011) 'How looked-after children are involved in their care review process', *Child Indicators Research*, 4(2): 221–9.

Bragg, S. (2001) 'Taking a joke: learning from the voices we don't want to hear', *Forum*, 43(2): 70–73.

Briggs, J.L. (1970) *Never in Anger: Portrait of an Eskimo Family*. Cambridge: Harvard University Press.

Burman, E. (1994) *Deconstructing Developmental Psychology*. London: Routledge.

Calhoun, C., Rojek, C. and Turner, B.S. (2005) *The Sage Handbook of Sociology*. London: Sage.

Clarke, C., Ghosh, A., Green, E. and Shauriff, N. (2009) 'Media portrayal of young people: impact and influences', available at: www.open.ac.uk/researchprojects/childrens-research-centre/files/crc-pr/file/ecms/web-content/clarke.pdf (accessed 17 October 2013).

Cunningham, H. (1991) *The Children of the Poor*. Oxford: Blackwell.

Evans, R.J. (1997) *In Defence of History*. London: Granta Books.

Fielding, M. (2001) 'Students as radical agents of change', *Journal of Educational Change*, 2(2): 123–41.

Foucault, M. (1980) 'Two Lectures', in C. Gordon (ed.), *Power/Knowledge: Selected Interviews*. New York: Pantheon Books.

Freeman, D. (1983) *Margaret Mead and Samoa*. Cambridge and London: Harvard University Press.

Freeman, M. (2009) 'Children's rights as human rights: Reading the UNCRC', in J. Qvortrup, W. Corsaro and M.S. Honig (eds), *The Palgrave Handbook of Childhood Studies*. Basingstoke: Palgrave Macmillan.

Frones, I., Jensen, A. and Solberg, A. (1990) *Childhood as a Social Phenomenon: Implications for Future Social Policy*. Vienna, Eurosocial Report no 36/1.

Giddens, A. (1995) *Sociology*. Oxford: Polity Press. Hall, P. (2001) 'The Evolution of Economic Policy' in H. Machin (ed.), *Developments in French Politics Vol II*. London: Palgrave.

Hart, R. (1992) *Children's Participation: From Tokenism to Citizenship*. Florence: UNICEF.

Hendrick, H. (1997) 'Constructions and reconstructions of British childhood: An interpretive survey, 1800 to present', in A. James and A. Prout (eds), *Constructing and Reconstructing Childhood*, 2nd edition. Basingstoke: Falmer Press.

Heywood, C. (2001) *A History of Childhood*. Oxford: Blackwell

Hoyle, E. (2000) 'Micropolitics of educational organisations', in A. Westoby (ed.), *Culture and Power in Educational Organisations*. Milton Keynes: Open University Press.

Humphries, J. (2010) *Childhood and Child Labour in the British Industrial Revolution*. Cambridge: Cambridge University Press.

Hyder, T. (2002) 'Making it happen: Young children's rights in action', in B. Franklin (ed.), *The New Handbook of Children's Rights: Comparative Policy and Practice*. London and New York: Routledge.

James. A. (1999) 'Researching children's social competence: Methods and models', in M. Woodhead, D. Faulkner and K. Littleton (eds), *Making Sense of Social Development*. London: Routledge, in association with The Open University.

James, A. and Prout, A. (1990) (eds) *Constructing and Reconstructing Childhood*. London: Routledge.

James, A. and Prout, A. (1997) (eds) *Constructing and Reconstructing Childhood*, 2nd edition. Basingstoke: Falmer Press.

James, A., Jenks, C. and Prout, A. (1998) *Theorizing Childhood*. Cambridge: Polity Press.

John, M. (1996) *Children in Charge: The Child's Right to Resources*. London: Jessica Kingsley.

John, M. (2003) *Children's Rights and Power: Charging Up for a New Century*. London: Jessica Kingsley.

Kehily, M.J. (2010) 'Childhood in crisis? Tracing the contours of crisis and its impact upon contemporary parenting practices', *Media Culture and Society*, 32(2): 171–85.

Kellett, M. (2011) 'Empowering children and young people as researchers: Overcoming barriers and building capacity', *Child Indicators Research*, 4(2): 205–19.

Kirby, P. and Gibbs, S. (2006) 'Facilitating participation: Adults' caring support roles within child-to-child projects in schools and after-school settings', *Children & Society*, 20(3): 209–22.

Lansdown, G. (2005) *The Evolving Capacities of the Child*. Florence: Innocenti Research Centre.

Lodge, C. (2005) 'From hearing voices to engaging in dialogue: Problematising student participation in school improvement', *Journal of Educational Change*, 6: 125–46.

Lundy, L. (2007) '"Voice" is not enough: Conceptualising Article 12 of the United Nations Convention on the Rights of the Child', *British Educational Research Journal*, 33(6): 927–42.

Mayall, B. (2000) 'Conversations with children: Working with generational issues', in P. Christensen and A. James (eds), *Research with Children: Perspectives and Practices*. London: Routledge Falmer. pp. 120–35.

Mead, M. (1928) *Coming of Age in Samoa: A Psychological Study of Primitive Youth for Western Civilisation*. New York: Dell.

Mead, M. (1930) *Growing up in New Guinea*. New York: Morrow Quill Paperbacks.

Nijjar, R. (2012) 'Investigating 11–12 year olds views about their learning environments in an English middle school', available at: http://childrens-research-centre.open.ac.uk (accessed 4 January 2013).

Priyasha (2010) 'Is homework affecting extra-curricular activities?', available at: http://childrens-research-centre.open.ac.uk (accessed 4 January 2013).

Qvortrup, J., Bardy, M., Sgritta, G. and Wintersberger, H. (eds) (1994) *Childhood Matters: Social Theory, Practice and Politics*. Aldershot: Avebury.

Reddy, N. and Ratna, R. (2002) *A Journey in Children's Participation*. Bangalore: The Concerned for Working Children.

Richardson, John T.E. (2011) *Howard Andrew Knox: Pioneer of Psychological Testing at Ellis Island*. New York: Columbia University Press.

Rousseau, J. (1762) *Emile, or On Education*, transl. Allan Bloom. Harmondsworth: Penguin (1991).

Rudduck, J. and Flutter, J. (2004) *How to Improve your School: Giving Pupils a Voice*. London and New York: Continuum.

Sayer, T. (2008) *Critical Practice in Working with Children*. Basingstoke: Palgrave Macmillan.

Shahar, S. (1990) *Childhood in the Middle Ages*. London: Routledge.

Shier, H. (2001) 'Pathways to participation: Openings, opportunities and obligations', *Children & Society*, 15(2): 107–17.

Terman, L.M. (1925) *Genetic Studies of Genius*. Stanford University, USA.

Treseder, P. (1997) *Empowering Children and Young People*. London: Save the Children.

United Nations Convention on the Rights of the Child (UNCRC) (1989) Geneva: United Nations.

Uprichard, E. (2008) 'Children as being and becomings: Children, childhood and temporality', *Children and Society*, 22(4): 303–13.

Webster, L. (2007) *Development and Evaluation of the 'Getting Sorted' Workshops for Young People with Diabetes*. Faculty of Health, Leeds Metropolitan University.

Webster, L. and Newell, C. (2008) *Development and Evaluation of the 'Getting Sorted' Workshops for Young People with Asthma*. Faculty of Health, Leeds Metropolitan University.

Wood, D.J., Bruner, J.S. and Ross, G. (1976) 'The role of tutoring in problem solving', *Journal of Child Psychiatry and Psychology*, 17(2): 89–100.

Woodhead, M. (1999) 'Reconstructing developmental psychology – some first steps', *Children and Society*, 13(1): 3–19.

Zelizer, V. (1985) *Pricing the Priceless Child*. Princeton: Yale University Press.

2 What is Research with Children and Young People?

Sandy Fraser, Rosie Flewitt and Martyn Hammersley

Research with children and young people has a long history, going back at least to the end of the nineteenth century (de Landsheere 1988). However, its character has changed over time, and become more diverse. This reflects the range of different areas and disciplines involved, such as the study of health and education, of psychology, anthropology and sociology. In this chapter we will look, first of all, at the nature of *research*: the aim will be to give you an initial sense of different approaches to inquiry that you will find in the literature about children and young people, the ideas underpinning them, and the debates that surround them. You will be introduced to these in more detail in later chapters. In the second half of the chapter we will look at what it means to do research *with children and young people*. In particular, since it has become very influential, we will pay close attention to what is referred to as 'participatory research'. As will become clear, this kind of work highlights some important methodological, ethical and political issues.

What is research?

Our starting point is the idea of scientific inquiry, and how this was initially interpreted in psychological and social research. At the end of the nineteenth century, and for a large part of the twentieth century, research concerned with children and young people was strongly influenced by the model of inquiry offered by the physical and biological sciences. In order for an investigation to be treated as scientific research – and therefore distinguished from journalism, from the everyday kinds of 'research' that we all might do in getting the information we need, or even from the sorts of account to be found in philosophy and the humanities – it had to be able to demonstrate that it had approximated to the rigorous methods of science. This implied a number of distinctive features: the systematic pursuit of knowledge, treated as of value in itself; a sceptical questioning of commonsense ideas; and, above all, a concern with *empirical investigation*.

Empirical inquiry

The word 'empirical' here means that primary reliance is placed upon setting out to discover facts about the world through observation, and/or through collecting testimony from witnesses – rather than relying upon existing commonsense knowledge, religious or political belief. In other words, science requires active investigation of the world: searching for whatever relevant data already exists, or producing new data through observation, experiment, or some other means. What is referred to as the scientific revolution of the seventeenth century is often seen as having first introduced this empirical approach – it was argued that only this can give us reliable knowledge, or at least knowledge that we *know* to be reliable (Shapin 1998; Principe 2011). And, in the wake of this revolution in the natural sciences, there were attempts to apply a scientific approach to understanding human psychology and also people's political, economic and social lives.

For example, some early research on children, especially in the nineteenth century, relied upon detailed observation of their development, with the idea of documenting the various stages through which babies and young children pass on the way to becoming adults; and, of course, there was also some interest in the illnesses characteristic of childhood, and how these could be treated. There were also broader investigations into the poverty to be found in the new towns and cities of the industrial age.

Other features of the natural sciences model

Because physics was widely regarded as the science in which the most remarkable progress had been made, people's ideas about the nature of rigorous empirical research were strongly shaped by the experimental approach characteristic of that discipline. This was seen as involving two key features:

1   The manipulation of variables to gauge their effects on outcomes of interest (for example, children's health or learning);
2   The attempt to measure these variables accurately, using tests and scales – thereby opening the way for quantitative analysis of the data.

Experiments in physics involved trying to isolate the processes of interest from interference by external influences, and then altering what was seen as the causal variable (for example air pressure) in order to document how this affected the outcome variable (for instance, temperature at which water boils). Scales were developed to measure key physical variables, as were techniques for carrying out measurements: the history of thermometers is a good illustration (Knowles Middleton 1966).

Under the influence of this model there were attempts to render the process of psychological and social measurement analogous to physical measurement, in the sense of treating people and their relations with one another as objects existing in the world, whose stable characteristics could be captured and analysed reliably. But, of course, the specific methods used in physics could not be applied when studying human beings. In psychology, for example, scales and tests had to be developed to measure mental characteristics. A case in point is the development of intelligence tests, which were subsequently used, for instance, in allocating children to different schools, and to different classes within schools. The techniques of measurement involved here were necessarily very different from those employed in measuring the properties of physical phenomena. For example, the children and young people being tested had to be given instructions about what they were to do, their responses were often verbal (rather than simply physical), and their behaviour could not be controlled to the same extent as the phenomena dealt with by physicists or chemists. Moreover, in social research it was frequently not possible to manipulate variables experimentally. Instead, there were attempts to employ comparative analysis as a means of 'controlling variables' in order to discover what caused what: by looking at cases where the variable suspected of being the cause was high by comparison with those cases in which it was low, and where other variables that might affect the outcome were at the same level.

So, even at its early stages of development, psychological and social research differed significantly from natural science at this time, but it nevertheless inherited key methodological ideas, not least the assumption that human behaviour must be conceived as subject to stable, causal laws.

Reliance on explicit procedures

Another important feature of the notion of scientific research, as it was widely understood in the first half of the twentieth century, and continues to be treated today in some quarters, was the requirement that empirical investigations should be carried out in ways that are made explicit, so that other people can understand exactly what was done and evaluate the likely validity of the findings on this basis. Closely related to this was the belief that it is necessary for researchers to follow a predetermined set of procedures in order to minimise the danger that their own distinctive individual characteristics (preconceptions, preferences, beliefs, etc.) will shape what they do and thereby distort the data and findings they produce. In other words, it came to be seen as important to minimise any effects that the particular researcher involved might have on the data and findings.

Replication (in other words, repeating an experiment to see whether the same outcome occurs) was often viewed as the main means of checking the validity of findings. Equally important was assessing the extent to which measuring instruments, for example psychological tests, provided consistent results when applied by different people or in different contexts. The idea of using explicit, predetermined procedures, whose reliability had been checked, developed only slowly in natural science (Shapin 1995), but in the twentieth century it came to be regarded by many as an essential feature of the scientific approach to psychological and social research.

For example, this is one reason why, in carrying out social survey interviews (whether face-to-face or online), the exact ordering and wording of the questions is laid out in the form of a pre-tested questionnaire. Interviewers are generally required to follow the instructions to the letter: only using the words specified, and employing predefined probe questions when interviewees fail to respond to a main question. In effect, the aim was to mechanise the data collection process, eliminating the effects of the particular characteristics of the interviewer in order to discover causal processes that were assumed to be universal or general. In addition, the aim was to ensure that the data produced by multiple interviewers, and coming from many respondents, would be comparable and open to quantitative analysis designed to detect causal relationships. While it was widely recognised that the process of data collection could not be completely mechanised, the argument was that approximation to this model would minimise potential error.

Objectivity, subjectivity, and the study of human beings

A concept closely associated with this approach is 'objectivity': it was believed that through proceduralising the research process 'subjective' factors, which were regarded as a major source of error, could be eliminated or minimised. However, what is meant by the word 'objectivity' here is complex (see Hammersley 2011). The term has at least two distinct meanings:

- The word 'objective' can be applied as an adjective to phenomena to indicate that they actually exist, rather than being a mere appearance or figment of imagination. Here 'objectivity' is a property of such phenomena, and the contrast is with the 'subjective' realm of imagination, fiction, myth, etc.
- Alternatively, 'objective' can mean that a thing belongs to the 'external' world that is publicly observable, not to the 'internal' or psychological world of a subject. In this sense, whereas tables are objective, thoughts and feelings are not; even though both may be real rather than mere appearances – that is, objective in the first sense.

Much thinking about scientific inquiry in the late nineteenth and early twentieth centuries conflated these two senses of the term: it was believed that we can only gain scientific understanding of the world (of objective phenomena in the first sense) through reliance on evidence that is objective in the second sense of being publicly observable, rather than a matter of 'subjective' intuition or insight. So, subjective factors – such as prior assumptions, imaginative conceptions, attitudes, and so on – were seen as a source of error in science whose effect had to be eliminated or minimised. It was precisely because observations could be distorted by subjective factors that it was insisted that scientific research requires the use of explicit, and standardised, procedures.

While this way of thinking perhaps made sense in the context of natural science, it generated problems when it came to studying people, because in important ways their behaviour is necessarily motivated by 'internal' or 'subjective' factors (Taylor 1964). Some psychologists, known as behaviourists, nevertheless sought to apply this approach in a relatively strict fashion. As its name implies, behaviourism tried to restrict psychological investigation to the observation of external behaviour, and aimed at explaining variations in this through showing links to external stimuli of various kinds. This approach was first applied to animals, seeking to understand the processes of learning through which their behaviour developed, but it was later applied to human beings as well. However, it proved impossible to study people's behaviour without ascribing perceptions and beliefs, intentions and motives, to them in order to explain what they do. As a result, it came to be believed by many that, somehow, it was necessary to find a way to study the subjective aspects of human behaviour in an 'objective' manner. One response, influential within both psychology and sociology in the first half of the twentieth century, was to develop standardised tests of psychological attributes – of intelligence, attitudes, etc.

There was a commitment to objectivity in other fields as well, but it took different forms. For example, in anthropology the scientific model led to an insistence that in order to understand 'primitive' societies it was necessary to abandon reliance upon the second-hand reports of travellers and missionaries, as nineteenth-century anthropologists had generally done, since these were likely to be biased by their preconceptions and prejudices. It was argued, instead, that it is necessary for anthropologists actually to go to these societies and engage in direct observation and careful questioning of people, in order to describe what they do and explain it. As part of this, the anthropologist was required to suspend her or his own prior cultural assumptions and prejudices in order to be able to grasp 'the native point of view' and the patterns of social behaviour which it generated (Malinowski 1922). As should be clear from this brief discussion, the word 'objectivity' came to take on a variety of meanings within psychological and social research.

Challenges to the natural sciences model

So, what was taken to be the model of scientific inquiry, derived from the physical sciences, was modified in various ways when applied in the human sciences. Moreover, increasingly over the course of the twentieth century, questions came to be raised in a challenging way about the scientific model, and how it had been interpreted. It was pointed out that the results of many studies in social science were of doubtful validity, and/or were in conflict with one another. It began to be argued that the distinctive nature of human beings and their lives requires a radically different approach. For example, anthropologists came increasingly to emphasise the difficulties faced in understanding other cultures, that a process of intercultural communication and interpretation is required which cannot be reduced to following explicit procedures. And cultural diversity also raised fundamental questions about whether there are universal or general scientific laws that apply across all human groups, and about the political implications and consequences of social research based upon the assumption that there are (see e.g. Geertz 1973; Clifford and Marcus 1992).

In addition, the prestige of natural science declined somewhat from the middle of the twentieth century and there was growing uncertainty, or even scepticism, among ordinary people about some of its findings. In physics, with the rise of relativity theory and quantum mechanics, the knowledge produced about physical reality no longer matched people's common, everyday experience of the behaviour of physical objects. There was also increasing concern about the consequences of applying science through technology: in light of the devastation caused by modern warfare techniques, the pollution generated by industry, and so on (Hesse 1972: 275).

In the second half of the twentieth century, the problems of applying the natural science model in studying human beings, and the shift in the prestige of science, encouraged psychologists and social researchers to explore a wider range of approaches to understanding human behaviour and social institutions, often ones which no longer involved any demand for experimental manipulation and control, or any constraint on investigating 'subjective' phenomena such as people's experiences and beliefs. It was insisted that individuals' behaviour cannot be properly explained simply as responses to external stimuli. Instead, the focus came to be placed upon understanding how people make sense of themselves, their actions and their surroundings, and how this shapes and is shaped by the processes of social interaction in which they are involved. Many researchers insisted that this sort of understanding requires a much more flexible and sensitive approach than that modelled on physics, one that draws upon researchers' human capacity for communication and learning, and their experience of sociocultural worlds.

Frequently, these new approaches to research involved the use of qualitative data; in other words, open-ended descriptions of patterns of action, and exploration of the accounts that people offer about their lives and circumstances. Moreover, these were collected in 'naturalistic' situations, rather than ones largely controlled by the researcher, with the idea that this would lead to more nuanced understandings of people's actions, attitudes, beliefs, etc. than the older, scientific approach. So, observation was carried out in the everyday situations in which people live their lives. And, increasingly, interviews tended to be open-ended and conversational in character, designed to explore people's experiences, perspectives and beliefs.

Furthermore, the concept of objectivity often came to be rejected, or at least redefined in ways that were felt to be more appropriate in the human sciences. For example, some commentators emphasised the importance of 'reflexivity': of researchers trying to remain aware of how they are shaping, or have shaped, the data and findings they produce, and making this explicit in research reports. A few moved beyond this, to the idea that research inevitably reflects the individuality of the researcher and the contingent character of the research process.

However, while these developments represented a shift in ideas about what 'being scientific' means, and while some qualitative researchers even rejected the very idea of psychological or social *science*, most social scientists retained a belief in the importance of systematic, sceptical, empirical investigation as the main source of reliable knowledge.

Ethical and political issues

As noted earlier, the changing public status of science was not just a matter of increasing scepticism towards its findings, equally important were ethical and political concerns about the *consequences* of scientific knowledge. Moreover, in the case of psychological and social research, the concern was not just about the consequences of knowledge but also about *the research process itself*. It had long been recognised that research could harm people or infringe their rights, and that precautions needed to be taken to minimise this. However, research ethics came to be interpreted by many researchers, not least in the field of Childhood Studies, as playing a more central role in the research process than previously.

One aspect of this was rejection by some of the idea that the production of knowledge is worthwhile in itself, and there came to be increasing insistence that, to be of value, research must contribute to improving policy or practice: for example by making the lives of children and young people better. Some saw this as being achieved through research showing which health treatments, social work interventions, or educational strategies are effective and which are not. But many emphasised the role of research in *challenging* policy or practice, for instance through amplifying the voices of children and young people, and/or through offering critiques of the assumptions on which it is based.

Often also involved here was a concern about the role that science had come to play in modern culture: as claiming to offer the only true account of the world, and as providing techniques for manipulating the behaviour of populations. This was viewed by some as a form of domination and as an infringement of people's autonomy. And these political and ethical ideas also came to be applied to the process of research itself. Important here were ethical and political ideas about the rights of participants in research, especially of children and young people.

The issue came to be raised of whether research should be carried out 'on' children and young people, or whether it should instead be carried out 'with' or 'by' them. Questions were prompted about the quality of data likely to be produced in research relationships where researchers are in control: deciding what to investigate and how to do this, how to analyse the data, and how to disseminate the findings. It was argued that such research would be biased by adult perspectives, and would therefore fail to grasp the experience of children and young people. Equally important, treating people as 'objects' to be studied seemed to many to be unethical. A consequence was arguments in favour of participatory models of research, in which children and young people were directly involved in the methodological decisions being made, albeit to varying degrees and in various ways. In the next section we will consider what it means to do research *with* children and young people.

Empirical research with children and young people

The second aspect which we cover in this chapter concerns the use of the phrase 'research with children and young people'. What exactly does 'with' mean in this context? In the past, social and psychological researchers often saw young children as not competent to describe or understand their own world:

> children [are] often denied the right to speak for themselves either because they are held incompetent in making judgements or because they are thought of as unreliable witnesses about their own lives. (Qvortrup et al. 1994: 2)

Similarly, children have often been valued and understood only in terms of being 'a work in progress' towards adulthood, the concern being with what, as already stated in this book, they might become and not who they presently are. Such an approach undermines the status of children in society, and sheds doubt on how relevant research findings can be, if these fail to take into account the perspectives of the people whose lives and experiences they are investigating.

Margaret Donaldson (1978) and others criticised the highly influential work of Piaget (1896–1980) as being defective because it failed to take sufficient account of the experimental conditions under which his observations of young children's behaviour and competences took place. Donaldson's work showed how, under different conditions, children were capable of the kinds of logical reasoning that Piaget had asserted occurred at a much later stage in their development. Consequently Woodhead and Faulkner argued that Donaldson's studies 'helped developmental psychologists recognise that children's true competencies are revealed *only in situations which make sense to them*' (Woodhead and Faulkner 2008: 26, emphasis added). If children and young people are competent in a way that has previously been ignored, and yet they are not listened to, then the evidence-based development of our education and social policies risks being misguided. Indeed, some researchers argue that any theoretical framework that concerns the lives of children and young people, but which does not reflect their viewpoints and experiences, may be misleading.

Much of the recent literature on research with children and young people argues against treating them as 'objects', and argues for viewing them as participants, as young citizens with rights that must be respected. This implies an approach to conducting research, rather than a specific method.

Research 'with' children involves a range of approaches towards research and towards children. At one end of this spectrum, children might be encouraged and supported to carry out research for themselves, with minimal adult involvement, or, at the other end of the spectrum, adults might carry out research in which the involvement of children is restricted to their providing interview or documentary data. The key is that the research helps us to understand children's lives. Many research studies with children fall between these two extremes, but are united by a common thread that children and young people are recognised as the experts in their own lives. So, in carrying out research with children and young people, a variety of methods can be used. Sometimes this might mean that the adult acts as the primary researcher, while at other times children might be more actively involved in forms of participatory research.

To illustrate how children and young people can act as active participants in the research process, and to give an idea of a spectrum of involvement, we have selected two examples where children and young people were involved to a greater or lesser extent in research. The first example is what is called the Mosaic approach, and shows how researchers enabled children to play an active part in revealing their 'worlds' but in a context where the research agenda was set by the researcher. The second example introduces an action research project, where young people in Bangalore became actively involved in a research-based process of change, influencing how the study was designed and its outcomes.

The Mosaic approach

The Mosaic approach was developed by Alison Clark and Peter Moss (e.g. Clark and Moss, 2001, 2005) (also see Chapter 12). This research is one of a growing number of studies to actively engage with young children as 'experts in their own lives' (Langsted, 1994) in order to gain new understandings about how young children connect to their environment:

> Surveys and audits, questionnaires and interviews are all excellent techniques to record information, but sometimes they are not appropriate to explore the subtle and hidden feelings that connect us with a place. They do not reveal the experiences and memories of childhood and youth that contribute to creating a sense of place. (Adams and Ingham 1998: 149)

The Mosaic approach uses a range of participatory visual methods, alongside observation and interviewing, to build up new understandings of young children's views and experiences of early childhood environments. Children under 5 are invited to take a researcher on 'tours' of their nursery, taking photographs and providing a 'running commentary' on their routine activities. They are asked to indicate who they typically meet and where they meet them, which rooms they have access to or not, and so on. The children are placed in charge of the tour and how it is recorded: by photograph, audio recording or drawings. Combining the results from this and the other research tools in the Mosaic approach can lead to a process of discovery at an individual, institutional and professional level.

There can be tangible and immediate benefits for individual children involved, in terms of understandings gained about children's interests and concerns within a particular space. At an institutional level, the first study using this approach discovered the importance of the children's private spaces within the nursery, as well as the need to involve the children in planning the use of external play areas. In a subsequent study that focused on the design and review of learning environments (Clark 2010), the Mosaic approach revealed data that challenged professional assumptions about young children's capabilities and perceptions. One example arose over the understanding that primary colours were appropriate for a nursery, and related to assumptions about young children's limited awareness of subtleties of tone. Children's comments about the differences in tone between the colour of a piece of furniture shown in a photograph they had taken and the actual object challenged this assumption which had long been held by architects.

This example illustrates how engaging with the perspectives of research participants can enrich the findings of empirical research. Such engagement may require that 'at times more established' methods of data collection are adapted to become more inclusive of children and young people to enable their participation at different stages of the research process.

Participatory research by children in Bangalore

The second example we have chosen illustrates how research with children and young people can challenge expectations and be a tool for change, making visible perspectives that run counter to the dominant power structures. The focus here was young people's perspectives on poverty and urban living. The majority of children and young people in the world grow up in circumstances and expectations that are quite different from those in minority-world countries. In these countries children live in contexts where there are less stable economic, legal and political institutions, and children and young people can find themselves caught between the influence of the affluent West and the uncertainty and difficulties of living in poverty.

In some countries, such as India, where this second example is set, the gradient between wealth and poverty can be very steep. Throughout the last decade, India's economy has grown rapidly, and a sustained and steady rate of growth has contributed to a reduction in poverty. According to the World Bank, the rate of poverty in India has fallen from 41.6 per cent of the population in 2005 to 32.7 per cent in 2010, with a definition of poverty based on a daily income of $1.25 (World Bank, India 2012). Of course, while income is important, poverty is multi-dimensional. For example, power is also important: children and young people at the sharp end of poverty are relatively powerless to challenge their conditions of life. When governments, charities and other international agencies seek to deal with such issues, the voice of children and young people is often left unheard. A research study which sought to redress this balance is the *Growing Up in Cities* (GUiC) project sponsored by the United Nations Educational, Scientific and Cultural Organization (UNESCO). GUiC research included many different projects throughout the world, one of which was in Bangalore, India.

In 'The Growing Up in Cities Project: Global Perspectives on Children and Youth as Catalysts for Community Change', Louise Chawla and David Driskell (2006) outline children's lives in Sathyanagar or 'Truth Town', a suburb of Bangalore:

> Like many urban settlements in India and throughout the developing world, Sathyanagar is a place that outsiders – including many middle-class Indians – would describe as dirty, squalid, poverty-stricken and depressed. It is, both in the classification scheme of the state bureaucracy and in the local nomenclature of its residents, a slum. (Chawla and Driskell 2006: 186–7)

The methodology used to research children and young people's lives in this study was Participatory Action Research (PAR), in which the children themselves became the primary researchers and producers of research and knowledge, rather than being 'researched upon'.

What emerged from analysis of the data was that despite the governmental and local designation of Sathyanagar as a 'slum', and despite the reality of living in a 'poor and environmentally degraded place', Sathyanagar was seen by these children and young people as 'culturally and emotionally rich, [allowing] happy lives, in a community that possessed a number of advantages: some apparent, and some perhaps invisible to the eyes of its adults' (Chawla and Driskell 2006: 187). This result was surprising and interesting, and the authors noted that:

> During the several month process of conducting the participatory research activities, not a single child in Sathyanagar was heard to utter the phrase 'I'm bored.' Indeed, the issue of 'idleness', often associated with underemployment and typically identified as a source of youth dissatisfaction and crime in many slums and low income communities, was nonexistent for these young people. (Chawla and Driskell 2006: 190)

The *Growing Up in Cities* project existed in order to do two things. First, it allowed the views of children and young people to be fed into local planning processes, local authorities and/or non-governmental agencies, highlighting problems and solutions identified by children and young people themselves. Secondly, such research sought to document obstacles to the proposed changes and to community development. While the children of Sathyanagar were imbued with resilience and a positive attitude, they were also clear about what Truth Town needed. Their concerns alighted on improvements to public sanitation and water supply. The data also highlighted what the children saw as obstacles to this improvement:

> While the stories shared by young people in Sathyanagar were infused with a grounded optimism about the future, their stories also told of first-hand experience with official neglect, broken promises, wasted resources and squandered opportunities, casting an unflattering light not only on inefficient, ineffective and sometimes inept or corrupt bureaucracies and politicians, but also on misguided development agencies and mismanaged non governmental groups. (Chawla and Driskell 2006: 192)

The authors go on to explain how this PAR project became reshaped over time to meet the agendas of sponsoring agencies, both governmental and non-governmental. What needed to change was not only that the viewpoints of children and young people needed to be included in the research process, but also that 'the way in which local decision makers understood and prioritised local issues' needed to be changed (Chawla and Driskell 2006: 192):

> Perhaps most disheartening was the near complete lack of connection between what local officials viewed as the needs of local young people (more opportunities for sports

and recreation) and what young people expressed as their needs (adequate clean water and sanitation). (Chawla and Driskell 2006: 194)

Despite these obstacles there were some successes, the need for a Study Centre for the children of Sathyanagar was identified and met. Yet, at the heart of this example of research with children and young people, there are two messages. The first is that good empirical research which features young people taking a primary role is possible. The second is that it can be politically resisted and downplayed due to the interests of others, such as the finding that the grounded optimism of Sathynagar's youth struck an awkward chord with NGOs, whose *raison d'être* required projects with definable and 'achievable' objectives. It might have been that provision of sports and recreation facilities were easier to accomplish and less politically and economically sensitive than provision of better public health infrastructure. Frequently, research with children and young people can be political in a wider sense.

From these two examples we can see how participatory research with children and young people can be carried out in different ways, with different roles taken on by the young researcher participants, and with different results that reflect the varying aims of the individual projects. What links both projects is that they each gave rise to findings which surprised the adult researchers and members of established organisations who were responsible for planning aspects of the young people's lives. They also both challenged long-held views about the perspectives and competences of the children and young people involved in the studies. At a deeper level, the Mosaic approach acted as a thinking tool, providing a context in which children and adults could use not only words but also images and artefacts to construct and reflect on knowledge, for example about a particular place. The *Living Spaces* study was an action research project which was not only about revealing power differences but about attempting to readdress some of these differences by exploring democratic forms of knowledge building (Reason and Bradbury 2006). Both are examples of participatory research, which set out to actively engage participants throughout the research process and to give status to the knowledge created.

Notions of child 'competence' in research

In the past it has been argued that young participants may lack the appropriate vocabulary and understanding to 'make sense' of research aims or of the research process. Yet this can also be true of adults. There is no necessary reason why an adult should have a more adept vocabulary for research than a child or young person. However, it is arguable that an adult will have a greater 'stock of experience' to draw upon which could provide relevant conceptions for empirical research. And it is equally possible that some children or young people will have had a more diverse stock of experiences and a greater facility with different languages than some adults.

Clark's research example of the Mosaic approach, for example, has also shown how symbolic tools other than language can be used to gain rich insights into young children's perspectives, such as asking children to take photographs and to make artefacts, and then to talk with them about the objects they have made. This exemplifies how the negotiation of meaning may unfold by using particular types of data collection methods that children engage with readily, such as drawings, photography, diaries and other innovative techniques. Yet these methods are not only effective with young participants – they can help to unlock the thoughts and perceptions of research participants of any age (see Reavey 2011).

This implies something else: the way in which research can be negotiated with children and young people, or indeed participants of any age, will differ according to habits and mores which the child or young person has learned. Recognising this involves taking into account the power relationships to which the child or young person is already subject. For example, within the time pressures and hierarchical power structures of a school, teachers may not necessarily be familiar or in agreement with a researcher allowing children the time or space to be active co-researchers in their own class environment. As a result, there will be great diversity in negotiated research relationships – a quality also found in research with adults because, like 'adults', 'children and young people' are not a homogeneous mass, but are diverse in their competencies and their freedom. Therefore, negotiating the terms of a 'research space' can be a practically challenging procedure (see Chapter 4).

Part of the practical difficulties may involve the political context – that is, the network of power relationships that a child or young person is already part of before any research begins. This can be in terms of the pattern of peer relations, family processes or institutional relationships, for example, being in school or in a residential care home. Moreover, the research may concern children and young people but it would be unusual if they were the only stakeholders involved. This may constrain a researcher's ambition to achieve equal partnership. It might be argued that children and young people can never be the sole voice that is heard within any piece of research; other stakeholders should be represented in the research too.

Research with children and young people can therefore be seen as different from research with adults, not necessarily because of young people's ability or understanding, but as a consequence of their perceived roles in the community, society and culture within which they find themselves. Samantha Punch (2002) argues that there are clear differences between research with children and young people as compared to research with adults, and suggests: 'There has been a tendency to perceive research with children as one of two extremes: just the same or entirely different from adults' (Punch 2002: 322). Elsewhere she notes:

> It is somewhat paradoxical that within the new sociology of childhood many of those who call for the use of innovative or adapted research techniques with children, are also those who emphasise the competence of children. If children are competent social actors, why are special 'child-friendly' methods needed to communicate with them? (Punch 2002: 321)

So called 'child-friendly' methods are sometimes negotiated compromises that allow communication between the different conceptual outlooks of children and young people on the one hand, and those of researchers on the other. We propose that using the term 'child-friendly' to describe data collection techniques may wittingly or unwittingly undermine the principle that young people must be considered competent experts in their own lives. There is nothing inherently or essentially 'child-friendly' about such techniques; they are all contingent to the frames of cultural reference of researchers and participants. Such techniques are 'participant-friendly' rather than 'child-friendly'. Even if created to be appealing to children, the same research methods are often also found to be highly motivational for adult participation as well, such as those that involve the use or creation of artefacts (photographs, film, etc.) or embodied enactment as a basis for discussion or exploration of experience.

Concluding remarks

In this chapter we have looked at two aspects of *research* with children and young people. We started by examining the notion of research. Initially, psychological and social inquiry was modelled on work in the natural sciences. However, over time various parts of this scientific model came to be questioned, for example on the grounds that studying people's lives places quite different demands on the researcher from those faced by natural scientists. There were arguments here about what sorts of methods are required if we are to produce sound knowledge not only about human beings, but also about the ethical and political aspects of psychological and social science. At the same time, for the most part the core idea was retained that research demands systematic, empirical investigation of the world in which many currently-taken-for-granted ideas are questioned, rather than reliance upon, say, common sense or the pronouncements of political or religious authorities.

In the second half of the chapter we examined ideas about what is distinctive about carrying out research *with* children and young people, showing respect for their competence and knowledge. There is variation in the form that such 'participatory' research takes, ranging from studies aimed at documenting the perspectives of children and young people, at one end of the spectrum, to studies where children and young people are more fully involved in the research process, from the early stages of identifying relevant research questions, through carrying out data collection and analysis, to the dissemination of research findings. Although participatory research is by no means the only way to conduct empirical research into the lives of children and young people, it can lead to highly original insights and can improve the credibility of the knowledge produced.

Bibliography

Adams, E. and Ingham, S. (1998) *Changing Places: Children's Participation in Environmental Planning*. London: Children's Society.

Chawla, L. and Driskell, D. (2006) "The Growing Up in Cities Project", *Journal of Community Practice*, 14(1–2): 183–200.

Clark, A. (2010) *Transforming Children's Spaces: Children's and Adults' Participation in Designing Learning Environments*. Abingdon: Routledge.

Clark, A. and Moss, P. (2001) *Listening to Young Children: The Mosaic Approach*. London: National Children's Bureau (2nd edition 2011).

Clark, A. and Moss, P. (2005) *Spaces to Play: More Listening to Young Children Using the Mosaic Approach*. London: National Children's Bureau.

Clifford, J. and Marcus, G. (eds) (1992) *Writing Culture: The Politics and Poetics of Ethnography*. Berkeley, CA: University of California Press.

de Landsheere, G. (1988) 'History of educational research', in J. Keeves (ed.) *Educational Research, Methodology and Measurement: An International Handbook*. Oxford: Pergamon.

Donaldson, M. (1978) *Children's Minds*. London: Fontana.

Geertz, C. (1973) *The Interpretation of Cultures*. New York: Basic Books.

Griesel, R.D., Swart-Kruger, J. and Chawla, L. (2002) 'Children in South Africa can make a difference: an assessment of "Growing Up in Cities" in Johannesburg', *Childhood*, 9(1): 83–100.

Hammersley, M. (2011) 'Objectivity: a reconceptualisation', in M. Williams and P. Vogt (eds) *The Sage Handbook of Methodological Innovation*. London: Sage.

Hesse, M. (1972) 'In defence of objectivity', Proceedings of the British Academy, 4 October.

Knowles Middleton, W. (1966) *The History of the Thermometer and its Use in Meteorology*. Baltimore: Johns Hopkins University Press.

Langsted, O. (1994) 'Looking at quality from the child's perspective', in P. Moss and A. Pence (eds), *Valuing Quality in Early Childhood Services: New Approaches to Defining Quality.* London: Paul Chapman Publishing, 29.

Malinowski, B. (1922) *Argonauts of the Western Pacific: An Account of Native Enterprise and Adventure in the Archipelagos of Melanesian New Guinea.* London: Routledge and Kegan Paul.

Principe, L. (2011) *The Scientific Revolution.* Oxford: Oxford University Press.

Punch, S. (2002) 'Research with children: the same or different from research with adults?' *Childhood*, 9(3): 321–41.

Qvortrup, J., Bardy, M., Sgritta, G. and Wintersberger, H. (eds) (1994) *Childhood Matters.* Vienna: Europe Centre.

Reason, P. and Bradbury, H. (eds) (2006) *Handbook of Action Research.* London: Sage.

Reavey, P. (2011) (eds) *Visual Methods in Psychology: Using and Interpreting Images in Qualitative Research.* New York: Routledge.

Shapin, S. (1995) *A Social History of Truth*, 2nd edition. Chicago: University of Chicago Press.

Shapin, S. (1998) *The Scientific Revolution.* Chicago: University of Chicago Press.

Taylor, C. (1964) *The Explanation of Behaviour.* London: Routledge and Kegan Paul.

Woodhead, M. and Faulkner, D. (2008) 'Subjects, objects or participants? Dilemmas of psychological research with children', in P. Christensen and A. James (eds), *Research with Children: Perspectives and Practices*, 2nd edition. London: Routledge Falmer. pp. 10–39.

World Bank, India (2012) Available at: http://data.worldbank.org/country/india (accessed March 2013).

3 Designing Research for Different Purposes

Victoria Cooper

There is no single or most effective way in which to conduct childhood and youth research but a range of approaches can be used which have evolved across many different disciplines. Consequently, there are contrasting, and at times conflicting ideas about what childhood and youth means as well as the methods best suited for research with children and young people. There is also the rhetoric of impact, which assumes that research can in some way influence the lives of children and young people by producing knowledge which can inform policy and practice.

This chapter focuses on the wide-ranging purposes for research and encourages you to consider the diverse contributions that investigations can make to how we understand children and young people and how such knowledge can influence policy and practice. To address each of these themes I draw upon traditional research examples as well as more contemporary studies that colleagues and I have been conducting at The Open University in conjunction with partner institutions; including the University of Oxford *Young Lives* study, and the University of Worcester *Work-based Research Project*. Each example illustrates a distinct methodological approach and research purpose and draws upon different combinations of academic discipline, spanning education, health and social care. Despite their differences, they each share a commitment to developing greater understanding of the lives and experiences of children, young people and their families.

Diverse research perspectives and purposes

Childhood and youth is a broad field which has been investigated over the years through qualitative, quantitative and mixed methods approaches. This opening section sets the scene for on-going discussion throughout the chapters in this book regarding the variety of purposes served by childhood and youth research;

how investigations are shaped by different disciplines and how such a diverse body of research can influence how we think about and work with children, young people and their families.

In this first section I concentrate on research within the area of family life. By focusing on one aspect of childhood and youth, I address the different ways in which researchers set about their studies with distinct purposes; how they are important in very different ways and connect with theory, policy and practice.

Research exploring the family

As Douglas (2004) indicates, family experiences may be understood from a variety of perspectives which address genetic and blood-tie relationships, social and cultural dynamics, economic and legal aspects of family life and draw upon diverse academic disciplines including psychology, sociology and anthropology.

Historically, psychologists interested in children and young people applied quantitative approaches to produce knowledge about how and why children and young people behave in particular ways, often using experiments to test a particular hypothesis or evaluate relationships between variables. A variable is something that can be changed or manipulated, such as the attributes of age or gender, and these are generally examined in psychological investigations to determine if changes to one or more variables result in different research outcomes. Psychological research has tended to focus on discrete aspects within family life, such as parenting style (Baumrind 1966), and children's social and emotional development (Erickson 1968), with a strong emphasis upon developmental trajectories (Piaget 1962) which mark out childhood as a period of socialisation and as a transition to adulthood. Much quantitative research has concentrated on family structures to examine, for example, parent and child separation and the impact of parent divorce and separation upon children and young people (Dunn and Deater-Deckard 2001).

Take for instance Bowlby's well-known study of attachment. Bowlby (1969) was interested in exploring how families interact. Whilst working as a psychiatrist he noted a relationship between early separation and later emotional problems in the children he worked with, and he devised a quantitative study to examine this. He selected 88 children (aged 5–16) and interviewed their parents, questioning them about early experiences of separation. The children were divided into two groups. Group 1 comprised 44 children who had a criminal record for theft. Group 2 comprised 44 children who Bowlby classified as 'disturbed' but 'emotionally functional'. Bowlby found that 14 of the child thieves displayed an 'affectionless' temperament, characterised by limited affection, shame, or responsibility for their actions. Almost all of these children had experienced early separation from their mothers in foster homes or during times spent in hospital. Only seven children from Group 2 had been separated from their mothers. The evidence appeared to support Bowlby's hypotheses that affectionless temperament was caused by maternal separation in early life, however the evidence was not conclusive. Biographical details about each child had been collected retrospectively, based on what parents could recall. In addition, the evidence, whilst inferring a correlation, did not confirm causation.

Critiques of Bowlby's early work suggest that whilst an association may have been evident, affectionless temperament could be influenced by a range of other factors which had not been considered during the study (Rutter 1979; Schaffer and Emerson 1964), such as the nature of the child's relationship with their parent and other family members as well as the child's experiences of care and support during periods of separation from their caretakers. Other variables, such as education, diet and parental income may also impact upon a child's social and emotional development. This is not to point out the failings of Bowlby's theory, but rather illustrate the many complex factors which are important within family experiences and the different ways in which research can examine family life.

Sociological researchers typically employ a number of methods to examine how children and young people experience family life within interconnected social systems. Through survey studies, for instance, which allow for the broad analysis of large populations, sociological research into trends in family demographics has demonstrated that family structures are exceptionally diverse and include extended, single parent, foster parent and stepfamilies (Morrow 2009). In contrast, ethnographic approaches, which build upon a long history of anthropological research, tend to gather in-depth data about smaller research cohorts, in an attempt to gather perspectives through case study analysis of lived experience. For example, sociological studies that have adopted an ethnographic approach have looked at contrasting family structures across cultures to reveal the complex social and emotional ties that make up family experiences (Carsten 2004). Through these diverse methodological approaches, and in contrast to the psychological research by Bowlby cited earlier, sociological research has revealed that experiences of family life can depend on a host of interrelated factors, including individual personality, sibling relationships and social and cultural contexts. Family structures can alter for a variety of reasons, reflecting changing circumstances such as war, famine and poverty. Families may be nuclear, extended, polygamous – when a man lives with several wives – and in rare cases polyandrous – when a women lives with several husbands (Montgomery 2009).

Early psychological and sociological research typically relied on adult interpretations of the family and did not include the views of children and young people – it was mostly research on rather than with children and young people. The field of Childhood Studies, as discussed in the introduction to this book, evolved from interdisciplinary work across sociological, psychological and anthropological research to recognise children and young people as active, competent social beings (Prout and James 1997) who can impart important messages about their own experiences. Morrow (2009) claims that the emergence of Childhood Studies represented a significant shift from examining children and young people and how they are socialised *within* families to include approaches which appreciate children and young people's agency in influencing their own lives; constructing their own meanings about family life and so providing opportunities for them to share their own views on issues such as parental separation (Brannen et al. 2000) and stepfamily life (Mayall 2002). Related to this, Roberts (2004) traces developments across policy and practice which promote the rights of children and young people to be consulted on issues which influence their everyday lives.

Despite, and perhaps partly because of, differences across the academic disciplines, childhood and youth research has produced rich insights into family life. Bowlby's work, for example had a profound impact upon our understanding of the significance of caretaker and child separation. This work provided a firm foundation for later research, carried out by Robertson and Robertson (1989), which has contributed to making changes to the support of children and young people during hospital care, and acknowledges the importance of minimising child and caretaker separation. These research insights have contributed to changing views of family life and are reflected across national and international policy and practice frameworks. For example, The Convention on the Rights of the Child treaty (United Nations 1989) sets out basic human rights – for all children, without discrimination – to survival, protection from harm, abuse and exploitation, the right to develop to their fullest potential, and the right to participate fully in family, cultural and social life (Ivan-Smith 1998). There are now a range of services within the UK which acknowledge the diversity of family living and the importance of providing support and guidance (Foley and Rixon 2008). Family centres within the UK have been established in recent years to provide a cohesive and integrated system of support on issues related to health care, education, family welfare and youth justice.

Research across the disciplines of psychology, sociology, anthropology and childhood and youth studies have contributed to a growing understanding of children and young people. Using the example of the family, you can begin to appreciate the varied purposes for research. This chapter does not promote one approach as more effective than any other but is organised to illustrate the distinct ways in which researchers can study aspects of childhood and youth and how their work can be influential in different ways. Research can influence the way we think about and understand children and young people and is reflected across policy and practice developments. The relationship between research, theory, policy and practice however, is complex. Our perspectives of childhood and youth have changed and research continues to add to our understanding in ways which contribute to existing knowledge. But how is this achieved?

How can research influence knowledge and understanding?

There are many ways in which research can inform how we think about and understand children and young people, some of which are discussed in Chapters 1 and 2. Investigations can add to existing bodies of knowledge which explain how and why children and young people behave in certain ways, providing new ways of understanding things which perhaps had not been considered before. Investigations can also challenge what we consider to be basic common sense. In addition, research can explore different ways of engaging with children and young people. Such a range of choices and possible avenues for investigation naturally incur disagreements. Rather than being a shortcoming, such disagreement can present researchers with a number of opportunities to advance knowledge through discussion and debate (McKechnie and Hobbs 2004). This leads on to another issue; how research ideas are shared within and across different academic, professional and policy focused communities. These themes are introduced here, using an example of one research study which explored children's literacy practices. This example illustrates how research can find new ways of studying children's experiences, enrich research knowledge and lead to the sharing of that knowledge through research dissemination.

Example 1: Inclusive early literacy practices

In this project the researchers, Flewitt, Nind and Pahl (2009) set out to explore the communicative experiences and literacy practices of three 4-year-old children identified with special educational needs who each attended special and mainstream early education settings, as their parents felt this combination would offer their child 'the best of both worlds'. To better understand the complicated lives these children led, and how they communicated and interacted in the very different environments of their home, a special setting and a mainstream setting, the researchers decided to use ethnographic, video case studies along with detailed analysis of how the children communicated not just through words, but through multiple 'modes', that is, through their gestures, body movements, facial expressions and gaze direction. Some of the research findings about one of the young children, Mandy, are discussed below.

Flewitt et al. (2009: 214) argue that for many young children identified with special educational needs during the early stages of their lives, it is often not clear what levels of literacy they may achieve. A 'skills-based approach' to understanding and exploring literacy assumes a 'normative pace' in which children move through stages of literacy development, often according to age and what is perceived as appropriate to their cognitive development. In much academic literature, language and literacy are defined by well-established traditions within psychology, with a strong emphasis upon developmental trajectories. As a consequence, language and literacy development are often viewed as universal processes. This view is reflected in policy and practice within the UK where literacy is emphasised as a curricular goal underpinned by the development of competencies in the skills of reading and writing. Such a perspective can be potentially limiting, but there are alternative approaches, as Flewitt et al. (2009: 212) suggest:

> If literacy is viewed as embedded in social practice rather than as a set of technical skills concerned with reading and writing, then separating children from literacy experiences due to perceptions of their cognitive ability effectively devalues how they construct meanings in the social worlds they experience ...

Flewitt et al. (2009) propose that a broader analysis of literacy as a social process focuses on how young children use a range of shared sign systems in their meaning making, and that these vary according to the interpersonal and social settings they find themselves in. Multimodality draws on linguistic theories of communication known as social semiotics (Halliday 1978). This approach considers how we all make choices when we are communicating, and these choices depend on how we perceive the social situation we are in. In early years research for example, this approach has been used to illustrate how children learn to communicate and become literate in many different ways, not just through language, but through learning to use combinations of different modes, such as gesture, gaze, movement, etc.

In order to capture the in-depth data that is required to explore and better understand the literacy practices of young children with special educational needs, the researchers in this study applied a qualitative approach, using observations, interviews with parents and staff, and diary notes completed by researchers and parents. Video observations were conducted both at home and in the different educational settings that the children attended. This allowed the researchers to capture the multi-modal nature of Mandy's interaction and meaning-making across each setting rather than limit the analysis to more language-focused conceptualisations of communication.

The research revealed contrasting perspectives on what could be regarded as a literacy practice and showed how some definitions can potentially limit how children such as Mandy are perceived. These contrasting perspectives are reflected in the title of this research article ('If she's left with books she'll just eat them'):

> ... Mandy's mother acknowledged her daughter's less conventional exploration of books: 'If she's left with books she'll just eat them'. At this time in Mandy's young life, books were literally indigestible for her if left on her own, although she tried her best to devour them. However ... with guided support in inclusive literacy events, books and other literacy artefacts became a rich source of mutual enjoyment and shared multi-modal meaning-making. (Flewitt et al. 2009: 214)

Flewitt et al. raise an important issue as they reflect on the design of their research which considered literacy in its broadest sense and enabled the research to move beyond solely addressing 'talk'. The research reveals different viewpoints in terms of how literacy events are conceptualised, how they are practised in education and care settings and also how they are interpreted through research. Relying upon psychological models of cognitive development can create a narrow focus and limit opportunities to examine a much broader understanding of communication and literacy. This research challenges conventional ways of thinking about literacy and has implications for how literacy is defined and understood by researchers, academics, practitioners, parents and others interested in language and literacy. It also addresses methodological issues in terms of how researchers design their studies to produce knowledge about literacy practices which can include all children and not just those who rely on 'talk'. If the researchers in this study had only paid attention to the children's language, then they would not have been able to gain these insights.

The researchers in this study also built upon the relationships with parents, practitioners and academic colleagues that they had developed throughout the investigative process to communicate their findings in a variety of ways. This research was disseminated through academic journal articles, chapters in books and articles in popular magazines that are bought by parents and practitioners. It therefore influenced knowledge and understanding about the literacy abilities of young children with special educational needs by contributing to on-going academic and public debates about how the abilities of young children with learning difficulties can be overlooked and about the nature of literacy practices, how they are defined and how they are studied. Reaching out to different audiences for their research and sharing their findings with parents, academics and professionals was an important consideration for these researchers.

Research of this kind offers scope for practitioners to consider their own practice and how children are conceptualised in relation to their education and care labels, which shape and often limit practitioners' and professionals' expectations of what children can achieve – how they can be 'enabled' by those around them rather than 'disabled'. This research also examines how professional practice can be developed to be more observant of and responsive to individual children's capabilities. In this way, research can contribute directly to professional practice.

However, the relationship between research and practice is not always clear-cut and closer inspection reveals issues concerning the application of research to practice. Edwards (2004: 258) states that sharing research is not simply a matter of making research 'accessible and available as commodities' but rests upon a complex process within research practice, where researchers must reflect carefully upon which issues are likely to be deemed relevant and of interest to policy-makers and practitioners.

How can research contribute to professional practice?

Many authors have drawn attention to the tendency within social science to examine issues that do not always reflect the experiences or interests of practitioners as well as children, young people and their families (Crivello and Murray 2012). Research findings rarely feed directly into practice (McKechnie and Hobbs 2004) and it is often difficult to generalise from knowledge which reflects distinct and at times idiosyncratic aspects of professional practice. Sharing knowledge is a complex process. How then can research be designed to contribute to practice in ways which might be beneficial to practitioners by representing issues which resonate to those most affected and which can be shared in ways which are productive?

Professional practice has and continues to be the focus of research across many fields, including education, health and social care. The analysis of professional practice can be undertaken by academic researchers, policymakers and practitioners. The next example discussed here details research undertaken by myself and colleagues in collaboration with practitioners at the University of Worcester (see Cooper and Ellis 2011) and draws upon the reflections of one practitioner researcher, Carole. Practitioner research refers to the gathering of data by practitioners, within case study/professional contexts, with the intention of developing greater knowledge and understanding about their own practice and/or about the practices that operate in the setting where they work (see this volume, Chapter 11). The idea is that by critically analysing practice, practitioners can action change and develop their practice based on greater insight (Tricoglus, 2001). Practitioners can draw upon a wealth of different approaches to critically examine their own practice, including action research and ethnographic enquiry, for example. As an experienced practitioner working within an education/social care context, Carole reflects on the value of ethnographic practitioner research for identifying service user needs and how the identification of need provides the impetus to develop and improve practice within multi-agency professional contexts.

Example 2: Enhancing paternal engagement in a fathers' group at a Children's Centre

My aim is to raise paternal engagement and I need to find out what are the barriers or problems that stop fathers from engaging in services we currently offer … (adapted from Ellis 2007)

As an experienced family support worker within a multi-agency professional team supporting family engagement with local services, Carole was keen to explore why fathers did not engage with the services on offer at their local Children's Centre. She set out to design an ethnographic research project, using observation, interview and questionnaire analysis, which could address the feasibility of establishing a 'fathers' group'.

Carole's research was situated within policy frameworks which recognise the need for professionals to support families (*Every Child Matters*, DfES 2004) and promote fathers' participation and engagement (*The Children's Plan*, DCSF 2007; *Aiming High for Children: Supporting Families*, DfES 2007). Fathers are a 'hard-to-reach' group, as Carole acknowledges upon reflection of her experience within her workplace where father engagement was low:

Our services offer early education integrated with child care, family support and outreach to parents and children and we should be engaging with fathers who previously have been excluded from services and whose children are at risk of poor outcomes … (Ellis 2007: 5)

A key question for Carole was how she could gather evidence which would allow her to consider the viability of establishing a fathers' group when she had such little contact with fathers. She drew upon her own professional knowledge working in the local community with other multi-agency social, education and healthcare professionals to establish contacts with local ante-natal groups, where fathers were present, along with church-led community fathers' groups.

Carole designed her research so she could establish contact, build relationships and through these relationships gain insights into fathers' views and experiences. Carole utilised her regular contact with other service users, particularly mothers, with whom she had regular contact, to devise a questionnaire which she could distribute to fathers within her setting via their partners. She also extended her ethnographic approach to observe and gather field notes in various fathers' groups which were well-established within her local community:

> Attendance at a fathers' direct conference gave me many issues to consider and reflect on, the first and foremost was to address my personal view of paternal engagement and would my views prohibit me from actively encouraging fathers to engage in sessions that we run from the centre ... The research has contributed to a greater understanding of a father's engagement from a male perspective ... Attendance at fathers' groups gave me insight into issues men face. (Ellis 2007: 8)

By accessing and observing within different groups and gaining some insight into how fathers felt in relation to engagement, Carole was able to consider some of the issues fathers face and to identify how she could use these insights to inform her own professional practice. This was particularly evident in her description of a critical incident when joining a local community fathers' group:

> Being in this male environment was sometimes uncomfortable. I heard a comment that was directed at me deliberately by one respondent who said, 'we don't have mums here, it's for dads only'. I found that this made me empathise with fathers who access services that we provide that are predominately female environments and how acceptance into a group is important to feeling valued and welcome. (Ellis 2007: 14)

Carole presents a personal account of what she learnt during her research and demonstrates how she was prepared to be challenged, to be critical of herself and to make changes where necessary. She reflects on how research enhanced her early years professional knowledge and enabled her to examine her personal practice and personal views. It also involved looking at change that would improve the quality of the services she offered to the families she supported.

By researching her own practice and addressing the views of fathers, Carole recognised the need to develop more paternal engagement, which she felt would enhance the child-focused family support provided within her own professional setting. Carole used her research findings to share more widely within her professional setting. Exchanging ideas and sharing local knowledge are important aspects of multi-agency professional practice. For Carole, this was a key feature of her professional role within the Children's Centre. Carole reflected on the value of exploring and scrutinising her own practice and the needs of the families she supported in order to consider how she could develop her practice to respond to diverse needs. She used her local knowledge to share with colleagues within her setting.

This example illustrates one way of conducting practitioner research which can inform professional practice. It is by no means the only way. The research conducted by Flewitt, Nind and Payler also had an impact on local practice, and has been read by a wide practitioner audience, with potential wider impact. On a more local scale, ethnographic research, like Ellis' study, provides opportunities for practitioners to examine their own practice. Through in-depth critical analysis practitioners can examine the needs within their own professional settings and consider different ways of meeting such needs. The value of any research rests upon how it can influence and inform. This can mean how it is useful within a particular local context or how it can be useful for others across different professional contexts. Research does not necessarily provide answers or indicate ways of working which can be transposed neatly across different contexts, but what it can do, as Nias (1993: 146) suggests, is provide ways of 'looking forward'.

Debates have questioned how research about any one setting or field of professional practice can be generalised and be relevant to other quite different professional sites and contexts (Schofield, 1993). The value of research for professional practice rests upon its capacity to offer insights and understandings which can transform ways of working (Edwards, 2004). Of course not all research is useful in exploring ways to develop and improve professional practice, and not all research will necessarily have positive outcomes. For example, Hammersley and Scarth (1993) draw attention to the misuse and misrepresentation of research in practice. Policies and professional practice designed to support children, young people and their families have been criticised for drawing upon research approaches which define childhood and youth in universal terms and neglect contextualised, local and cultural experiences (Durand 2010). Furthermore, policy is not always underpinned by robust research findings and the process through which research findings become translated into policy is neither linear nor straightforward.

How can research feed into policy?

The relationship between research and policymaking is multifaceted, and research findings may often be at odds with policy initiatives. Policymaking reflects a politically charged arena where decisions are often made in the interests of what is deemed 'best for' children, young people and their families in the absence of research evidence (Crivello and Murray 2012). In recent years there has been mounting pressure to ensure practice and policymaking is more evidence based (Roberts 2004). But who decides on the issues which are important? Do adult researchers and policymakers share the same concerns as children, young people, their families and the practitioners who implement policies? How are the rights of children and young people situated within research practice?

The next research example details the longitudinal *Young Lives* (*YL*) international study of poverty. This project (www.younglives.org.uk) provides a unique example of a longitudinal international study (2001–2017) which seeks to explore the local realities and experiences of 12,000 children and young people living in Ethiopia, India, Peru and Vietnam (see Chapter 14 for a researcher's account of one aspect of this study). *YL* uses a combination of approaches and methods to examine experiences of poverty across a range of local and global perspectives, and it promotes the rights of children and young people to contribute to research on matters which may affect their lives.

Example 3: Researching young lives

> If *Young Lives* research is to contribute to policy change that translates into visible grass-roots impacts for children and their households, it will be important to invest in fostering in-depth, longer-term relationships. (Thi Lan and Jones 2005: 8)

The *YL* international study contributes to an existing body of literature which recognises the barriers and sometimes poor linkages between research, policy and practice. It sets out to strengthen these linkages through careful research design and dissemination, and by focusing on three broad themes; the dynamics of childhood poverty, experiences of poverty and transitions.

In order to examine experiences of poverty and how these can be improved, the *YL* research team designed a longitudinal research project which could explore the life paths that children, young people and their families follow, in order to understand diverse needs and what strategies may help to support and break the 'cycle of poverty'. During the early stages of research planning, the *YL* team recognised the importance of building long-term relationships with policymakers, practitioners, children, young people and their families.

The emphasis upon relationships within research practice is important here and reflects the way in which the *YL* project has been devised to promote 'ongoing consultation' and 'discussion of relevance', throughout the research process, and to maintain a clear dialogue between researchers, policymakers and practitioners, as well as children, young people and their families (Crivello and Murray 2012: 2). Consultation recognises the importance of multiple views and stakeholder interests. The emphasis upon establishing relationships is also evident in the channels of communication that are implicit within *YL* and which enable all stakeholders to share their ideas and feed their views back throughout the study. Crivello and Murray (2012) suggest that this approach re-conceptualises dissemination and shifts the emphasis away from sharing research findings as outcomes at the end of the research process, towards regarding dissemination as an on-going process of consultation, negotiation and knowledge exchange.

As a collaborative project, *YL* draws upon expertise across a number of academic disciplines, including anthropology, economics, education, health, psychology and sociology in consultation with local community families, children, young people, practitioners and policy makers. This promotes a holistic approach which recognises the importance of studying individual children and young people and how their experiences and views of poverty are shaped by personal, social and cultural contexts; for example, how the influences of family life, school, leisure time, healthcare, work and economic forces combine to impact upon experiences of poverty.

YL combines quantitative data collection – a survey of all 12,000 children, young people and their primary caregivers – in conjunction with qualitative analysis with a smaller, sub-sample, in order to:

> … share some of the children's own perspectives on the world and their reflections and responses to our research – in their own words. This is an essential part of the *Young Lives* approach – to ensure children's voices are heard and their participation is a core value of the study (www.younglives.org.uk/what-we-do)

Longitudinal projects like *YL* are based on engagement and repeated observation of the same children, young people and their families over long periods of time. Applying a combined, mixed-method approach facilitates a broad-based understanding of the range of issues and experiences of growing up and experiences of poverty. Repeated observation enables researchers to examine the same children, young people and their families and how their experiences of poverty change in relation to life transitions. In this way, the *YL* team set about building in-depth case studies of local experiences across international contexts.

The significance of longitudinal research rests upon its capacity to unveil patterns of change and development in the lives of selected groups of people and so provides insight into everyday life. The *YL* project has developed various approaches to engage with children and young people. Thi Lan and Jones (2005: 12) describe two forms of participation developed in Vietnam as part of their research:

> In Young Lives Vietnam, children have been given opportunities to express their concerns and those of their families and communities to local policy-makers. Two major forms of child participation have been developed: provincial Children's Fora and Young Journalist Clubs. By involving children in the Young Lives project, the aim is to produce more reliable information about children because no one can understand children and children's needs better than themselves. Moreover, children's voices will constitute a very good reference resource not only for policy-makers and the community, but also for future revisions of the Young Lives surveys and research.

In order to represent the childhood voices, *YL* carried out a series of participatory projects. This led to the making of a film 'Voicing Experiences' (www.younglives.org.uk/what-we-do/children's perspective/india-participation-film) which derives from a series of theatre workshops held with children and young people from three different communities in Mahaboobnagar and Hyderabad in India, portraying their lives over a period of six months. It uses children's and young people's own words and performances to communicate their own views on poverty in which drug and alcohol abuse, domestic violence, parental injury and pressure to drop out from school and work are just some of the topics raised.

Longitudinal research projects, such as *YL*, are exceptionally far reaching in terms of their scope. They provide data and insights which are relevant across education, health and social care sectors and so are of interest to parents, policymakers and practitioners, as well as children and young people. Longitudinal research can achieve such broad reach by virtue of addressing a number of themes, working with a large participant sample across an extended period of time over which change and development can be observed.

This type of research not only focuses on views but acknowledges the possibility that children and young people may raise themes and share experiences which perhaps would not be considered from an adult researcher perspective. During their analysis in Ethiopia on the effects of poverty following bereavement, Crivello and Murray (2012: 3) describe how the everyday concerns of young people whose parents had died tended to centre around the risks and impact of poverty rather than their 'status as orphans', and this finding challenged the researchers' own assumptions. Similarly, the book *Changing Lives in a Changing World: Young Lives Children Growing Up* (Van der Gaag with Pellis and Knowles 2012) provides a series of 24 stories from *YL* children and young people who describe the issues affecting their lives. Seble's story provides a unique insight into a young woman's experience growing up in Ethiopia. Seble and her mother talk about girls' decisions to marry and how these are set against cultural assumptions and practices such as female genital cutting. *YL* continues to explore how many Ethiopian girls insist on getting married young or undergoing female genital cutting. Traditionally, both practices are perceived as a way of protecting girls and keeping them safe from sexual activity outside of marriage, which is regarded as socially unacceptable.

Seble's story offers a glimpse into aspects of her life experience and how this has changed since getting married. She also touches upon social practices within her culture, such as her relationship with her mother since marrying and the protection that marriage affords. Personal reflections such as these enable *YL* to explore children and young people's experiences as they interact with diverse social and cultural influences. This provides the capacity for further research to identify the needs of young people, such as Seble, and to focus on the systems of support that are in place.

The *YL* research project illustrates how research can be designed to address the importance of relationships within research practice and how these can be maintained to accommodate knowledge sharing, consultation and dissemination as an ongoing process. Longitudinal research has the capacity to combine methods and approaches over an extended time period which allows researchers to track and examine in-depth experiences as they change and respond to social and cultural forces.

This chapter has provided brief examples of three very different research projects to illustrate that issues related to policy and practice can be addressed in a variety of ways (Nutley et al., 2002). Research can take many forms and in this chapter you have considered how contrasting approaches, including longitudinal, survey and ethnographic case studies produce knowledge in different ways and consequently influence how we understand and work with children and young people. If policy and practice are to be informed by research, then we need to explore possible connections, such as how research can address questions that are considered important or useful to practitioners and policymakers at particular moments in time, and research which represents the views and experiences of children, young people and their families (Edwards, 2004). We also need to reflect on how investigations can be designed to examine local and global issues and how knowledge is shared across diverse academic, policy and practitioner communities.

Summary

Childhood and youth research represents a broad interdisciplinary field and draws upon a variety of different ways to produce knowledge about children and young people. Research can be designed in a variety of ways to serve different purposes, and in so doing can make distinct contributions. Research continues to advance new ways of thinking about children and young people and contributes to existing and well-established bodies of knowledge. Through careful consideration of how investigations can build relationships which represent service users as well as service providers, research can develop as a process of negotiation, knowledge building and sharing, and provide clear linkages between research, theory, policy and practice. Such a process has the capacity to produce knowledge which can deeply influence the lives of children, young people and their families.

References

Baumrind, D. (1966) 'Effects of authoritative parental control on child behaviour', *Child Development*, 37(4): 887–907.
Bowlby, J. (1969) *Attachment: Attachment and Loss (Vol. 1)*, 2nd edition. New York: Basic Books.

Brannen, J., Heptinstall, E. and Bhopal, K. (2000) *Connecting Children: Care and Family Life in Later Childhood*. London: Routledge Falmer.

Carsten, J. (2004) *After Kinship*. Cambridge: Cambridge University Press.

'Children's perspectives', www.younglives.org.uk/what-we-do/childrensperspectives/children's-voices (accessed 4 April 2013).

Cooper, V.L. and Ellis, C. (2011) 'Ethnographic practitioner research', in S. Callan and M. Reed (eds), *Work-Based Research in the Early Years*. London: Sage.

Crivello, G. and Murray, H. (2012) 'Why strengthening the linkages between research and practice is important: Learning from Young Lives', *Young Lives Policy Brief* 19. Oxford: Young Lives.

Department for Children, Schools and Families (DCSF) (2007) *The Children's Plan*. Nottingham: DCSF.

Department for Education and Skills (DfES) (2004) *Every Child Matters: Change for Children*. Nottingham: DfES.

Department for Education and Skills (DfES) (2007) *Aiming High for Children: Supporting Families*. Nottingham: DfES.

Douglas, G. (2004) *An Introduction to Family Law*. Oxford. Oxford University Press.

Dunn, J. and Deater-Deckard, K. (2001) *Children's Views of their Changing Families*. York: Joseph Rowntree Foundation/YPS.

Durand, T.M. (2010) 'Celebrating diversity in early care and education settings: Moving beyond the margins', *Early Child Development and Care*, 180(7): 835–48.

Edwards, A. (2004) 'Education', in S. Fraser, V. Lewis, S. Ding, M. Kellett and C. Robinson (eds), *Doing Research with Children and Young People*. London: Sage.

Ellis, C. (2007) 'A feasibility study into the enhancement of paternal engagement at a fathers' group in the Children's Centre', unpublished foundation degree thesis in early years, University of Worcester.

Erickson, E. (1968) *Identity: Youth and Crisis*. New York: Norton.

Flewitt, R., Nind, M. and Payler, J, (2009) '"If she's left with books she'll just eat them": Considering inclusive multimodal literacy practices', *Early Childhood Literacy*, 9(2): 211–33.

Foley, P. and Rixon, A. (2008) *Changing Children's Services: Working and Learning Together*. Bristol: Policy Press.

Halliday, M.A.K. (1978) *Language as Social Semiotic: The Social Interpretation of Language and Meaning*. London: Edward Arnold.

Hammersley, M. and Scarth, J. (1993) 'Beware of wise men bearing gifts: A case study in the misuse of educational research', in R. Gomm and P. Woods (eds), *Educational Research in Action*. London: Paul Chapman.

Ivan-Smith, E. (1998) Appendix 3: 'The United Nations Convention on the Rights of the Child – history and background', in V. Johnson, E. Ivan-Smith, G. Gordon, P. Pridmore and P. Scott (eds), *Stepping Forward: Children and Young People's Participation in the Developmental Process*. London: Intermediate Technology Publications. pp. 310–12

Mayall, B. (2002) *Towards a Sociology for Childhood: Thinking from Children's Lives*. Buckingham: Open University Press.

McKechnie, J. and Hobbs, S. (2004) 'Childhood studies', in S. Fraser, V. Lewis, S. Ding, M. Kellett and C. Robinson (eds), *Doing Research with Children and Young People*. London: Sage.

Montgomery, H. (2009) 'Children and families in an international context', in H. Montgomery and M. Kellett (eds), *Children and Young People's Worlds: Developing Frameworks for Integrated Practice*. Bristol: The Policy Press.

Morrow, V. (2009) 'Children, young people and their families in the UK', in H. Montgomery and M. Kellett (eds), *Children and Young People's Worlds: Developing Frameworks for Integrated Practice*. Bristol: The Policy Press.

Nias, J. (1993) 'Primary teachers talking: A reflexive account of longitudinal research', in M. Hammersley (ed.), *Educational Research: Current Issues*. London: Paul Chapman.

Nutley, S., Davies, H. and Walter, I. (2002) *Evidence Based Policy and Practice: Cross Sectors Lessons from the UK*. ESRC UK Centre for Evidence Based Policy and Practice: Working Paper 9.

Piaget, J. (1962) *The Language and Thought of the Child*. London: Routledge & Kegan Paul.

Prout, A. and James, A. (1997) 'A new paradigm for the sociology of childhood', in A. James and A. Prout (eds), *Constructing and Reconstructing Childhood: Contemporary Issues in the Sociological Study of Childhood*, 2nd edition. London: Falmer Press.

Roberts, H. (2004) 'Health and social care', in S. Fraser, V. Lewis, S. Ding, M. Kellett and C. Robinson (eds) *Doing Research with Children and Young People*. London: Sage.

Robertson, J. and Robertson, J. (1989) *Separation and the Very Young*. London: Free Association Books.

Rutter, M. (1979) 'Maternal deprivation, 1972–1978: New findings, new concepts, new approaches', *Child Development*, 50(2): 283–305.

Schaffer, H.R. and Emerson, P.E. (1964) 'The development of social attachments in infancy', *Monographs of the Society for Research in Child Development*, 29(3), serial number 94.

Schofield, J.W. (1993) 'Increasing the generalizability of qualitative research', in M. Hammersley (ed.), *Educational Research: Current Issues*. London: Paul Chapman.

Thi Lan, P. and Jones, N. (2005) 'The ethics of research reciprocity: Making children's voices heard in poverty reduction policy-making in Vietnam', *Young Lives Working Paper* 25. Oxford: Young Lives.

Tricoglus, G. (2001) 'Living the theoretical principles of critical ethnography', *Education Research*, 9(1): 135–48.

United Nations (1989) *Convention on the Rights of the Child*. New York: United Nations.

Van der Gaag, N. with Pells, K. and Knowles, C. (2012) *Changing Lives in a Changing World: Young Lives Children Growing Up*. Oxford: Young Lives.

4 Doing Qualitative Research with Children and Young People

Sue Bucknall

Introduction

Over recent decades there has been a significant change in the roles that children and young people have been able to play in research. This change has been especially marked when their own lived experiences have been the focus for investigation. So, while child-related research does not always involve children and young people as active participants, research *with* them rather than research *on* them is increasingly common. This chapter considers some of the issues that have been brought to the fore by this shift. It begins by looking at why and how research with children and young people has evolved, before attending to the complex and pervasive notion of children's voices and the related issues of silence, representation and representativeness. The research relationships which adults might build with children and young people as 'other' to themselves provide the focus for the final section. Throughout the chapter, the need for researchers working with children and young people to reflect critically on their research is highlighted, supported by examples of reflective practice.

The evolution of research with children and young people

The recognition of children and young people as competent social agents has challenged views of adults as the experts on children's lives and of children as unreliable informants, incapable of understanding the research process or of making decisions about participating, as discussed in previous chapters (Morrow 2005; Woodhead and Faulkner 2008). Particularly relevant to this shift in thinking are Articles 12 and 13 of the United Nations Convention on the Rights of the Child (CRC). Encompassing children's rights to access information and to have their views sought and given due weight in all matters affecting them, these pave the way for children to voice their opinions on activities and decisions which shape their lives. Since it is intended that these rights should be exercised in all areas of children's lives, it follows that children should be offered authentic choices and opportunities for the expression of views during research into their lives and experiences. Information and choice, for example, are crucial elements of the process of gaining informed consent from child participants. Indeed, the revised ethical guidelines offered by the British Educational Research Association (BERA 2011) make specific reference to CRC Article 12 in requiring that children should be facilitated to give fully informed consent.

Despite the implications of the CRC, opportunities for children and young people to receive information and to make choices regarding their participation in research are usually mediated by adults. Nevertheless, while power inequalities in adult–child relationships will always be present in some way, in some spheres of social science research children increasingly take an active part in the research process as participants or as co-researchers. Participatory research has begun to show that children of primary-school age are aware of community, national and global issues, and would like to be involved in helping to solve problems and to be better informed (Taylor et al. 2008).

Despite research methodology traditionally being considered too difficult for children and young people to learn and to implement, Kellett argues that the attributes of researchers 'are not synonymous with being an adult' (2005: 9). There now exist many reports in the literature in which adult researchers attest to the high levels of competence displayed by young co-researchers and examples of research projects successfully led by children and young people of different ages and abilities are also increasingly reported (Kellett 2011; Bucknall 2009, 2012). One such project is described in Research Example 1.

Research Example 1

In 2011, 70 children and young people living and working in four rural communities in northern Nicaragua conducted research with the aim of addressing social problems that they had identified as causes of concern to them, notably violence and alcohol abuse. Their research was facilitated and supported by CESESMA, an independent NGO, but young people, aged between 9 and 19, led all stages of the research process. As a result of their research findings, the young people were able

(Continued)

> *(Continued)*
>
> to make recommendations and to draw up action plans. A crucial element of these plans was the identification of 'areas of influence' where their recommendations could be shared. Although their reports acknowledge that it is too soon for the impact of their studies to be evaluated (something that is planned for the future), their research is described as having considerable impact on the young researchers involved and on the adults in their communities, especially in terms of recognition of the young people's competences and of their potential to effect change (CESESMA, 2012).

By highlighting an example of active research *by* children and young people, I am not suggesting that such research is more valuable than that conducted by adults. Rather, it demonstrates how children and young people's expertise on their own lived experiences can drive research, how their involvement can help them to understand the purpose of research in seeking to make a difference, and just how far levels of children and young people's participation in research can extend. While this particular level of engagement in research is still unusual, it does help to illustrate why it is not acceptable to view children and young people only as passive sources of data.

The voices of children and young people

It is widely acknowledged that, historically, children have lacked a voice in the writings of sociologists, historians and anthropologists and have relied upon adults to describe and account for their lives and experiences. More recently, increasing recognition of children's rights and social status together with concerns about the power and control implicated in the ways adults access children's perspectives have prompted a move towards attending to the voices of children and young people. This is now seen as imperative when child- or childhood-related research is carried out. Certainly, it seems that the introduction of new participatory research methods is likely to increase the potential for children and young people to express their views on matters under investigation and to relate their own experiences. The requirement of Article 12 that 'due weight' be given to what children and young people say is significant in this context, signalling that voice is not only about expression but, perhaps more importantly, about being listened to and being heard: it is about being taken seriously.

The notion of voice, however, is problematic. As researchers, we need to understand and acknowledge the complexities of voice work and to adopt a critical approach to a process which, superficially, might suggest that it is enough to merely listen to, record and report what children and young people have to say.

The oft-heard phrase 'giving children a voice', for example, suggests that voice is a gift, attainable only through the generosity of adult others. The assumption that 'giving children a voice' in research will address inequalities in child–adult power relationships thus presents something of a paradox since participative opportunities for children and young people are, indeed, in the gift of the adults leading the projects, who control not only what can be talked about but also the methods employed. Providing children and young people with information about the focus and purpose of the research and the means by which their views might be sought – and, crucially, offering participation as a choice – allows them some control and are important elements of a researcher's ethical behaviour. This is important in settings such as schools where opportunities for children to question adult decisions are unusual.

A further point for consideration is that voice is not an autonomous production. As Maybin (2006) explains, we all communicate by using the words of others. She cites Bakhtin, the Russian philosopher, who argued that our voices are not neutral, but are imbued with the voices of other people and with the social contexts and settings in which they were used. When we speak 'in our own words', our utterances are reconstructions, crafted to meet our own intentions from the utterances and intentions of others. Bakhtin spoke of the 'struggle' we have to make meaning from the different connotations and associations of the words and phrases we use. Thus, voice is work and it is social, arising from and influenced in its reproduction by different discourses and practices. As researchers, we need to avoid the danger of '[taking] for granted that children have message-like thoughts that can be exchanged, and intentions that match the situations defined by adults'. Instead, we need to recognise 'the complexity of communication as a local interactional activity' (Komulainen 2007: 25). This means understanding that data is co-constructed, a result of what is asked and the responses the research participant makes according to her or his understanding of context and setting. For this reason, adopting the term 'data construction' rather than 'data collection' seems to make more sense, the latter suggesting that data is just 'out there' waiting to be gathered in rather than the outcome of joint enterprise between the researcher and the researched.

The role of the CRC in promoting the voices of children and young people gives rise to a further paradox. Since its implementation, critics have argued that, by focusing on 'the child', the CRC apparently ignores the many different ways in which childhood is experienced across the world. As a result of this oversight, 'projects that aim explicitly at children's empowerment through voice-giving may unintentionally mask, bury or silence their experiences and views' (Kallio 2012: 82). Research Example 2 illustrates that even when children and young people have been afforded the right to voice their opinions and to seek information, this is likely to be challenging in social and cultural contexts where their voices are more usually subdued.

Research Example 2

The Child Mobility Research Project aims to provide evidence that will improve transport policy in three countries in sub-Saharan Africa: Ghana, Malawi and South Africa (www.dur.ac.uk/child.mobility) and in particular, the mobility constraints which restrict access by children and young people to goods and services, including health and education. Such an undertaking is seen to be particularly challenging, not least because, in Africa, transport policy and practice is not only male dominated but focuses on construction and maintenance rather than social need. Consequently, while the concerns of the poor and of women have rarely informed policy development, the mobility needs of children are 'almost invisible' (Porter and Abane 2008: 155).

Academics involved in this project have reflected on the ethical responsibilities of researchers when children are engaged in active participatory research roles 'where local cultural constructions of childhood and associated economic imperative ... help shape the attitudes of adults to children's rights and responsibilities and inter-generational power relations' (Porter et al. 2010: 215). Porter and her colleagues point out that, although children have considerable responsibility in terms of labouring to support and care for family members, for example, the ways in which childhood tends to be culturally constructed in Africa means that children are positioned at the bottom of family hierarchies and expected to respect their elders. The inclusion of children under the age of 14 as research protagonists, therefore, was likely to 'subvert the traditional view of children's proper role as supporters, not leaders' (Porter et al. 2010: 217). An additional concern was that teenage male protagonists might be seen as a potential threat and cause of disruption since in some communities, earlier youth action and violence as a response to the anti-apartheid struggle affected how older generations perceived those that were younger. Porter et al. (2010) suggest two ways in which such concerns might be addressed. The first is to ensure that young research protagonists hold realistic expectations about the potential impact of the research in which they are involved. This means planning advocacy strategies involving young researchers that will obviate them being 'ignored, ... spurned, ridiculed or accused of arrogance' (Porter et al. 2010: 225). Facilitating the inclusion of child researchers' presentations in periodic 'consultative group meetings' with influential adults who are aware of the project aims, for example, has already met with some success. The second is to help older generations to value the work the young people have carried out by taking care to include them, as well as the young people involved, in the sharing of the research findings. In this way, Porter and her colleagues hope to prompt a new receptiveness to the roles young people can play in research in their communities.

Porter and her colleagues have signalled the ethical responsibility of adult researchers in taking steps to help ensure the voices of children and young people are listened to and taken seriously when the participatory roles young people have been encouraged to adopt might make them vulnerable to negativity in their communities. Reflection on these potential difficulties and on possible solutions – before, during and after research – seems imperative if participatory roles are to offer authentic opportunities for the voices of children and young people to make themselves heard.

Silence

Like voice, silence is not neutral but communicates meaning. It might, for example, signify unwillingness to participate at all, unhappiness about answering particular questions or misunderstanding of what is being asked or required. In research involving child voice, then, we need to account for ' ... why and how children's silences were recognised, noted, responded to and interpreted' (Lewis 2010: 19). Since silence can be more informative about children's perspectives than what is said (Spyrou 2011), it is clear that silence needs 'listening to' as carefully as other expressions of voice. Nevertheless, silence is not always the consequence of active choices made by participants. The actions of researchers, too, can be responsible for the production of silence, even if unintentionally. In Research Example 3, we see how reflection on their experiences helped two Swedish researchers to draw some conclusions about the complexities of silence.

Research Example 3

Alerby and Kostenius (2011) report on a research project which set out to investigate the psychosocial health of children and young people living in the Arctic. Responsible for conducting the research in Swedish Arctic regions, these two researchers adapted the World Health Organization (WHO) Cross-National Survey to gather data from 440 schoolchildren. Each question offered a range of possible responses alongside 'tick boxes' where students could indicate which aligned most closely to their opinions or experiences. Only responses placed correctly within the boxes were to be deemed valid during the process of analysis.

During this process, however, the researchers noticed that more than half of the completed questionnaires contained unanswered questions, had notes written by respondents in the margins and/or extra tick boxes inserted by respondents between or alongside those offered (these sometimes being accompanied by written messages). Alerby and Kostenius describe how these unexpected responses provided them with an opportunity to reflect on the use of questionnaires as research tools when the aim of research is to voice the perspectives and experiences of children and young people. A second round of analysis was decided upon, this time using a qualitative rather than a quantitative approach, in order to develop an understanding not only of the notes in the margins but also of the reasons why some items had not been completed. As a result of this analysis, Alerby and Kostenius identified two significant patterns: one accounting for messages that were 'silent' and another for those that were 'silenced'.

Silent voices

As Alerby and Kostenius (2011) discuss in their report, there are many reasons why questionnaire items might not be answered, including, for example, lack of interest in the topic, lack of time, carelessness or simply perceiving the question to be too personal or intrusive. The crucial point here, though, as they argue, is that 'non-messages' communicate meaning even if that meaning is not always readily apparent. It might be impossible to interpret non-responses in research situations, but to ignore the messages they might convey is to ignore the very voices that child voice research seeks to hear. Reflection on the research practices which may have prompted them is important.

In interview situations, silence as a response might be a little easier to read. After all, we recognise many of the ways meaning is communicated that do not rely on the spoken word and are adept at reading facial expressions, gestures and body language. We usually recognise when silence is comfortable and when it is threatening and understand that the meaning communicated by a challenging stare is very different from that suggested by a complete lack of eye contact or a hung head. In research interview situations, the noting and interpretation of silence is as important as the attention paid to the words spoken, just as it is during the process of analysis.

Our interpretation of silence during interviews will, of course, influence how we respond. There are often pressures associated with having to complete interviews, whether with individuals or groups, in the time allocated; covering all that we intend to poses the danger of us interrupting the very silences which might allow our participants to reflect on what they are being asked and to frame considered responses. Individual tolerances of the length of silence come into play here, as do cultural norms and the norms of behaviour in specific settings. Schoolchild interviewees who are familiar with the rapid responses expected by their teachers in class might feel they have to respond quickly to an interviewer, saying, 'I don't know', perhaps, when, given (or taking) more time, their response might be rather different. Alternatively, they simply might not want to respond (for further discussion, see Chapter 8, 'Interviews'). As researchers, then, we must consider how we are going to respond to children's silences. One useful strategy, as indicated, is simply to 'allow' silence rather than jumping in with a further question or utterance. Another, 'practical', strategy is to provide interviewees with cards that they can use to indicate the reason why they have not responded to a question immediately; they might hold up one to indicate that they do not want to answer the question, for example, or another to indicate that they are thinking about what they want to say (Bucknall 2012). Strategies such as this offer children choice and, at the same time, respect for their right to remain silent.

Voices that are silenced

In relation to the research described in Research Example 3, Alerby and Kostenius (2011) account for voices that were silenced through the use of their questionnaire. They explain that the first round of analysis did not take into account instances where children had amended or annotated the document because the range of possible responses offered did not allow them to express their own responses accurately. In one particularly apposite example, a child had responded to the question *How often do you play with friends after school?* by ticking the box indicating *1 day a week* but, underneath, wrote *Dammed taxi cab* [sic], thereby suggesting that there was a reason why he was unable to play with his friends after school. This, and similar instances, prompted Alerby and her colleague to question the use of survey-type questionnaires since they do not allow researchers to understand the reasons for participants' responses. When designing questionnaires, I have found it useful to provide space where children and young people can explain or expand on their responses to preceding 'tick box' responses if they want to. Without such opportunities, the illuminating clarifications I have sometimes been offered would have been silenced (see Figure 4.1).

Group interviews or focus groups, too, while promoted as methods which might diminish the inequalities involved in researcher–researched relationships, can silence the voices of children who choose to keep their own views to themselves in order not to contradict the majority views of their peers. As one 10-year old focus group participant explained to me after a session in which she had spoken very little, '... you are sort of in that place where you think, well, I think this but I really want to fit in with them'.

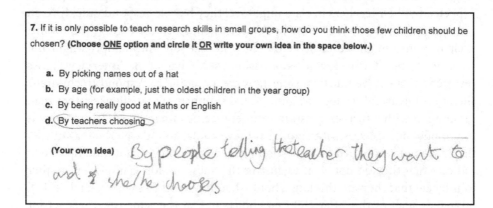

Figure 4.1 Extract from questionnaire completed by child

The uncritical use of any research instruments, however, is not the only way in which voices are silenced in research. While voice implies a participatory process, for some, silence and suppression are more likely outcomes. Young children and those with disabilities (especially those with speech and communication impairments) are often deliberately excluded from engaging in research initiatives by adult gatekeepers, as are those, particularly in schools, who are not well-equipped to articulate their views in ways that are seen to be appropriate. Bragg, for example, confirms that many reports accounting for voice research in schools ignore the fact that, in order to be listened to, students must enter an 'implicit contract' which requires them to 'speak responsibly, intelligently and usefully' (2001: 73); the voices of those who are unwilling or unable to comply are, consequently, silenced.

These voices, and the voices of those with language impairments or poor literacy skills, the very young or those who do not speak the majority language, are not always easy to 'hear'. In her study of the different ways in which very young children communicated meaning at home and in a pre school setting, for example, Flewitt (2005) identified a wide variety of non-verbal communicative strategies through which children and adults co-constructed meaning. As researchers, we can help to ensure that the voices of young children are not silenced by acknowledging, and developing strategies which take into account, the different ways in which they communicate. The 'Mosaic approach', discussed elsewhere in this volume, has proved effective in allowing the very young to give voice to their experiences and perspectives by harnessing the multimodal nature of their communication.

Reflection on our approach to hearing both voice and silence and acknowledgement of how some voices might be silenced during our research, even if inadvertently, are vital parts of an ethical and respectful research process. Related to this are the issues of *representation* and *representativeness*, and these provide a focus for the following section of this chapter.

Representation and representativeness

The terms *representation* and *representativeness* are used to convey different meanings in the context of research but both relate to how we strive to represent those we research in ways that are responsible and truthful. The distinction between these concepts often becomes blurred; nevertheless, in this section, we consider each separately.

Representation

In participatory research which purports to address the inequalities of power inherent in adult–child relationships, what happens to the data generated with young participants is particularly important, especially as it remains comparatively unusual for children and young people to have any control over the analysis, interpretation and reporting stages of research, although as the chapters in this book discuss, there is an increasing trend towards participatory approaches throughout the research process. As researchers, then, we have the responsibility of representing the voices of those we have researched to the audiences of our work. Increasingly, representation is referred to in the literature as *(re)*presentation or re-presentation. This is not the representation of participants in some kind of ambassadorial role (although in voice research this might, indeed, be an underlying role the researcher seeks to adopt), rather the concern is with recreating, for example, observed behaviour or spoken words in some form of transcription, and using that as a basis for the interpretation of data. The issue here is *how* this is done.

The wholesale reproduction of data generated during a research project is not practicable when producing reports. It is the role of the researcher to select data that respond to the research questions, this selection being informed both by the research literature and by the researcher's increasingly expert knowledge of the field. Neither is it possible to reproduce participants' quotations, for example, and let them stand alone without discussion, since the drawing out of themes is needed in order to guide the reader and to draw conclusions. Researchers, then, need to select which views to (re)present. So, while quotes given in research reports might be faithful records of participants' utterances, they are usually chosen by the researcher to illustrate a particular point. Such choices need to be subject to explicit critical reflection (James 2007). Furthermore, while we have a responsibility to listen carefully to – and make meaning from – what participants say, we have a concomitant responsibility to acknowledge that our interpretations of the data are driven inevitably by the research questions and the research literature and are as subjective and context-bound as the data itself. The perspectives or experiences voiced by children, whether these are vocal or expressed though other modes, will be those which they have chosen to share in response to how they perceive the purposes of the research in which they are participating, the relationship they have with the researcher and the context or setting in which the research is carried out.

It is widely acknowledged that adults can be guilty of misunderstanding, misrepresenting and sometimes disregarding children's perspectives. This is a particular danger when these conflict with the researcher's own experiences, interests and interpretations (Woodhead and Faulkner 2008). The concepts and categories which adult researchers identify in the data often correspond to the knowledge they bring to the study; they are not always generated by children and young people although they can be. In ethnographic research, for example, themes often emerge through interviews with participants which are participant generated even if the research is not participatory. Nevertheless, it is clear that even when the aim of research is to privilege the voices of children and young people, those voices can still be misrepresented or silenced during the processes of data selection and representation. Adults are not necessarily guilty of doing this deliberately; rather, they might find it problematic to interpret what children say (Sinclair 2004). The involvement of children and young people in the analysis and interpretation of their own data might help here but is not often feasible. Researchers need to explain how they have developed their categorisation schemes and to be open to other possible interpretations. Audiences of research can then decide for themselves whether or not the interpretations and conclusions offered are convincingly grounded in and supported by the data. All research papers are open to critique in this respect.

Representativeness

Representativeness in research involves asking two questions: 'How representative is the data presented in research reports in relation to the data generated during the research being reported?' and 'How representative were those involved as research participants in relation to the population they are deemed to represent?' These two separate but related issues are important considerations, for example, when the aim of research is to inform policy and practice in relation to a particular group of children or young people.

Selective processes are inevitably implicated in the choice of research participants and, no matter how the researcher plans to address issues of inclusion, they are often at the mercy of gatekeepers. It is worth bearing in mind here that when children are given a choice of participating or not, it is often those who are articulate, confident and interested who come forward. So, while choice is an important ethical consideration and itself an expression of voice (Bucknall 2012), such children cannot be representative of all children or even of the peer group to which they belong. As is often pointed out, no one child's voice can speak for all. Researchers need to be aware that attending to children's views, experiences and perspectives can, in fact, involve exclusionary practices which fail to recognise how diverse these can be, even when target populations have other characteristics in common. Identifying selection criteria which would help to ensure that the diversity of the target population is represented in the sample and discussing the desirability of inclusive research practices with gatekeepers are two ways in which researchers can seek to increase representativeness.

It could be argued, however, that no matter how research participants have been selected, they can only be representative of those who have consented to participate. Similarly, the data generated in response to a questionnaire item, for example, can only be seen as representative of those who chose – or were able – to complete that particular item. Such complexities are unavoidable but aiming for inclusivity through adopting a range of research tools and means of communicating information that meet the needs of diverse potential participants can go some way towards addressing them. What researchers can also do is be honest about how they hoped to select their samples, about what actually happened and why, and about the impact this might have had upon the conclusions that can be drawn or the claims that can be made regarding the group whose views, perspectives or experiences they seek to represent. What is needed, as Silverman (2001) summarises, is for researchers to demonstrate to their audiences why their claims should be believed. This is important if the findings of a particular study seem likely to be transferable to similar populations in other sites. It is also vital that, while identifying and representing data relevant to the study, examples that run counter to any conclusions that might be drawn are not excluded. The following research example demonstrates the impact of such exclusions on the outcome of one participatory project.

Research Example 4

Mand (2012) reports on a participatory arts-based project conducted with 9- and 10-year-old children of Bangladeshi origin attending two London schools. Part of a wider research study which sought to discover how children from South Asian families experience mobility across places, and, importantly, to develop innovative methods in migration research, the project involved the children in producing sketches of images they related to home and, separately, to being away. These were then used as raw material for the production of graffiti boards by a local 'spiritual' artist whose background was similar to those of the children. Although this participatory approach was intended by Mand to include children's voices within the research, she reports her unhappiness when discovering that the children would take a passive role in the production of the graffiti. Due in part to the artist's expressed need for consistency across the different panels, this was also, and more significantly, because the artist ruled out some of the images the children had produced. These were, he considered, controversial.

Mand describes how this selection process, carried out by an artist who she had chosen because of his apparent understanding of the project, 'stifled' some of the children's voices and 'felt like the antithesis of participatory practices': children's perspectives were 'moulded to fit a particular version of Islam based on an "adult" perspective' (2012: 156, 158). As part of the planned research output, the graffiti boards, along with banners produced using the children's pictures, were displayed by a well-known museum. These, however, were hung according to strict display rules which stipulated that they were to be placed out of children's reach. Their detail was thus rendered difficult to decipher. Other images were rejected by the museum as lacking visual impact. Moreover, it was a requirement of the museum that the text accompanying the exhibition be written by the researcher following strict museum-imposed criteria, a process, Mand states, of 're-inserting the authority of the researcher' (2012: 158). In spite of Mand's participatory approach, children's voices were subdued 'at the point of representation in the public space of the museum' (2012: 159).

While it might be interesting to consider what Mand would – or should – have done if she herself had considered any of the images to be controversial (this, itself, raising questions about the ethical responsibilities of researchers when faced with representing views that are overtly offensive), this example highlights the importance of honest and critical reflection on the processes which might lead to failures of representativeness. The audiences of our research need to know just *how* representative our data is of the *range* of views and perspectives offered by our participants.

Children and young people as 'other': positioning the researcher

No matter how childhood and adulthood are constructed culturally and socially, children will always be 'other' to adults. By implication, adults are 'other' to children. 'Otherness' lies in the inevitable power differentials between adult researchers and their young participants and in the undisputable fact that, while the former were all once children, it is not possible for them to enter the childhood worlds of today *as* children. This has implications for how adult researchers approach child-centred research, although, of course, the researcher–researched position as 'othered' does not come into play only in adult–child research. It can be argued, for example, that men are no more able to orient to the perspectives of women (and vice versa), the able-bodied to those of the disabled or those of one culture to those of another. The crux of the matter for all researchers is this: they must consider how they can best meet, or position themselves in relation to, their participants in order to build a rapport and thus help to address 'otherness'.

It is clear from reports of ethnographic research that adult researchers engaging in participant observation have adopted a variety of stances in relation to the children who have been the focus of their research in attempts not to disrupt their research settings. Perhaps the most widely cited example is Mandell's (1991) 'least adult' role. Adopted by Mandell during her study of 2–4-year olds' interactional behaviour in day care centres in the United States during the 1970s, this 'completely involved' role developed as she spent a considerable time alongside children as they played. Deliberately involving herself in situations where the children were not under direct staff supervision, she sought to resist exercising any authority over them. Instead, through her actions, she tried to minimise the social differences between herself and the children, to show that she believed the children's social worlds to be as important as those of adults and to attempt to find shared meaning through their social activities. By letting the children correct her when she 'broke the rules' she built not only a picture of how the children interacted with each other, but also trusting relationships between herself and the children. Together with establishing positive relationships between herself and other adults the children trusted, Mandell identifies this as essential in aiding her admittance to the children's worlds.

This strategy has been criticised for attempting to '[wish] away the complexity of the differences and similarities between children and adults' (Christensen 2004: 173) and ignoring the institutionally and contextually dependent understandings of children about what or who an adult is. In my own school-based research, children have often interrogated my identity, asking where I am from, what I do, whether I am a teacher, etc. Indeed, Christensen argues that responses to such questions, which help both researcher and researched to work out how they relate to one another, are critical in enabling 'children's genuine participation' (2004: 166). I have certainly found that honesty and openness have been vital in building trust with my young participants: in this, positioning myself as 'other' to the adults the children encounter in their daily lives at school seems to have been equally important in facilitating dialogue. One 10-year-old interviewee told me that, 'If you're working with people from school you say what they expect and not express your opinion, you say what they want to hear but if you're talking to [people from outside school] you can say what I want to this person [sic]'. Christensen poses two questions which she considers researchers need to ask themselves in order to address 'otherness': '[Are] the practices employed in the research process in line with and reflective of children's experiences, interests, values and everyday routines?' and 'What are the ways in which children routinely express and represent these in their everyday life?' (2004: 166). Whether or not children are or become willing to engage in research in positive and productive ways is in their gift. It is the responsibility of the researcher to try to meet them on their own terms.

Summary

The issues which have provided the focus for this chapter are those which are particularly pertinent to more recent understandings and practices in the field of research with children and young people. Far from being vulnerable, incompetent and unreliable, children are now widely acknowledged to be competent and rights-bearing social actors whose voices increasingly appear in social research. Nonetheless, we have also seen that such developments have not been – and should not be – accepted uncritically and need to be problematised if effective research with children and young people is to continue to evolve in a positive direction. Of particular significance here are the complexities of voice and the critical attention which needs to be paid to the ways in which this might be accessed, expressed, represented or silenced. Lahman, whose words I have chosen to end this chapter, summarises most eloquently the dilemmas faced by researchers working with children and young people and draws attention to the two elements which seem to me to be crucial facets of child-focused research, and which are articulated, implicitly or explicitly, throughout this chapter, that is, the need for constant critical reflection and respect:

> ... the moment we feel our research has captured an understanding of childhood we are on the shakiest ground. As long as we remain in a posture of questioning findings, reflexively considering the research process, acknowledging the power of our memories of childhood experiences over research interpretations, and respecting children, we are on firmer ground. (Lahman 2008: 283)

References

Alerby, E. and Kostenius, C. (2011) '"Dammed taxi cab" – how silent communication in questionnaires can be understood and used to give voice to children's experiences', *International Journal of Research and Method in Education*, 34(2): 117–30.

BERA (2011) *Ethical Guidelines for Educational Research* [online]. Available at: www.bera.ac.uk/publications/EthicalGuidelines (accessed 15 January 2013).

Bragg, S. (2001) 'Taking a joke: Learning from the voices we don't want to hear', *Forum*, 43(2): 70–73.

Bucknall, S. (2009) 'Children as researchers: Exploring issues and barriers in English primary schools', unpublished PhD thesis, Milton Keynes, The Open University. Available at: http://oro.open.ac.uk/23332/ (accessed 19 September 2012).

Bucknall, S. (2012) *Children as Researchers in Primary Schools: Choice, Voice and Participation*. London and New York: Routledge.

CESESMA (2012) *Learn to Live without Violence: Transformative Research by Children and Young People*. Matagalpa, Nicaragua, CESESMA, in association with The Centre for Children and Young People's Participation, University of Central Lancashire, UK.

Christensen, P. (2004) 'Children's participation in ethnographic research: Issues of power and representation', *Children & Society*, 18(2): 165–76.

Flewitt, R. (2005) 'Is every child's voice heard? Researching the different ways 3-year-old children communicate and make meaning at home and in a pre-school playgroup', *Early Years*, 25(3): 207–22.

James, A. (2007) 'Giving voice to children's voices: Practices and problems, pitfalls and potentials', *American Anthropologist*, 109(2): 261–72.

Kallio, K. (2012) 'Desubjugating childhoods by listening to the child's voice and childhoods at play', *ACME: An International E-Journal for Critical Geographies*, 11(1): 81–109.

Kellett, M. (2005) 'Children as active researchers: a new research paradigm for the 21st century?' [online]. Available at: http://oro.open.ac.uk/7539/ (accessed 9 November 2012).

Kellett, M. (2011) 'Empowering children and young people as researchers: Overcoming barriers and building capacity', *Child Indicators Research*, 4(2): 205–19.

Komulainen, S. (2007) 'The ambiguity of the child's "voice" in social research', *Childhood*, 14(1): 11–28.

Lahman, M. (2008) 'Always othered: Ethical research with children', *Journal of Early Childhood Research*, 6(3): 281–300.

Lewis, A. (2010) 'Silence in the context of "child voice"', *Children & Society*, 24(1): 14–23.

Mand, K. (2012) 'Giving children a "voice": Arts-based participatory research activities and representation', *International Journal of Social Research Methodology*, 15(2): 149–60.

Mandell, N. (1991) 'The least-adult role in studying children', in F. Waksler (ed.), *Studying the Social Worlds of Children: Sociological Readings*. London: Routledge Falmer. pp. 38–59.

Maybin, J. (2006) *Children's Voices: Talk, Knowledge and Identity*. Basingstoke: Palgrave Macmillan.

Morrow, V. (2005) 'Ethical issues in collaborative research with children', in A. Farrell (ed.), *Ethical Research with Children*. Maidenhead: Open University Press. pp. 150–65.

Porter, G. and Abane, A. (2008) 'Increasing children's participation in African transport planning: Reflections on methodological issues in a child-centred research project', *Children's Geographies*, 6(2): 151–67.

Porter, G., Hampshire, K., Bourdillon, M., Robson, E., Munthai, A., Abane. A. and Mashiri, M. (2010) 'Children as research collaborators: Issues and reflections from a mobility study in sub-Saharan Africa', *American Journal of Community Psychology*, 46(1–2): 215–27.

Silverman, D. (2001) *Interpreting Qualitative Data: Methods for Analysing Talk, Text and Interaction*. London: Sage.

Sinclair, R. (2004) 'Participation in practice: Making it meaningful, effective and sustainable', *Children and Society*, 18: 106–18.

Spyrou, S. (2011) 'The limits of children's voices: from authenticity to critical, reflexive representation', *Childhood*, 18(2): 151–65.

Taylor, N., Smith, A. and Gollop, M. (2008) 'New Zealand children and young people's perspectives on citizenship', *International Journal of Children's Rights*, 16: 195–210.

Woodhead, M. and Faulkner, D. (2008) 'Subjects, objects or participants? Dilemmas of psychological research with children', in P. Christensen and A. James (eds), *Research with Children: Perspectives and Practice*. London: Routledge. pp. 10–39.

5 Ethics

Priscilla Alderson

Introduction

This chapter begins by briefly considering the development of research ethics and its regulation, then outlines three main frameworks or approaches to thinking about ethics: principles, outcomes and rights. Some limitations and criticisms of research ethics are summarised, followed by sections on why research ethics matter, and on applying to an ethics review committee. The rest of the chapter reviews some of the key questions and processes related to ethics that arise throughout research projects, from first plans onwards. These include harm and benefit, privacy and confidentiality, information and consent. Concern with research ethics began in medicine, but besides healthcare this chapter also relates to research in education, welfare, youth, criminal justice, commercial and many other services and topics that affect children and young people.

Practical ethics

You might like to make a list of the problems that relate to ethics in the following hypothetical example, before you read the rest of the chapter. While this relates to only one kind of research, it raises questions that apply much more widely. Later, when you have read the chapter, you could decide whether there are any further points in this example that you could add to your list. Some of the main points are set out as basic ethical standards at the end of the chapter.

> Alisha worked in schools for a counselling support agency. The agency director, Dr Pete Wilson, was asked by one of their main funders to conduct an evaluation of their work and outcomes. The director wanted to video some of Alisha's sessions. Alisha asked about privacy and consent from the children and parents. 'They have given consent when they agreed to have the counselling, and evaluation is just a routine part of high quality work', Pete replied.
>
> *(Continued)*

(Continued)

When Alisha arrived for her next session with Kwame, aged 11, the video camera was already set up and partly concealed, and Dr Wilson was welcoming Kwame before leaving. Somehow Kwame began talking quickly about his dream before Alisha could mention the camera and she felt more and more awkward. What would Kwame think if she told him about the camera? Would it destroy the fragile trust that had slowly grown between them over past weeks? Would it be better just to ignore the camera and to hope that he need never know about it? Nervous and uncertain, she tried to concentrate on Kwame, who talked revealingly about his dream of his father who was in prison.

Dr Wilson wrote the report for the funders and presented it, with video clips, to a meeting of the funders and some of the teachers. Alisha was very troubled to see clips of Kwame talking so emotionally and eloquently, with Dr Wilson highlighting the 'successful communication'. Later, when Alisha talked to Dr Wilson about anonymity, he said it was too late to alter the report and presentation, but he would alter names in the paper he was writing for a research journal.

The next week, Kwame shouted at Alisha, 'I'm not coming any more. You told my tutor about my dream! He talked about it in front of my whole tutor group and they laughed. How could you do that?'

Development of research ethics

Professional ethics has a long history, stretching back to ancient codes such as the medical Hippocratic Oath from the fifth century BCE. However, formal concern about research ethics is much more recent. During the 1940s, publicity about Nazi research forced awareness that medical research could no longer be seen simply as part of the routine medical care of patients. The Nuremberg Code (1947), written by lawyers, stressed the dangers of research and the importance of respect for research subjects' informed, unpressured consent or refusal. Children were assumed to be too immature to be able to consent, and were therefore banned from taking part in research projects.

Yet in the early 1960s, many babies were born with deformed limbs after their mothers took thalidomide during pregnancy. This tragedy led doctors to insist on the vital importance of medical research to develop and test treatments for childhood conditions and problems; they stressed the dangers of using under-researched treatments. The Declaration of Helsinki (World Medical Association, 1964/2008), written by doctors, set out detailed ethical research standards, many of which apply to all kinds of research involving people. Slowly, doctors accepted that they have extra duties to patients who take part in research. All professionals, including teachers and social workers, have different duties when they are being either researchers or practitioners. When they do research with children they already care for, they have to be extremely careful to ensure the children understand the nature of their different and separate roles and relationships.

During the 1970s, US lawyers and philosophers developed the new discipline of bioethics (Beauchamp and Childress, 2008). Their ideas have spread around the world, through the research professions and disciplines, and the formal review networks of research ethics committees (RECs) and, in the US, institutional review boards (IRBs). These serve as gatekeepers and determine whether particular projects can go ahead in medical, psychological and, increasingly, all areas of social research, including welfare and education. Over the latter part of the twentieth century, researchers in many disciplines gradually agreed research ethics standards and these are now regularly updated (for example: British Educational Research Association 2011; British Psychological Society 2010; British Sociological Association 2004; Cochrane Collaboration 2012; Economic and Social Research Council 2010; Graham et al. 2013; Nursing and Midwifery Council 2007; Social UK Research Integrity Office 2009; United Nations 2005). Professional and academic associations and also funders of research usually refer to research ethics standards on their websites. Unethical, fraudulent and sometimes dangerous research affecting children, however, continues to be reported (Beder 2009; Boseley 2010; Goldacre 2009; Kolch et al. 2010; Sercombe 2010; Sharav 2003; Slesser and Qureshi 2009).

Views vary on the relevance of research ethics and of ethics regulation. Some have doubts about formal ethics regulation, and some believe that focusing on the task of producing knowledge should be the priority (Hammersley 2009). Some emphasise the importance of working to resolve specific ethical problems as they arise (for theoretical models and practical examples of situated ethics, see Simons and Usher, 2000). Others see all research as value-laden (Sayer, 2010). With the great potential of research, through its processes and influences, to harm or benefit children and adults, and to misuse power, researchers should consider the morals of their work as carefully as the methods. Certainly, the present high failure rates in schools, when over 40 per cent of young people leave without qualifications, indicate that more critical educational research, concerned with respect and justice, is urgently needed (Allen and Ainley, 2007).

Three frameworks for research ethics

Rules for ethical research stem from three main frameworks or ways of thinking about what is 'good' research. These mainly emphasise *principles*, *outcomes* or *rights*. They all address similar concerns, but analyse and justify the ethics in different, though complementary rather than conflicting ways. They are often combined, though they tend to appeal to people's various preferences for seeing life in terms of principles, outcomes or rights.

Principles involve doing 'good' research because it is the right, correct thing to do. Standards include always respecting children as sensitive, dignified human beings, trying to be fair, and to conduct excellent research. The four mainly cited *principles* are: respect for personal integrity and autonomy; justice; avoiding harm; and beneficence or doing good.

Research based on *best outcomes* means working out how to avoid or reduce harms and costs, and to promote the hoped-for benefits of research, to contribute to knowledge, inform policy and practice, or help to promote effective services.

Rights based research, like principled research, is based on respect. Children's rights in the 42 main Articles of the Convention on the Rights of the Child (United Nations, 1989) have been grouped broadly into the '3 Ps' (Alderson 2008; Franklin 2002; Percy-Smith and Thomas 2010), and each one relates to research ethics. *Provision* of basic needs includes the best attainable healthcare, education, and other services, where 'best' is partly defined by 'well-researched', carefully designed and tested services. *Protection* from harm, abuse, exploitation, neglect or discrimination is central to ethical research. And *participation* rights, crucial to ethical research, require that children are well-informed and have their own views listened to and respected by adults. Increasingly, children are active participants and also researchers in their own right (Christiensen and James 2008; Kellett 2010).

There are other frameworks such as virtue ethics, feminist ethics and situated ethics. These can support rich, useful analyses of questions about ethical research. Yet underlying them all is attention to principles, rights and/or outcomes. The main approaches have been listed here to help you to identify which approach you tend to prefer, and which ones inform the research reports that you read, or see reported in the mass media, whether or not the chosen approaches are clearly stated.

There are doubts about when children become old enough for ethics; for example, when does respect for their autonomy and personal integrity begin to matter in research with them? Psychological research with premature babies by Heidelisa Als (1999) observes standards set by the three main ethical frameworks. Als respects the babies in her study as sensitive, dignified human beings, whose bodies and reactions, their signs of suffering or pleasure, express a 'language' that can be 'read'. She aims to discover, through immensely detailed observations, the babies' expressed 'views' about what harms or helps them, and how their care can become more humane and effective, less painful and distressing. Als' work illustrates how researchers who intended to benefit children have to relate closely and respectfully to them, and learn from them at every stage of the project. She observed how the babies in her study tried to wriggle into the corner of their cot, which helped them to curl and rest in a contained foetal position, and how the nurses would replace them neatly on their backs in the centre of the cot, where they sprawled uncomfortably, stressed and dazzled by the bright lights. Als' findings now inform an international movement (NIDCAP, 2012) of 'baby-led' routines and policies in neonatal units, which aim to prevent harms and promote benefits (Als et al. 2012). For example, the staff reduce the light and noise levels, nurse the babies in womb-like fabric nests, promote family-centred care, and do all they can to help the babies to relax and rest, working out with each one their preferred forms of care.

Limitations of research ethics

The main approaches to ethics outlined earlier all have strengths and limitations, which are widely debated. One problem is that principles and outcomes are left fairly vague and offer considerable scope for disagreement: what exactly does 'respect' or 'harm' mean? Much is left to researchers and review committees to determine.

The 'golden rule' of respect is to treat others as you would wish to be treated yourself, but adults' personal preferences may not always match children's choices. A researcher is likely to be keen to take part in a research interview, when a child might be reluctant. There are dangers when researchers assume that they know best how to edit and report children's views without noticing how they might misrepresent them, as discussed in Chapter 4.

Another problem is that truth-telling is noticeably missing from the four principles (respect; justice; avoiding harm; and beneficence). Although truth is crucial in every aspect of ethical research, it is only implied in talk of respect, and adults might justify withholding some details, hoping to protect children from confusion or anxiety.

There can be conflict between science (sound rigorous research methods) and ethics. For example, taking care not to upset an interviewee might lead researchers into avoiding vital but probing questions, or into excluding vulnerable children altogether, so that they are silenced and the eventual findings may be limited and misleading. One purpose of research ethics is to prompt researchers to consider such conflicts carefully, instead of assuming there is a single correct answer.

Ethics guidelines do not provide simple answers (Hammersley and Traianou 2012). Instead, the aim is to encourage researchers to reflect on, work towards, and justify the standards they value, and to be accountable to their participants as well as to their sponsors and colleagues. This can involve balancing different aims, or searching for the least harmful option. Principles can sometimes conflict, as can rights, such as respecting children's decisions but also protecting them from harm – their autonomy versus their protection rights.

This chapter on ethics therefore does not set out a definite format to follow or list to tick. Instead, it offers the above long-debated principles and values for researchers to refer to, reflect on, select, try to balance, and decide how to apply to their work. The chapter briefly introduces a few of the moral questions raised at every practical stage of research projects, but does not prescribe precise answers. Sometimes there are no clearly agreed solutions. Ethical research involves the process of researchers pondering moral questions, sometimes with colleagues, participants or advisers, recognising disagreement and uncertainty, searching for the best way forward, or at times the least harmful way, and working out how to prevent or reduce harms and to promote hoped-for benefits. This may sound a vague perhaps pointless process, and the next section considers why it matters.

Why research ethics matters

Whereas law sets basic standards for researchers to follow, research ethics helps to promote high standards. This section reviews how ethics draws attention to researchers' obligations and to potential problems and harms in order to help to prevent or reduce these.

Researchers have different obligations to their subjects or participants than practitioners such as teachers or nurses. Whereas services are designed to offer benefits *to* their users, research obtains data *from* people. Participants might enjoy and gain from taking part in research, but that is not the main purpose of research and it cannot be assured. Research means collecting, analysing and reporting data. It may be designed to produce new knowledge, which can contribute to a collective good, if the findings are published, read, implemented or have some influence. However, whilst a great deal of research is published, only rarely are *all* these outcomes achieved. More reliable outcomes are that research benefits the researchers who obtain the data and other advantages, such as a qualification or employment. Researchers therefore need to treat research participants with at least as much, if not more, care and respect than service providers do.

Formal research ethics committees and reviews of protocols only became routinely required for much social research during this century, twenty years or so after medical ethics committee review became routine. Some social researchers say that ethics is vital in medical research, because that might cause physical harm, seriously in extreme cases, but it is unnecessary in social research. Yet, however skilled and well-intentioned they may be, social researchers can still do harm. The ethical principle 'do no harm', aims to avoid distressing or embarrassing people, betraying their confidences, damaging their prospects or reputation, misunderstanding or misreporting them, which can deeply wound and wrong

some people. Emotional and social harms may matter more to people than specific physical harm. Many of the parents who protested that their deceased children's organs were removed for research purposes without their consent, said
they would have agreed to the organs being removed had they been asked. They
were shocked and angry because their consent, and their responsible relationship
to their child, had been ignored and disrespected (see http://en.wikipedia.org/
wiki/Alder_Hey_organs_scandal).

Before discussing how ethics needs to be taken into account throughout all
stages of research projects, the chapter now considers the processes of formal
ethics review before a project begins.

Research ethics review

Formal ethics review by RECs/IRBs does not ensure that problems will be prevented. Yet it offers encouragement and a specific request to researchers to consider problems and risks carefully, with the aim of avoiding or reducing them.
Formal review is intended to protect research subjects, to protect researchers
from later possible complaints, and to protect the high standards and reputation
of research generally. Committees decide whether to approve each project or to
ask for revisions.

Critics of REC/IRB formal review and governance oppose the power this can
exert over researchers (Hammersley 2009; Wald 2004). Orton-Johnson (2010),
for example, reviews restrictions imposed on online research. Some argue that
bureaucratic RECs undermine researchers' own ethical standards and personal
responsibility, and if committees approve substandard projects, this gives an
excuse or licence to researchers to work to lower standards. Others regret opposition between researchers and review committees (Israel and Hay 2006, though
they also review the problems), since they share similar aims and standards.
Ethics governance can be over-dominant and bureaucratic, acting to protect
universities and funding bodies from litigation. Yet its purpose is also to represent the interests of the least powerful group, to try to prevent research participants being treated as subjects without their knowledge or consent and to redress
a potential researcher/researched power imbalance.

In contrast to those who argue that RECs/IRBs have too much power, some
critics contend they are not simply weak, but, in healthcare and psychological
research for example, that they unduly support research sponsored by science-
related industries such as pharmacology and genetics (Evans et al. 2011;
Hedgecoe 2010; Petersen 2011; Sharav 2003). Critics show how university RECs
are under pressure to approve research which brings income to universities, sala-
ries for researchers, and potentially prestigious reports and influence.

Serious problems still occur and there is a case for strengthening critical ethics committee review, with stronger lay membership to represent the views of the research subjects. The move that most of all transformed medical ethics was when patients joined RECs/IRBs and represented very different views from the ones that doctors had assumed were sufficient. Agencies that conduct international research may sometimes exploit lower standards of ethics governance in Africa, Asia and South America, causing great harm to children (Boseley 2010; Kolch et al. 2010).

When they apply to a research ethics committee, many researchers working with children and young people may feel fairly powerless: they might be doing degrees, or independent or freelance projects, or working in teams, within ever tighter budgets and deadlines. To have to apply to a REC or IRB can feel like a heavy, extra, time-consuming demand to busy, stressed researchers, already facing many challenges. If ethics approval is delayed, this can wreak havoc with staffing and funding contracts and timetables. In response to problems and complaints, RECs have improved their systems over recent years and have increased prompt, fast-track and 'light-touch' reviews. For example, healthcare RECs have broadened their remit, and recruited members with more understanding of qualitative and other social research methods (NRES 2012).

In Britain, each university or other research agency should advise researchers on where and how to apply for ethics approval. Researchers usually have to submit an ethics form to their own university and sometimes to external agencies, such as the National Research Ethics Service (www.nres.nhs.uk/). RECs are especially concerned with any particular ethical concerns raised by the project, and also with information sheets and consent forms for participants (the NRES site gives a helpful example with advice).

Ethical questions through the research process

Besides thinking about ethics when applying to an REC/IRB, researchers need to think about ethics questions at every stage of the research, from early planning right through to dissemination. A few questions are reviewed in the following sections (and see Alderson and Morrow 2011 for many more).

When planning research or reading other researchers' reports, to picture the model of the child in the researchers' minds can help to identify their ethical relationship with children in the project, and how the relationship influences the research. Examples include: the innocent child needing protection; the child at specific Piagetian stages (see Chapter 1); the deprived disadvantaged child needing resources and services; the criminal child requiring control and reform; the 'ignorant' child who needs education; the excluded child who may need special shelter or opportunities; the disabled child seen either as the victim of personal tragedy or of a rejecting society; and, far less often, the strong resourceful child who shares in solving problems and creating new opportunities. In all but the final example, it is as if we put children into a small glass cage called childhood, and then examine how they perform within its restrictions, instead of looking critically at the cage itself, its causes and effects. Almost inevitably, research findings reinforce the original model. Researchers find what they are looking for – vulnerable or immature or competent children – and their reports contribute towards public attitudes that either exclude and confine children, or else respect and include them in mainstream society.

In the book *Games People Play*, Eric Berne (1967) shows how people tend to be drawn into an unhappy destructive triangle of playing the victim, the rescuer or the persecutor. Research about children can re-enact this game. Berne proposes the solution of everyone moving beyond the game and working together towards ethical, honest and mutually respectful relationships. In research, this involves moving beyond simple stereotypes of children as victims or villains to see that everyone, children and adults, has needs and strengths, failings and skills. Researchers can then work respectfully with and for children and young people to explore their complex and wide-ranging views and experiences. Researchers might, for example, combine reports of children's social, political and economic state with children's own views about these broad matters, as discussed in Chapter 18.

Early plans, research design

The first questions for researchers to ask include: What is the point of the project? Does it aim to answer worthwhile, new questions, or older questions that need to be re-thought or re-tested? Is the research worth doing? Numerous small studies research children's play or learning – will a new study really produce new knowledge? Has there been a thorough literature review to check that the proposed research does not simply repeat published studies? Can new theories and ideas be brought into this topic area? Further questions include: Do the chosen methods fit the question? In whose interests is the research being planned? Who is intended to benefit from any findings?

Harm and benefit

Other early questions include: What might be the potential harms or inconvenience to children in the study? Are they justified by the hoped-for benefits of the knowledge to be gained? Experimental or comparative research, for instance of different support programmes for young asylum seekers, might involve exposing one group to a seemingly inferior programme, although this is not yet certain, and the point of the research is to discover which is best. Researchers need to explain and evaluate the general risks and perhaps modify the design.

Some risks might seem to apply less to young children. Are they aware enough to feel embarrassed or betrayed? Does it matter if babies are taken from their mothers to see how quickly they become upset; or if children are told not to eat some sweets – for no given reason – and then left alone and secretly filmed to see for how long they resist temptation; or if children are prompted to talk or behave in ways they feel awkward about revealing? In several ways children are at higher risk. From the earliest years they can feel shame about disapproval and anxiety about relationships they sense are deceptive and mistrustful (Dunn 1988; Murray and Andrews 2000; Winter 2011). Young children are most vulnerable to being exploited or labelled, and least able to defend themselves or to correct misreports. Small incidents in childhood can have long effects.

Rights to privacy and confidentiality

Privacy involves ensuring that no one except the primary research team sees identifiable data or personal records and all reports are anonymised. Confidentiality means that each person's responses and identifiable data will not be discussed with anyone else in the study, including parents or teachers, but only among the research team. Increasingly, researchers are expected to avoid taking photos and videos which include images of children's faces. They should also ask children who take photos for the research not to include faces, or they could blur or pixilate the faces if they publicise photos or films of the children (Plowman and Stephen 2008). The aims are to avoid exploiting and publicising children without valid consent and for child protection purposes.

Online research is increasingly used by academic researchers, and far more by market research (Savage and Burrows 2007). Commercial companies spend massive budgets on games, digital recording, cookies, data-mining, peer-to-peer marketing and 'cool hunting', to collect billions of personal details about family and friends from children at ever younger ages (Beder 2009; Save the Children 2007). Kozinets (2010) contends that netnography, or online ethnography, enables the respectful study of cultures and communities and immersion in people's lives, and it is an economical, effective and unobtrusive means of studying 'naturalistic' data. Kozinets proposes 'looser' ways to resolve ethical problems when researching adult online groups sometimes without their knowledge or consent. His discussion raises questions about secrecy and exploitation that have extra complications in research with children.

Questions about privacy also include: Are all publicised records and reports anonymised? Are standards in the 1998 Data Protection Act respected and all data kept in a lockable storage space? Are researchers careful not to discuss any interviews with other participants, unless there is concern that a child might be seriously harmed?

Information

Ethics committees require that information leaflets are written for adults and children to see, to help them to decide whether to take part in the research (NRES 2012). Leaflets should explain the nature and purpose of the research: Why is it being done? What are the main questions? Who might benefit from the findings? What might participants gain – if anything? Any risks or problems should be explained, with a brief summary of the methods and timetable, and any activities participants will be asked to do. Leaflets should explain how and where to contact the researchers (address, telephone and email) and should name the ethics committee that approved the project. Several points can be headed 'Your rights', as suggested in Figure 5.1.

Even if an ethics committee does not require information leaflets, it is good ethical practice to write them for the children, young people and adults involved in the project. Besides helping potential participants to know and decide whether to take part in a project, writing a leaflet can help researchers to think very clearly

---

Research and your rights

- It is for you to decide if you want to talk to me. You do not have to say 'yes'.
- If you do say 'yes', you do not have to do the whole interview.
- We could stop when you want to, or have a break.
- If you do not want to answer some of the questions, you can just say 'pass'.
- Before you decide whether to help me, you might like to talk about this project with your parents or with a friend.
- I will keep recordings and notes of the interviews in a safe, lockable place.
- When I talk about the research and write reports, I always change people's names, to keep their views anonymous.
- I would not talk to anyone you know about what you have said, unless you tell me about the risk of someone being harmed. If so, I would talk with you first about what could be done to help.

Figure 5.1 Example from a research information leaflet for children

about the nature and purpose of their work, which in turn is likely to improve the standard of the research, and make it easier to explain to participants.

Adults can read and explain leaflets to young children or those with learning difficulties, or children themselves can read the leaflets. Plain English, or other first language, is vital, and diagrams and pictures can help. Large print, a pale background and non-glossy paper will help children with poor sight. Before research sessions such as interviews, researchers can go through the leaflet with the interviewee, who may not have read or remembered the leaflet.

Consent

Informed and voluntary consent is central to research ethics to ensure that people understand what is involved; they agree to any risks or inconveniences because they think the hoped-for benefits of the research are worth supporting; and they make a decision free from pressure or persuasion.

Consent can be particularly complicated in research with children and raises often unresolved questions. Do we always have to obtain parents' as well as children's consent, even for young people aged 12, 15 or 17 years, as some guidance advises? There is clear agreement that the young child's reluctance and refusal must be respected in some guidelines (listed in the end references). Parents can give vital support to children who wish to refuse, but should we be barred by parents' refusal when the children or young people want to join the research?

Teachers can grant access but cannot give consent, only people with legal parental responsibility may do that on children's behalf. In school research, every child in a school or class who might be observed should be informed about the research, and preferably be given a leaflet to take home for their parents/carers to read as well. It is complicated to research classes where a few children or parents have not given their consent. These children may need to have different activities during research sessions, and should not be observed, or recorded or have notes made about them. People have the right to refuse and should not be asked to give a reason. Researchers have to balance the risks of children being either coerced into joining a project, or else unwillingly excluded and silenced if they consent but their parents refuse, and these questions are still being debated.

Competence

When are children old enough to be competent to consent? There is no simple answer to this question. Much depends on each researcher's view of children's competence, along with each child's own experience and confidence, the type of research, and the skill with which researchers talk with children and help them to make unpressured informed decisions. Some people propose standardised tests to assess competence, but these tests may result in unduly high thresholds of competence that many children and some adults fail to reach. Instead, their competence to consent to research can be assessed by asking children how much they understand about the specific project, what they will be asked to do, and their relevant rights. This turns the session into a two-way test, not only of the children and young people, but also of the researchers' skill. How well have they informed and respected and listened to each potential participant? The session can also become a discussion that enables children to give a more informed and unpressured consent or refusal.

There is no certain law on children's consent to research and researchers are advised to also request the consent of the people with parental responsibility to research people aged under 16 or 18 when possible. Recent European law has undermined former respect in English law for competent children (Biggs 2010). Instead it relies on parents' consent, and now, for example, ignores the consent of everyone aged under 18 years to any research approved through NHS review committees (European Regulation 1901/2006; NRES 2009).

Social researchers, who have greater legal freedom than NHS researchers to respect children's consent, and who observe and talk with them, find that children are usually far more competent in their real everyday lives than they are in research laboratories. One example is how young children with diabetes have great understanding, and they share in managing their condition (Alderson et al. 2006). Another example is children aged 4 to 7 years who had been severely abused and neglected and were able to express their views and experiences and feelings of sadness and loss in profound interviews (Winter 2011). Instead of gazing directly and perhaps intimidatingly at the children, Winter sat beside them while they decorated small boxes with craft materials. The children showed on the outside how they thought they appeared to others, and on the inside their wishes and feelings. International research with young child workers in poorer countries is increasing childhood researchers' respect for all children's potential capacities. For instance, young children in Peru run their own businesses as street traders (Invernizzi, 2008), and children aged from 4 years agreed with their mothers that they could learn and earn more if they were on their own when selling goods. In remarkable contrast to children confined in Western nurseries, these competent young children raise vital questions about the age when children are able to give informed consent to take part in research. As discussed in other chapters, researchers increasingly involve young children in practical research methods: making maps, photos and videos, dramas and exhibitions about their daily lives, so that the methods reinforce the ethical respect for their competence.

Other stages of research

Further ethical questions about respect and justice, harm and benefit and rights arise throughout research projects. They apply when raising funds, selecting and arranging access to potential participants, and aiming to be inclusive (Morris 1998). They also arise during later stages when collecting, storing and analysing data, writing reports, publicising the work and, if possible, working with policy-makers and practitioners on ways to put the findings and recommendations into practice, so that all the former work becomes worthwhile.

If social research reports are disseminated effectively at local or national level, then they can sometimes greatly influence and reshape public opinion and policy, and powerfully affect people's lives for better or worse (Goldacre 2009; Slesser and Qureshi 2009). Among countless examples is research about methods of dealing with hyperactive children, young offenders and many other troubled and troublesome young groups.

Children and young people now share in planning, conducting and reporting research, and then meeting policymakers to see how it can be used. For example, through the Children's Rights Alliance for England (CRAE 2008), young people researched the state of children's rights in England and presented their findings to an impressed United Nations Committee on the Rights of the Child in Geneva. The Committee recommended that young people in other countries should be similarly involved when governments present their regular reports on progress in implementing the United Nations (1989) Convention.

Conclusions

This brief review has raised only a few of the many ethical questions that arise in research with children and young people. The aim has been to alert you to such questions and suggest ways to start addressing them. As mentioned earlier, ethics helps researchers to be more aware of hidden problems although it does not provide easy answers.

Often, the problems at first seem to be about conflicting opposites: science or ethics, encouraging children's participation or protecting children by excluding them from research. And yet ways to balance these seemingly opposite values can often be found. While working to complete projects on time and to budget, sometimes researchers also have to be ready to slow down and wait until children are ready to take part. This need not be a simple clash between scientific efficiency and ethical respect. Adjusting the pace to suit the children may help them to make a far more worthwhile contribution to the project. Ethics can strengthen scientific method.

Informing and involving children may block certain research methods, such as covert or deceptive research. However, if researchers rethink their questions and methods in more transparent and honest ways, they may gain more interesting and worthwhile findings. One example is not to do covert studies of children who 'truant' from school or 'abscond' from children's homes, but instead discuss the research with informed and consenting children and young people. The researchers may then learn far more about the motives and reasoning of the 'truants' or 'absconders' and how their problems and problem behaviours might be resolved, in an approach that respects children of all ages as meaning-making agents who can participate actively in research.

Ethics questions can also alert you, when you conduct research or read other researchers' reports, to underlying questions. What are the underlying values and interests? Who benefits? How is power used, misused or shared? Are children seen as problems, villains or contributors? Do the researchers aim to rescue, or criticise, or respect children?

Being aware of their moral relationship with children can guide researchers towards solving many ethical and practical problems that arise throughout the research process. Ethical standards, high or low, weave themselves into all parts of the research fabric and shape the methods and findings. Modern medical ethics has caused medical researchers to change their methods. They now generally do less risky research with children, and they inform, respect and protect children more. In my view, when all researchers take ethics more seriously, they might drop older covert methods, and continue to promote more participative ones.

Some of the missing ethical standards in the opening example:

- Respect and time for shared planning and working between senior and junior staff.
- Care with ethical standards for services, and for extra standards in research or other interventions that are not primarily intended to benefit the people concerned.
- Clearly agreed plans on the purpose and nature of the work, the methods of collecting, analysing, storing and reporting data, the hoped-for benefits, privacy, anonymity, and any risks or inconvenience to participants.
- Clear information leaflets and consent forms, with time for potential participants to discuss and form their decisions, knowing that that they can refuse or withdraw.
- Care with any public reports that might reveal people's identities.

References and ethics guidelines

Alderson, P. (2008) *Young Children's Rights*. London: Jessica Kingsley/Save the Children.

Alderson, P., Sutcliffe, K. and Curtis, K. (2006) 'Children's consent to medical treatment', *Hastings Centre Report*, 36: 25–34.

Alderson, P. and Morrow, V. (2011) *The Ethics of Research with Children and Young People: A Practical Handbook*, 3rd edition. London: Sage.

Allen, M. and Ainley, P. (2007) *When Education Make You Fick, Innit?* London: Tufnell Press.

Als, H. (1999) 'Reading the premature infant', in E. Goldson (ed.), *Developmental Interventions in the Neonatal Intensive Care Nursery*. New York: Oxford University Press. pp. 18–85.

Als, H., Duffy, F., McAnulty, G. et al. (2012) 'NIDCAP improves brain function and structure in preterm infants with severe intrauterine growth restriction', *Journal of Perinatology*, 32: 797–803.

Beauchamp, T. and Childress, J. (2008) *Principles of Biomedical Ethics*. New York: Oxford University Press.

Beder, S. (2009) *This Little Kiddy Went to Market: The Corporate Capture of Childhood*. London: Pluto.

Berne, E. (1967) *Games People Play*. Harmondsworth: Penguin.

Biggs, H. (2010) *Healthcare Research Ethics and Law: Regulation, Review and Responsibility*. London: Routledge.

Boseley, S. (2010) 'Nigeria: Drug trial tale of "dirty tricks"', *Guardian Weekly*, 17 December, and see www.cbsnews.com/8301-505123_162-42846951/pfizers-nigeria-scandal-doctors-without-borders-stirs-the-pot-to-little-effect/ 5 January 2011 (accessed 7 January 2013).

British Educational Research Association (BERA) (2011) *Ethical Guidelines for Educational Research*, www.bera.ac.uk/system/files/BERA%20Ethical%20Guidelines%202011.pdf (accessed 7 January 2013).

British Psychological Society. (2010) *Code of Human Research Ethics*, www.bps.org.uk/about/rules5.cfm (accessed 6 January 2013).

British Sociological Association (2004) *Statement of Ethical Practice*. Durham: BSA.

Christensen, P. and James, A. (eds) (2008) *Research with Children: Perspectives and Practices*, 2nd edition. London: Routledge.

Cochrane Collaboration (2012) www.cochrane.org (accessed 14 October 2013).

CRAE – Children's Rights Alliance for England (2008) *State of England's Children*. London: CRAE, and see www.crae.org.uk/protecting/un.html (accessed 7 January 2013).

Dunn, J. (1988) *The Beginnings of Social Understanding*. Oxford: Blackwell.

Economic and Social Research Council (2010) *Framework for Research Ethics*. Swindon: ESRC.

European Regulation (1901/2006) *Medicinal Products for Paediatric Use.* Brussels: EC.

Evans, J., Meslin, E., Marteau, T. and Caulfield, T. (2011) 'Deflating the genomic bubble', *Science,* 331(6019): 861–2.

Franklin, B. (2002) *The New Handbook of Children's Rights.* London: Routledge.

Goldacre, B. (2009) *Bad Science.* London: Harper.

Graham, A. et al. (2013) *Ethical Research Involving Children: International Charter.* Florence: Innocenti, UNICEF.

Hammersley, M. (2009) 'Against the ethicists: On the evils of ethical regulation', *International Journal of Research Methodology,* 12(3): 211–26.

Hammersley, M. and Traianou, A. (2012) 'Ethics and educational research', *British Educational Research Association On-line Resource,* www.bera.ac.uk/category/keywords/ethics (accessed 6 January 2013).

Hedgecoe, A. (2010) 'Bioethics and the reinforcement of socio-technical expectations', *Social Studies of Science,* 40(2): 163–86.

Invernizzi, A. (2008) 'Everyday lives of working children and notions of citizenship', in A. Invernizzi and J. Williams (eds), *Children and Citizenship.* London: Sage. pp. 131–42.

Israel, M. and Hay, I. (2006) *Research Ethics for Social Scientists.* London: Sage.

Kellett, M. (2010) *Rethinking Children and Research.* London: Continuum.

Kolch, M., Ludolph, A., Plener, P., Fangerau, H., Vitiello, B. and Fegert, J. (2010) 'Safeguarding children's rights in psychopharmacological research: Ethical and legal issues', *Current Pharmacological Design,* 16(22): 2398–406.

Kozinets, R. (2010) *Netnography.* London: Sage.

Morris, J. (1998) *Don't Leave Us Out! Involving Disabled Children and Young People with Communication Impairments.* York: Joseph Rowntree Foundation.

Murray, L. and Andrews, H. (2000) *The Social Baby.* Richmond: The Children's Project.

NIDCAP – Newborn Individualized Developmental Care and Assessment Programme (2012) www.nidcap.org/ (accessed 6 January 2012).

National Research Ethics Service, www.nres.nhs.uk/ (accessed 26 October 2012).

National Research Ethics Service (NRES) (2009) *Standard Operating Procedures for Research Ethics Committees: Version 4.0.* London: Department of Health. www.nres.nhs.uk/nres-publications/publications/standard-operating-procedures/ (accessed 10 July 2013).

Nuremberg Code (1947) http://ori.dhhs.gov/education/products/RCRintro/c03/b1c3.html (accessed 26 October 2012).

Nursing and Midwifery Council (2007) *The Code: Standards of Conduct, Performance and Ethics for Nurses and Midwives.* London: NMC.

Orton-Johnson, K. (2010) 'Ethics in online research', *Sociological Review Online,* 15(4).

Percy-Smith, B. and Thomas, N. (eds) (2010) *Handbook of Children's Participation.* London: Routledge.

Petersen, A. (2011) 'Can and should sociology save bioethics?', *Medical Sociology News,* 6(1): 2–14, www.medicalsociologyonline.org/resources/MSo-&-MSN-Archive/MSo-v.6/MSo-Volume-6-Issue-1.pdf (accessed 14 October 2014).

Plowman, L. and Stephen, C. (2008) 'The big picture? Video and the representation of interaction', *British Educational Research Journal,* 34(4): 541–65

Savage, M. and Burrows, R. (2007) 'The coming crisis of empirical sociology', *Sociology,* 41(5): 885–900.

Save the Children (2007) *Why Social Corporate Responsibility is Failing Children.* London: SCF.

Sayer, A. (2010) *Why Things Matter to People.* Cambridge: Cambridge University Press.

Sercombe, H. (2010) 'The "teen brain" research, *Youth & Policy,* 105: 71–80.

Sharav, V. (2003) 'Children in clinical research: A conflict of moral values', *American Journal of Bioethics,* 3(1): 1–99.

Simons, H. and Usher, R. (2000) *Situated Ethics in Educational Research.* London: Routledge.

Slesser, A. and Qureshi, Y. (2009) 'The implications of fraud in medical and scientific research', *World Journal of Surgery,* 33(11): 2355–9.

Social UK Research Integrity Office (2009) *Code of Practice for Research.* London: UKIR, www.ukrio.org/publications/code-of-practice-for-research (accessed 14 October 2014)

United Nations (1989) *Convention on the Rights of the Child.* New York: United Nations.

United Nations (2005) *Universal Declaration on Bioethics and Human Rights.* New York: United Nations.

Wald, D. (2004) 'Bureaucracy of ethics applications', *British Medical Journal,* 329: 282–5.

Winter, K. (2011) *Building Relationships and Communicating with Young Children: A Practical Guide for Social Workers.* Abingdon: Routledge.

World Medical Association (1964/2000) *Declaration of Helsinki,* Fernay-Voltaire, WMA, www.wma.net/en/30publications/10policies/b3/ (accessed 26 October 2012).

SECTION 2
METHODOLOGICAL APPROACHES TO RESEARCH WITH CHILDREN AND YOUNG PEOPLE

Introduction

In this section of the book, the chapters focus on some of the basic processes involved in designing research and producing data. Chapter 6 outlines what is involved in research design, and provides an overview of the various sorts of data that can be involved in research with children and young people. Research can vary both in how the design process is managed, for example whether it largely follows a fixed plan from the beginning or is more flexible, as well as in terms of the specific types of data it is planned to collect and the sort of analysis that is proposed.

Subsequent chapters examine methods of data production in more detail. Chapter 7 is concerned with participant observation, the central source of data in much ethnographic work in anthropology, sociology and other disciplines, and widely used in research with children and young people. This involves a researcher gaining access to particular settings, observing what goes on there participating in one role or another, as well as talking to other participants – with a view to understanding their perspectives and practices, these often being seen as constituting a distinctive culture that is adapted to the circumstances in which they live and work.

Participant observation is just one form that observation can take. It tends to be characterised by a relatively open-ended or unstructured orientation, with the researcher taking note of anything that might be significant for the research topic, or to the lives of the people being studied. Field notes may be jotted down and written up later, though increasingly audio- or even video-recording is also used. The main contrasting form of observational research is generally referred to as 'structured' or 'systematic' observation. This also often involves going to natural settings to observe what is going on. But this time the observational process is structured by use of a schedule that identifies types of event or action to be observed and counted or measured.

Interviews can also vary according to the degree to which they are structured, and this is central to the discussion in Chapter 8. At one end of the spectrum are survey-type interviews that employ a fixed set of questions, to be administered with each respondent in the exact words and the exact order specified, and with answers often provided from which respondents are requested to choose. At the other extreme are relatively unstructured interviews in which questions are formulated by the interviewer as the interview progresses. While they are usually designed to cover a set of topics relevant to the research questions, the particular questions asked will follow from what the informant says and be designed to stimulate further talk relevant to those topics. Other ways in which interviews can differ in character are also considered in this chapter, for example in terms of whether they are individual or group interviews, and whether or not they use stimulus material of some sort, such as photos.

The other main type of data employed in research with children and young people is documents and artefacts, these often containing text and/or images. Many of these are available prior to and independently of any particular study, and can be acquired and analysed by the researcher. Examples of such 'found' documents include school prospectuses, clinical notes and instruction manuals in hospitals, or photographs displayed on the mantelpiece in a home. Artefacts can vary even more in character, from objects like toys to buildings and rooms. Researchers also sometimes ask people to produce documents or artefacts for the purposes of research, for example requesting that they keep diaries, take photographs, or make videos. Chapter 9 discusses some of the considerations that surround the use of texts, images and artefacts for research purposes. As illustration, it examines a research project in schools that involved primary-age children producing posters and other artefacts relevant to an anti-bullying campaign.

The final chapter in the Section is concerned with methodological ideas. When they make decisions about what to investigate, what sources of data to use, how to go about obtaining the data, and how to analyse it, researchers do not operate within a consensually agreed framework, simply choosing whatever methods are most appropriate for their aims. They necessarily rely upon questionable assumptions about the nature of the phenomena they are investigating, including the children and young people involved, and about how a proper understanding can be gained. There is considerable disagreement among researchers about these matters, leading to rather different forms of research. The most obvious such division is between those who rely primarily or entirely upon qualitative data, those who use quantitative data, and those who 'mix' or combine the two sorts of data. In Chapter 10, four broad methodological philosophies are outlined – positivism, interpretivism, constructionism, and 'critical' research – and their implications for what to study and how this should be done are explored.

6 Research Design

Martyn Hammersley

The term 'research design' refers to the task faced by a researcher in formulating research questions and planning how to produce and analyse the data required to answer them. More specifically, it is concerned with how this task can be pursued most effectively, within appropriate ethical and practical constraints. Research design is a high priority in the early stages of a research project, but it continues to be of importance throughout the process. Moreover, research design plans often have to be restructured during the course of investigation, because of changes in the focus of the research, or as a result of obstacles encountered along the way.

While the research process cannot begin without some initial ideas about what question(s) are being addressed, these are not simply givens: formulating, clarifying, and perhaps even transforming research questions is part of the process of research design. So, in this chapter we will need to give some attention to how research questions arise, develop and change before we go on to consider other aspects of research design.

Sometimes research questions can be answered by drawing on previous research. This can be done through synthesis of the findings of earlier studies; and/or through secondary analysis of the data they produced, where this is available. There are now substantial amounts of data stored in data archives, and these may be open to use by researchers. Some assessment has to be made, then, about what data is already available and whether it would be sufficient for the purposes of the new study. However, often, a researcher will need to produce new data, and it will be necessary to plan how this can be achieved. This chapter will provide an overview of the methods used for obtaining data about the lives of children and young people.

Research design is not only concerned with the production of data required to answer research questions but also with how those data will be processed and analysed so as to generate potential answers, and to produce evidence about their likely validity. So, we will also need to outline the different forms of analysis that can be used.

Research questions

All research begins from some set of questions that are believed to be important, and to which answers are not currently known (or, at least, are judged to be not known with sufficient certainty). These questions may be very specific ones, for example concerned with whether the level of bullying in a school, or across all schools in a country, is increasing. Often, though, research begins from more vaguely formulated issues, for instance about the significance of children's use of social media in their lives today.

While potential research questions must be judged in terms of their importance, and according to the current level of knowledge about them, there is, almost always, scope for differences in view about both these matters.

As regards importance, some people argue that research must be geared to addressing questions that are of immediate significance for policy or practice. So, for example, it might be argued that topics such as the incidence of child abuse, its causes, and the effectiveness of policies dealing with it, should be at the top of the research agenda whereas others, for example studying the attitudes of skateboarders towards their sport, may be judged less important.

However, other commentators insist that researchers should be free to address any question that can be shown to be of general interest. They resist the idea of a single hierarchy of what are important research topics, or even the assumption that we can know with any certainty which topics are and are not the most important before we investigate them. It may also be argued that, in themselves, major public issues are rarely feasible research questions, since they are usually very complex. They may involve assumptions that need to be investigated, they will depend upon value commitments that research cannot validate on its own, and they cannot usually be addressed all in one go – research will often need to focus on parts of them whose investigation *is* viable. For example, the desirability or undesirability of children's involvement in paid employment is an important topic, but a single study could not address this effectively, across all the different contexts and different forms of work that are involved. Furthermore, no study can tell us, in itself, whether or not paid employment is desirable, only what the consequences of children's working, under various conditions, tends to be. Research can also provide other kinds of useful information, for example about what proportion of children within a particular national society are engaged in full- or part-time, work; what their attitudes towards and experience of it are; how it fits with the social organisation of their family lives; and so on. But separate studies may well be required for each of these topics.

Assessments of what is already known can also vary, and this is one of the reasons why published research findings are sometimes dismissed as trivial, or as restating what is already well-established. It is necessary to be cautious about such dismissals (Gage 1991). Take the claim, frequently made, that over the past 20 or 30 years in the UK and other Western societies young children have become increasingly sexualised. Some people regard the truth of this as quite obvious, but others are more sceptical. In part this hinges on differences in how the word 'sexualisation' is interpreted. It also depends upon one's views about the nature of childhood: a Freudian perspective carries very different implications from the idea that children are 'innocent'. Disagreement may also result from the fact that people can be focusing on different aspects of what comes under this heading; for example, the wearing of clothes that are in some sense sexually explicit, versus increased exposure of children to knowledge about sexual activity. These two things do not necessarily go together, so that an increase in one does not automatically imply an increase in the other.

It is also important to bear in mind that there is generally a difference between what is treated as sufficiently well-known for research purposes and what we take to be well-known in many other contexts. Usually, researchers demand more evidence, and more reliable evidence, than most of us would usually expect in making everyday judgements about the same matters, unless these relate to very consequential decisions. For this reason, there will often be differences between the assessments of researchers and others about what is and is not currently well-known.

In summary, then, researchers must ask themselves about the importance of the topic they are proposing to investigate, and also about whether the questions they are addressing are ones to which answers are currently not sufficiently well-established. Moreover, readers of research reports must also make judgements about these matters, and may of course come to different conclusions from the researchers themselves.

There is a third consideration that should be taken into account in formulating research questions. This is that it must be possible to answer them *given the resources likely to be available*. It is not uncommon for research projects to be over-ambitious, especially at the beginning – attempting to provide answers to questions where sufficient reliable evidence is unlikely to be attainable. Indeed, published research reports sometimes make excessive claims about the effectiveness with which ambitious research questions have been answered. So, during the research process researchers need continually to assess whether the initially proposed research questions seem open to effective investigation; and, if not, what modifications might be required to make the study viable. In addition, readers of research reports must consider whether the research questions addressed in a study are ones that it was possible to answer in research terms, in the circumstances, and given the resources available and the strategies used by the researchers.

As noted earlier, some projects are directed at testing hypotheses that have been closely specified right from the beginning, whereas in other studies the research questions will be less precisely defined and more open-ended or exploratory in character. This will partly reflect the stage of development of the relevant research field, for example how much is already known about how to frame fruitful research questions, and possible answers to them, about the particular matters at issue. It may also be related to the nature of the methods that the researchers intend to use. For example, carrying out a large-scale survey, using a fixed-choice questionnaire, requires much more precise specification of research design at the beginning than a smaller-scale study that will rely upon ongoing observation in a particular setting, and/or on a set of interviews.

While having some set of research questions, however loosely specified, is an essential starting point, it is important to recognise that, as already indicated, these may change over the course of inquiry. There are several reasons why this could happen:

1   The original questions may come to be seen as too ambitious, as not currently answerable given the resources available;
2   It could be concluded that the original questions were based on false assumptions;
3   It may be that more fruitful questions emerge during the process of investigation.

Inquiries, of all kinds, often have to be redesigned as a result of changes in the initial research questions. It is also important to recognise that, however precisely specified they are at the beginning of the process, a researcher's understanding of what those questions mean, and of their significance, may change over the course of inquiry.

So, even where researchers have a relatively clear sense of what they are investigating at the start of the research process, how they define the phenomenon of interest may still be clarified, or may change, notably through issues not initially seen as relevant coming to be recognised as important. This underlines the degree to which research is a process of discovery: one may find that one's initial assumptions need to be revised. And a similar sort of process can occur during the course of reading a research report, leading to a re-evaluation of the study concerned, and perhaps also to a significant change in one's views about the issue being investigated.

Types of research question

The questions that researchers study can take at least two main forms: descriptive or explanatory.

Descriptions are concerned with documenting the existence, features, variability, or frequency of some type(s) of phenomenon, as these occur in a particular context or set of contexts. So, descriptions can be about what happens in specific types of situation, what different people believe and how they act, how frequent particular sorts of event are, what proportion of people in a population share a certain type of attitude, and so on. For example, if we were to ask what proportion of children under 16 in a particular community engage in work, what types of work, and how much time they spend working, these would be descriptive questions.

Explanations are concerned with determining why some event, or pattern of events, occurred, or why an object or person possesses some property or displays particular variation in it. For example, if we were interested in what leads children to engage in work, or how this affects their schooling, or shapes their peer group relations, these would be explanatory questions.

Where the aim is description, there will need to be some attention to what would and would not be relevant. This will depend upon the nature of our interest: any set of objects can be described in many different ways. For instance, if we were aiming to document how many children in a community work, we would need to think about what boundaries to childhood we are assuming (up to 14 years' old, up to 18 years' old?) and also about what would count as work – how is this to be defined? Are we concerned only with paid work, or perhaps even more narrowly only with that which is officially registered? What about domestic chores that children carry out in their own homes, or work in businesses owned by their parents or other members of the family? What about work done in return for goods in kind? Researchers need to consider such matters so as to clarify the framework within which descriptions are to be produced. Similarly, readers of research reports need to understand how the researchers have interpreted the concepts that are central to their investigations, and the implications of this for the conclusions they can draw. They will also need to assess whether these judgements were reasonable.

In many research studies the aim is to answer questions that call for an explanation, not just a description. Producing an explanation always depends upon descriptions of what is to be explained and of those factors that might explain it. However, in addition, explanatory research demands that evidence be provided about what is likely to have caused the outcome to be explained, or how some particular series of events generated it. Here, we must ask what sort of evidence can be provided that would enable cogent conclusions to be drawn about these causal relationships. As we shall see, detailed investigation of processes occurring within particular cases and/or the comparison of cases may be required.

Having identified initial research questions, and determined their character, the next step in research design is to decide what cases need to be investigated if those questions are to be answered, and how access can be gained to data about these cases.

Case selection strategies

A wide range of case selection strategies are used in research with children and young people, but they belong to three broad types: individual case study, surveys, and experiments. Each of these strategies has distinctive strengths and weaknesses.

Individual case study: Here a relatively small number of cases is investigated in detail – and, typically, many aspects or features of each case are examined, the aim often being to gain a deep understanding of these cases. For example, in her research on children's play Woodyer (2010) studied 10 children in six households. Case study also often involves a relatively open-ended, exploratory approach, in which the aim is to document the distinctiveness of particular cases as well as their similarities with one another. Cases may be selected on a variety of grounds, from aiming to produce representative knowledge of some wider set of cases to choosing cases designed to develop and/or test some theoretical idea. Thus, Woodyer was interested in providing evidence relevant to currently influential arguments claiming that children's play has become distorted through the effects of new technologies and commercial pressures.

Surveys: Many social science studies involve the investigation of a relatively large number of cases, hundreds or even thousands. Surveys may involve the use of questionnaires or interviews, or structured observation by a large team of researchers. A common feature of surveys is that data are collected by means of some standard format: a set of questions for respondents to answer or a set of features for observers to count or measure. Cases will often be selected in a manner designed to produce a representative sample of a larger population, perhaps with statistical techniques used as a basis for maximising the chances that the sample matches the population in relevant respects. This was the case selection strategy used by Streuli, Vennam and Woodhead (2011) in studying early childhood and primary education in Andhra Pradesh, India: they drew on a sample of 2,000 children living in diverse communities throughout that Indian state, though this was also complemented by in-depth qualitative research. On the basis of the data produced, they sought to draw general conclusions about inequalities in access to early educational opportunities in India.

Experiment: There will often be difficulty in finding the particular sorts of case required to test explanatory hypotheses, and where possible one solution is to use an experimental strategy. In effect, this amounts to creating the various sorts of case required to investigate an explanatory question, in order to determine what seems to cause what. Cases where the candidate causal factor is present, or is at a high level, will be compared with others where it is absent, or at a low level; various strategies being used to rule out the influence of other factors. Experiments are used in much psychological research, for example in Donaldson's

(1978) experiments on the development of children's understanding of physical processes. This built on, but also criticised, the classic work of Piaget, showing that some of his inferences about what children were incapable of doing at early stages of development arose from a failure to recognise the potential for misinterpretation built into the experimental process: that experiments are social events, with all the scope for misunderstandings that are present in such contexts.

These three case selection strategies have varying advantages and disadvantages. For example, an experimental approach can sometimes provide much more powerful evidence about what causes what than can non-experimental research. However, there are threats to the validity of conclusions reached via experimental method, just as there are with any other method. In particular, there is the question of how closely the cases created under experimental conditions correspond to naturally occurring cases to which the explanation produced is intended to apply. Might children's behaviour be altered when they know they are participating in an experiment? The answer to this will usually be 'in some ways but not in others', and the critical question is how serious a threat to the validity of the conclusions of a particular study this sort of 'reactivity' poses.

Surveys have the advantage that they are often able to supply representative information about very large populations on the basis of studying samples. Furthermore, because a large number of cases is investigated there is a greater possibility of identifying probabilistic causal relationships, as compared with studies involving a small number of cases, whether experiments or case studies; in other words, it is possible to recognise general trends. However, usually, only a relatively small amount of data can be collected about each case in a survey, and there will be limits to how far the reliability of the data can be checked.

Case studies, like surveys, are sometimes used to provide descriptive information, and can provide considerable detail about many aspects of the case(s) investigated. However, they are also used in explanatory research. They are weaker in principle than experimental research in identifying causes, but the richness and reliability of information they provide about particular cases can be of great value. In particular, they will often supply in-depth knowledge of the perspectives of participants and of processes within cases occurring over time. Very often, research of this kind reveals hitherto unsuspected complexities, but it can also develop and sometimes test explanations effectively on its own.

It is possible to combine two or more of these case selection strategies within the same study. Furthermore, multiple studies using different strategies may be complementary in building up knowledge in a field.

It is important to recognise that there is often a discrepancy between the cases that it was originally planned to study and the cases that are actually investigated – as a result of practical difficulties. Devising experiments in such a way as to control relevant variables is a challenging task that is by no means always entirely successful, as we saw in the case of Piaget and Donaldson's criticisms of his work. In the case of surveys, it is extremely rare for all of the cases selected to be accessed successfully. For example, not all of the people selected as part of the sample will be contactable, and some will refuse to participate, so that the sample from whom data are collected will only be a proportion of the target sample, in some surveys it is less than 50 per cent. This is referred to as the problem of non-response. Similar problems are faced in case study research: gaining access to cases in order to obtain data can be difficult.

Given this, in reading and assessing studies it is important to get a clear sense of what cases were actually studied, as compared with the researchers' original intentions, and what the implications of this might be for the likely validity of the conclusions they reached. For example, in the case of surveys, the problem of non-response can raise questions about whether information about the sample can be generalised with confidence to the target population.

Each of these case selection strategies may involve collecting different types of data. So, another important question that needs to be taken into account in research design is what particular sorts of data might be needed in order to answer the research questions. This issue is independent of which case selection strategy is adopted. I will consider this in the next section.

Types of data

Data can come from three main sources: from observation by the researcher, from accounts elicited by the researcher from other people, and from documents (including material artefacts) of various kinds that are already available.

While the distinctions among these types of data capture important broad differences, each one includes considerable diversity in what it covers:

Observation

This requires the researcher to watch and listen to some course of action, and to record data about it. It can vary along at least two dimensions:

a **Detached observation versus participant observation.** Observation may be carried out in such a way that participants are unaware that it is taking place, for example through a two-way mirror or via CCTV cameras, or by 'lurking' in online sites. (Ethical considerations may arise here, of course.) Or participants could be aware of the observer but he or she plays no direct role in the proceedings, being simply a spectator. However, some observational research involves researchers taking on a role in the field, in other words becoming 'participant observers'. Or, alternatively, people who are already participants in a context may take on the role of researcher. Of course, there is likely to be variation in the character of observation according to the nature of the role adopted and the kind of setting involved. It is also worth noting that a researcher could plan one kind of observation but find that he or she is involved in a rather different kind. Thus, King (1984) intended to be a detached observer in a nursery classroom but the children had other ideas, drawing him into their activities.

b **Variation in the degree to which data are structured.** Some observation involves the use of observational schedules, requiring the occurrence of pre-specified types of event to be recorded, with the result that there is a relatively narrow and fixed focus. By contrast, other observational studies are more open-ended, with the observer focusing upon whatever is occurring that might seem relevant to the research topic, or that might be of broader significance, with the idea that what is relevant has to be *discovered*.

These two dimensions indicate the main ways in which observation can vary; and the various types of observation they identify differ in their advantages and disadvantages for particular purposes. For example, adopting a detached observational role may minimise the effect of the research on the people being studied if they are unaware that observation is taking place, but by contrast they may be affected more by a researcher they are aware of who is acting as a spectator than by a participant observer. Much depends here upon the context in which observation is taking place, as well as on people's expectations about the researcher, and the role he or she takes on.

Of course, it is possible for researchers to combine different forms of observation. The key consideration is what kinds of data are likely to facilitate answering the research questions, and what threats to the validity of conclusions are associated with each strategy. For example, Corsaro (1981) combined observation through a two-way mirror with participant observation in studying young children. The first enabled him to comprehend something of the overall pattern of children's activities when he was not involved, the second gave him more understanding of what particular children were doing, and of how they responded to others, both to one another and to him.

There can also be variation in strategies for recording data: from various kinds of manual recording (field-note writing, making counts of events, etc.) to forms of electronic recording (audio-recording, video-recording, photography).

Sometimes researchers invite participants to write records of what they have observed or experienced or to produce audio- or video-recordings. This may enable observational data to be obtained from settings to which the researcher does not have access (again, there may be distinctive ethical issues here). It can also provide insight into what participants believe to be important and relevant, as signalled by what they choose to record, and not to record. For example, in a study taking the form of 'participatory photography' the children chose to take photographs of the school toilets, because they were unhappy with their condition, something which led to some conflict with the school management, though also to improvement in the facilities (Kaplan 2008: 185–5).

Elicited accounts

One of the main strategies here is interviewing. This, of course, involves asking people questions and recording their answers, but in practice it can take several forms:

a **Informal versus formal interviews.** At one end of this spectrum, interviews may be snatched conversations taking place alongside or around other activities. At the other extreme, interviews will be meetings that are specially pre-arranged, in a particular place at a particular time, for the purposes of asking questions, and insulated as far as possible from surrounding activities. This is, of course, a dimension, so that interviews may vary in their degree of formality.

b **Structured, semi-structured, or unstructured interviews.** A structured interview involves closed questions with interviewees being asked to choose from a set of pre-specified answers, in much the same way as in fixed-choice questionnaires. By contrast, in unstructured interviews the questions are not decided beforehand, and are open-ended; and, for the most part, they will be designed to invite informants to talk at length about matters that could be relevant to the research topic. Again, what is involved here is a dimension, with more semi-structured kinds of interviewing lying between these two poles. These might involve a series of questions that all respondents are to be asked, but with other questions added in where appropriate; and respondents left free to answer the questions in their own terms. A single interview may combine structured, semi-structured, and unstructured questions, but usually one type predominates.

In addition, we might note that interviewing can be face-to-face, via telephone, or online, for example using video-conferencing software or email. The mode adopted may have important implications for the character of the data produced.

There are also group interviews as well as individual interviews. Here the responses may well be shaped by the fact that other people are the audience as well as the researcher. And the response of one person may prompt another into saying something that they might not otherwise have disclosed.

With interviews, as with observation, strategies for recording data can vary, from filling in an interview schedule during the course of the interview, through writing notes on people's answers and expanding these later, to audio- or video-recording.

Eliciting accounts may take other forms than interviews, for example:

- *Questionnaires:* These can be administered face-to-face, be sent by post or filled in online. We can also include under this heading the administering of psychological tests of various sorts.
- *Diaries, life histories,* or *blogs,* in which people report on and reflect about some aspect of their lives. These may be written, or audio- or video-recorded.

Already available documents and artefacts

These are data that have been produced by others independently of the researcher but are available for analysis. Documents may involve texts or images, or both. They may also be public or private. Examples include: official reports and diaries; photographs and drawings. The medium in which documents exist can vary as well: while many are paper-based, an increasing number are electronic.

Artefacts are material objects of some kind, but here again the medium can vary, as can the size. Those relevant in the study of children and young people include toys of various kinds, and also the physical layout of places like homes and schools.

Obtaining the necessary data is clearly very important in research, but equally significant is what is done with it. The final aspect of research design we will discuss is the analysis of data.

Modes of analysis

There is considerable variation in how researchers studying children and young people go about analysing data. In large part this will reflect the particular questions they are addressing and the circumstances in which the research is carried out. Also relevant will be whether the aim is to produce a description or an explanation, and the nature of the data available.

As already noted, most studies address explanatory questions. There are two basic analytic strategies for doing this:

- **Within-case analysis**: Here the focus is on processes and structures within cases, perhaps looking at how these change over time. The aim is to discover signs that might indicate what produced the outcome that the researcher is trying to explain.
- **Cross-case analysis**: Here there is a search across cases for patterns between potential explanatory factors and the outcome that it is hoped to explain.

Within-case analysis usually involves examining cases where the outcome that is of interest actually occurred, to look at what preceded it or what is otherwise associated with it, and to find out participants' understandings of themselves, their situation, and their behaviour that might be relevant to any explanation. The aim is to use the data to think about what processes could have generated the outcome, and to test out ideas about this.

Cross-case analysis can involve investigating cases where the type of outcome we are interested in has occurred, but perhaps also cases that are similar in many respects but where this outcome was absent. Researchers might also investigate cases where what they suspect is the key factor is present to find out whether the outcome also occurred there. The patterns discovered through comparing cases can suggest what causes what, and may also enable us to test our ideas about this. Doing this will often require comparing cases where other factors that might affect the outcome are constant.

There are advantages and disadvantages to both within-case and cross-case analysis: they provide different kinds of information. Given this, there is much to be gained from combining them, and a great deal of research does this.

Qualitative versus quantitative, versus mixed, methods?

In discussing each of the various aspects of research design, we have identified alternative strategies that researchers can use. It is common in accounts of research methodology for these strategies to be grouped into two overall categories – quantitative and qualitative. The implication of this division is that adopting a particular strategy to deal with one aspect of research design automatically requires that certain other strategies must be adopted to deal with the others; so that one either takes a quantitative or a qualitative approach.

In these terms, qualitative researchers would tend to adopt a flexible approach to research design, beginning from open-ended research questions that will only be made more specific towards the end of the inquiry process. They also tend to adopt a case-study approach, collect relatively unstructured data, and rely mainly upon within-case analysis. By contrast, quantitative research is more likely to specify hypotheses to be tested quite early on, to use an experimental or survey approach in selecting cases, to collect structured forms of data, and to rely upon cross-case analysis.

In this spirit, books on social research methodology typically have distinct sections dealing with qualitative and quantitative approaches (see e.g. Bryman 2012). And many researchers describe themselves as committed to either a quantitative or a qualitative approach, sometimes insisting that theirs is the only valid or legitimate one.

This distinction between qualitative and quantitative research relates closely to the question of the grounds on which researchers should decide which strategy to use in selecting cases, types of data, and forms of analysis. We have presented these decisions up to now as a matter of evaluating the relative advantages and disadvantages of each strategy in pursuing particular research questions. This is not completely misleading, but the issue is not as simple as this implies. This is because there are always assumptions already built into how researchers go about their work – they cannot start from a blank slate. In particular, there are presuppositions implicit in research questions, and in how researchers decide what are significant advantages and disadvantages associated with particular research strategies, and their relative importance.

These assumptions or presuppositions relate first of all to the nature of the social world – and in the case of the area of work we are concerned with in this book, most obviously ideas about the nature of children, young people and their relations with others, the institutions in which they are involved, and so on. There are also, necessarily, presuppositions about how we can best come to understand these phenomena, given what we assume about their character. Qualitative and quantitative approaches tend to be associated with rather different sets of assumptions about the nature of human beings and their social lives, and about how these can be understood – what we might call different paradigms or methodological philosophies.

However, what we find in the methodological literature is not an opposition between just two monolithic approaches. As we shall see in Chapter 10, there are more than just two sets of ideas about the nature of the social world and how it can be understood. Nor are the methodological philosophies that have shaped research concerned with children and young people's lives mutually exclusive in all respects. There are divergent interpretations of each philosophy, and there is some overlap between them.

Moreover, if one looks at actual research studies and how they are carried out, it is common to find that the various strategies we have identified in relation to different aspects of research design are combined in ways that do not correspond neatly to the qualitative/quantitative divide. For example, there is research that is exploratory in character, rather than being geared to hypothesis-testing, but uses structured data, while focusing on within-case analysis. There is also work that is more sharply focused at the start, but which uses relatively unstructured data for the purposes of cross-case analysis. Other studies involve separate qualitative and quantitative components that each contribute to their findings to varying degrees; for example, it is not unusual to find a survey involving structured data and cross-case analysis being used to complement an in-depth case study that employs relatively unstructured data and concentrates on within-case analysis. Indeed, the combining of 'qualitative' and 'quantitative' strategies has come to be championed in the past decade or so, under the heading of 'mixed methods research' (see Bryman 2008; Tashakkori and Teddlie 2010). Discussions of this have outlined the various ways in which research strategies can be combined, and the advantages and disadvantages of these (Cresswell and Plano Clark 2006).

Conclusion

In this chapter we have explored what is involved in research design. This is concerned with determining how to investigate a topic so as to produce sound knowledge, albeit within the limits of what is practically feasible and ethically acceptable. We looked at the formulation of research questions and at different types of research question. We noted that research does not necessarily require the collection of new data, but that often it will do so. Research design demands attention to what cases are to be studied and how they are selected, and to the type of data that would enable the research questions to be addressed effectively. Relevant here are the distinctive threats to validity associated with different strategies and types of data. Finally, we looked at different modes of analysis aimed at developing and testing explanations.

All these aspects of research design must be considered by researchers in the course of their work. Similarly, when we read research reports we must try to get a clear sense of what research questions were being addressed, how they were investigated, why a particular research design was adopted, and how effectively it can provide answers to those questions. It was noted, however, that there are some difficult methodological issues and debates surrounding the adoption of particular research strategies, and these too need to be examined. This will be the task in the other chapters making up this section of the book.

References

Bryman, A. (2008) 'The end of the paradigm wars?', in P. Alasuutari, J. Brannen and L. Bickman (eds) *Handbook of Social Research*. London: Sage. pp. 13–25.

Bryman, A. (2012) *Social Research Methods*, 4th edition. Oxford: Oxford University Press.

Corsaro, W. (1981) 'Entering the child's world – research strategies for field entry and data collection in a preschool setting', in J. Green and C. Wallat (eds), *Ethnography and Language in Educational Settings*. Norwood, NJ: Ablex.

Cresswell, J. and Plano Clark, V. (2006) *Designing and Conducting Mixed Methods Research*. Thousand Oaks, CA: Sage.

Donaldson, M. (1978) *Children's Minds*. London: Fontana.

Gage, N. (1991) 'The obviousness of social and educational research results', *Educational Researcher*, 20(1): 10–16.

Kaplan, I. (2008) 'Being "seen" being "heard": Engaging with students on the margins of education through participatory photography', in P. Thomson (ed.), *Doing Visual Research with Children and Young People*. London: Routledge.

King, R. (1984) 'The man in the Wendy House: Researching infants' schools', in R. Burgess (ed.), *The Research Process in Educational Settings: Ten Case Studies*. London: Falmer Press.

Streuli, N., Vennam, U. and Woodhead, M. (2011) 'Increasing choice or inequality? Pathways through early education in Andhra Pradesh, India', *Young Lives Project Working Paper* 58, University of Oxford. Available at: www.younglives.org.uk/files/working-papers/bvlf-ecd-wp58-india-increasing-choice-or-inequality (accessed 13 August 2012).

Tashakkori, A. and Teddlie, C. (eds) (2010) *Handbook of Mixed Methods in Social and Behavioral Research*, 2nd edition. Thousand Oaks CA: Sage.

Woodyer, T. (2010) 'Playing with toys: The animated geographies of children's material culture', unpublished PhD thesis, Royal Holloway College, University of London.

7 Participant Observation

Heather Montgomery

Introduction

It is always tempting with any research method to think that it holds the key to successful research: if only the method is right then the research will do well and the right techniques for working with children will provide the exact data that you want. Unfortunately this is rarely the case and this chapter does not provide a how-to guide on successful observational research with children. Instead it will discuss one particular method: participant observation. This is a central component of the ethnographic approach to research, and we will look at its strengths and limitations. The focus of the chapter will be on the theory behind participant observation, how it works in practice, and some of its benefits and problems. It will end with a discussion of the dilemmas that participant observation raises and its impacts on both researchers and those they research.

What is participant observation?

Participant observation is a research technique first pioneered by social anthropologists in the early twentieth century and is particularly associated with Polish-born anthropologist Bronislaw Malinowski (1884–1942) and his 1922 book, *Argonauts of the Western Pacific*. This was Malinowski's analysis of the life and culture of the people of the Trobriand Islands of Papua New Guinea, with whom he lived for four years. In this book he laid out the basic anthropological method which has remained an idealised model (albeit with numerous deviations and differences) ever since. Malinowski believed that this method contained two crucial elements. Firstly, in order to study and understand the patterns of life in other societies it was necessary to live and work alongside the indigenous people and this involved a period of immersion into a culture, known as fieldwork, during which one could make observations of daily life while also blending in and becoming a part of it. Malinowski describes his own experiences of participant observation in the Trobriand Islands as follows:

> Soon after I had established myself in Omarakana (Trobriand Islands), I began to take part, in a way, in the village life, to look forward to the important or festive events, to take a personal interest in the gossip and the developments of the small village occurrences ... I would get out from under my mosquito net, to find around me the village life beginning to stir. ... As I went on my morning walk through the village, I could see intimate details of family life, of toilet, cooking, taking of meals; I could see the arrangements for the day's work, people starting on their errands, or groups of men and women busy at some manufacturing task. Quarrels, jokes, family scenes, events usually trivial, sometimes dramatic but always significant, formed the atmosphere of my daily life, as well as of theirs. (1922: 7)

Malinowski claimed that behaving in this way meant that not only would you be on the spot if anything happened, but people would get to know you better and become less self-conscious about your presence. Eventually the Trobriand Islanders came to regard him, he claimed, as 'part and parcel of their life, a necessary evil or nuisance, mitigated by donations of tobacco' (1922: 8).

Secondly, he argued that it was necessary to view fieldwork as a science and participant observation as a scientific technique (comparable to experiments in chemistry or physics) by which anthropologists could collect and analyse their data and thus make a contribution to scientific knowledge. In the 1920s, when people outside the West were routinely derided as ignorant or childish savages, Malinowski argued that they were just as intelligent and logical as Westerners and must always be treated as such. The best informants about a particular way of life were, Malinowski believed, those who lived it. The anthropologist's purpose was to not to judge or ridicule others but to understand them and the logic and reasons behind their behaviour, thought and actions.

Malinowski claimed that anthropologists should record three types of data:

1 **Concrete, background information**. This included specific case histories, genealogies, numbers of children, harvest yields, etc.
2 **The 'imponderabilia of actual life'** (2002: 18). He coined this term to refer to those actions or beliefs that are so ingrained or commonplace that people do not think about them or think it necessary to explain them. Malinowski thought that these had to be observed, not asked about, but he also believed that sometimes anthropologists should stop taking notes and just participate in these ordinary activities to get a better feel for them.
3 **People's own explanations, stories, myths, etc.** These should be collected in their own words and in their language, in order that a collection of indigenous knowledge could be built up.

When this data has been collected, anthropologists critically analyse it in ethnographies (a word combined from the ancient Greek word *ethnos*, meaning people and *graphia* to write), which recount, explain and interpret unfamiliar cultural practices and belief systems. Ethnography therefore is both a research method, based on participant observation, and the outcome of this process in the form of an article or book in which the anthropologist attempts to explain and interpret the social and cultural lives of others.

Malinowski's account of participant observation retains its status as a seminal text which helped establish modern anthropology. Participant observation also remains an important technique throughout the social sciences and has been adopted by many other disciplines, such as sociology, cultural studies, childhood studies and education. Yet Malinowski's theories and practices have been much scrutinised and criticised, not least because Malinowski himself did not always follow his own methods or live up to his own ideals (the publication of his personal diaries in 1967, in which he recounted his less than flattering accounts of individual Trobrianders, led to much soul searching within anthropology about the nature and purpose of participant observation). His method has also been criticised for its impracticality. Few people today can spend years in the field, cut off from the outside world, and anthropologists now work within their own societies as much as they do abroad. The idea of a scientific discipline in which a lone, impartial, objective expert measures, counts or collects aspects of other people's societies and cultures has largely gone, to be replaced with a more nuanced and practical realisation of the possibilities and problems of participant observation. A later American anthropologist, Clifford Geertz (1926–2006), came closer to reality when he described participant observation as 'deep hanging out' (1998), a light-hearted but telling phrase which hints at the messiness and contradictions of this technique.

Participant observation with children

Participant observation with children involves many of the same processes as doing such research with adults. It involves engagement and 'deep hanging out' with children, understanding their lives, their experiences and how they make sense of the world. But doing participant observation with children also raises particular challenges and it is unwise to pretend that children are a subject like any other, or that, as a technique for researching children, participant observation is without problems.

Holistic studies of small-scale societies, such as those pioneered by Malinowski, described and acknowledged children's role in the family, while other famous anthropologists, such as Margaret Mead, focused their research on young people and lived and worked extensively alongside them, producing books such as Mead's *Coming of Age in Samoa* (1928), which is still in print today. American anthropologists focused much attention on child rearing practices and socialisation, analysing the ways children were raised in different societies and speculating on the long-term impacts of this (Montgomery 2009). Within sociology, for example, Carl Werthman and Irving Piliavin (1967) documented the perspectives and activities of gang members in the US and their relationship with the police. Yet, despite this work, many anthropologists and sociologists took it as axiomatic that children were not proper informants; they were seen as still learning the ways of their society, they were incompletely socialised and did not know enough about their culture to be worthwhile informants. British anthropologist Audrey Richards, in her authoritative account of girls' initiation rites among the Bemba of Zambia, written in 1956, pointed out that the one group of people she did not talk to were the girls themselves, on the grounds that they were 'the least interesting of the actors in it' (1956: 63).

By the 1970s this caution about using children as informants led to criticism that social scientists were uninterested in the lives of children and young people. This criticism is not altogether fair, however; as mentioned above there have always been individual anthropologists and other social scientists interested in childhood and there is a long tradition of studying child-rearing in the USA. Richards herself regretted not talking to the girls and acknowledged the gap in her analysis. Sociology too has seen many researchers studying and learning from young people, particularly in the fields of education and deviance (Franzese 2009). However in the 1970s and 1980s there were concerted attempts throughout the social sciences to focus more directly on children and young people and their own experiences and explanations; and, under the banner of 'New Social Studies of Childhood', researchers called for children's perspectives and understandings to be taken more seriously and for age to be acknowledged as an important organising principle in society, as worthy of study as gender or ethnicity. Childhood was understood as a culturally constructed social phenomenon which changed over time and place, and ideas about childhood as well as children's lives were recognised as important fields of study (James and Prout 1997).

This approach also raised methodological issues about how best to work with children and young people. While many participant observation techniques are the same for both children and adults, there are important practical and ethical issues that have to be overcome when researching children, such as language competency (it is difficult to use very young children who cannot speak as informants, even though, as other chapters in this book suggest, it is possible), concentration span, and the social norms of politeness and deference to adults which constrain many children. Thus social scientists have developed techniques which involve play, games, painting or drawing, which not only mirror children's everyday activities but also allow younger children to participate in research.

Puppets and dolls have been used by some researchers to encourage children to talk and to make interviews less intimidating. The researchers on one project which looked at deaf children's experiences in British classrooms asked children with hearing problems to talk to, or sign to, a puppet and asked them to tell the puppet what advice they would give to other children who were hearing impaired (Iantaffi et al. 2002). Other participant observation research with children has entailed giving them cameras and asking them to photograph people and places that are important to them. In his work among street children in Brazil, Tobias Hecht (1998) gave them recorders and asked them to interview each other as if they were journalists and then to bring the recordings back to him. By using this method he elicited information from them that they might not have felt happy revealing directly to adults. In my own research with young prostitutes who lived in a slum in Thailand, I would draw outlines of their bodies – 'body maps' – in the dust surrounding their houses and use these to ask questions about whether they were hurt or ill or if some parts of their bodies did not feel right to them. However my best interviews with the girls were done not by sitting down with a notebook and interviewing them, or even by observing them in their daily lives, but by becoming a part of everyday activities, well away from their work. I would let them play with my hair, paint my fingernails and would discuss my love life with them while listening to them tell me stories about theirs. It was important to share and reciprocate and I found this an essential component of participant observation.

Many of those interested in studying children have tried to find ways of reducing the distance between themselves as adults and the children they wish to research. Several have written explicitly about this dilemma, including Nancy Mandell (1991), who tried to overcome this distance by taking on a 'least-adult role', never correcting or directing the children's actions and trying to play down her adult status and her verbal and cognitive competence. William Corsaro (1985) has also worked extensively with young children in schools in Italy and America, and while he concedes that he will never be seen as one of them, he argues that it is possible to be assigned a special role by the children – in his case as 'Big Bill' – a non-adult-like adult:

Two four-year-old girls (Betty and Jenny) and adult researcher (Bill) in a nursery school:

Betty: You can't play with us!
Bill: Why?
Betty: Cause you're too big.

Bill: I'll sit down (sits down)
Jenny: You're still too big.
Betty: Yeah, you're 'Big Bill'!
Bill: Can I just watch?
Jenny: OK, but don't touch nuthin!
Betty: You just watch, OK?
Bill: OK
Jenny: OK, Big Bill?
Bill: OK
(Later Big Bill got to play)
(Corsaro 1981: 117)

Sociologist Gary Fine has suggested that there are four possible roles an adult outsider can play when researching children:

- *Leader*: The leader has authority over the children and also attempts to maintain friendly relations with them; popular teachers are leaders.
- *Supervisor*: The supervisor role involves authority over children, but without an attempt to establish friendly relations (e.g., authoritarian teachers).
- *Observer*: The observer in the ideal form of this role has neither positive contact with the subjects nor authority but simply records events without becoming personally involved.
- *Friend*: The friend role is an attempt to couple a positive relationship with a minimal amount of authority. To the extent this can be managed, this is identical to the traditional participant observational role used to deal with adults (Fine 1987: 223–4).

From this description it might seem that taking on the role of friend is the most productive way of observing, and even participating in, a child's world, but it is questionable as to whether an adult (especially one with a research agenda) can ever truly be a friend to a child. Furthermore, there are plenty of examples of adults retaining their adult role and nevertheless managing to generate illuminating data about the experiences and perspectives of children and young people. David Hargreaves carried out participant observation of school life in a boys' school in the UK in the 1960s, and in his 1967 book discusses the many dilemmas of participant observation. While never attempting to be the pupils' friend, and being clear with both staff and pupils about his role as an adult social scientist, his account of school life is very revealing and provides a plausible account of the positive and negative aspects of teenage male culture in the school he studied.

Others, however, argue that dismantling the hierarchies of age and power are important prerequisites for effective research. Anna Laerke (1998), in her work with British primary school children, tried to blend in with them, playing in the sand pit alongside them, dressing like them, sitting on the same small chairs, and allying herself with the children against the teacher and sometimes siding with one child against another. Eventually, she noted:

> The children stopped asking for my adult help or intervention; they began, in my presence, to tell secrets about whom they were in love with or whom they didn't want to play with; they began bullying me, and I sometimes found myself giggling along with those who bullied others. (1998: 3)

Yet, despite an awareness of the difficulties of taking on these various roles, it is still hard to anticipate how children and young people will respond. Some children might accept a non-adult adult in their midst and relate to a 'Big Bill' figure, but not all children will. Children may want to be friends and collaborators but it can be difficult for children to differentiate a friend from a researcher they know and like and they may enter into a relationship with the adult researcher that they do not have the full knowledge and agency to understand. Alternatively, they may choose not to be friends or may be embarrassed, confused or even intimidated by an adult sitting in the sand pit with them or sitting next to them at school. Young people, in particular, may well be mortified by an adult 'hanging out' with them, trying to be like them and wanting to find out things that they would rather share only with their peers.

There are also questions about the impact taking on these roles has on the researcher. Mary Jane Kehily, in her work with British schoolgirls, has written about some of the dilemmas of fitting in, while also attempting to retain her own personal and political identity.

> One day I found myself lying on the floor pinching my fat bits, comparing the wad of flab squeezed between thumb and forefinger with that of other girls in the room. There were moans, waves of disgust and shrieks of laughter. Her tummy, my upper arms and, oh my god, look at that blubber around the thighs. Was this a scene recalled from adolescence or a more recent memory – a moment of weakness on a girlie night in with your mates? It actually happened during a research encounter not so long ago, while I was doing an ethnographic study in a primary school. The girls I was working with were age 10 at the time and I was, er, about 42 and three-quarters. After years of involvement in feminist politics and a few more years as a feminist researcher, I thought I had acquired something of 'the knowledge' – that unique blend of theoretical insights and feminist sensibilities that equip 'us women' for social situations. But knowing what I know about body image, fat and self-regulation, why was I engaging in such an activity? (Kehily 2004: 366)

While sharing many elements of Malinowski's account of participant observation – joining in with the mundane and ordinary and doing what your informants do – this account suggests a more ambivalent relationship between researcher and informants. Gone is the scientific detachment and in its place an acknowledgment that research can have problematic and even painful impacts. Ten years after carrying out her research, Anna Laerke eloquently expressed her feelings of uncertainty and distress over her research role. She claims that it 'broke her heart' (2008: 144) and that:

> While writing has been an exorcism, of sorts, of a fieldwork identity that literally made me sick, a reconstituted and properly dislodged 'me' has yet to materialize. Ten years on, I am still in the grip of it … writing about [my fieldwork] has produced a gradual sedimentarisation of two feelings: anger and sadness. (2008: 144)

Interpreting observation

There is, of course, no such thing as a perfect research relationship where there are no differences in size, age, or power, and, although working with children highlights some of these imbalances, they are not issues which are unique to studying childhood. Participant observation with all informants poses challenges and dilemmas, both theoretical and practical, and building up a complete picture of every aspect of children's lives is rarely achievable. Outside the industrialised West, many anthropologists have written ethnographies, based on participant observation, which focus on children who live on the street or who work in illegal and often dangerous jobs. Yet it would be impossible for an adult outsider to enter into an illegal sweatshop in order to work alongside or even observe a child worker; and living on the street with street children could well attract unwelcome attention and create further problems for them. As someone who wanted to understand child prostitution in Thailand, I inevitably found it impossible to observe or participate in this part of the children's lives. I was reliant on what I was told, not on what I observed, which meant that the aspect of children's lives I most wanted to understand was hidden from me.

A partial solution is to participate in and observe as much of the children's lives as possible and then ask questions about those areas to which you cannot, and maybe should not, gain access. It is possible to obtain life histories when children look back on their lives so far and tell you what has happened, and to compare these with those of their siblings. Parents too are an important source of information and help. While memories are often unreliable, and people tell life narratives in particular ways, asking multiple people the same questions makes it possible to build up a picture of many aspects of a child's life, even if you have not directly observed or participated in them.

The use of language also remains a central issue for researchers with children, but again different problems emerge when speaking to adults and children. In the classic fieldwork scenario envisaged by Malinowski, it is the researcher who is linguistically incompetent, trying to learn a new language with sufficient fluency to understand, interview and analyse what is going on. When working with children, however, it may well be the informants who do not have full command of the language and cannot express themselves (see Waller and Bitou 2011).

It is noticeable that most 'child-centred' anthropology has focused on older children who can talk, state their opinions and act as informants; and that there is less work done with younger children. Some researchers see participant observation with very young children as pointless and reject the notion that such children can ever act as informants. Fine and Sandstrom argue:

> Part of the difficulty with achieving a reflective and interpretative understanding of the world of young children is that children are not able to articulate reflexively (at least in 'adult' modes of discourse) the way their world appears to them when questioned by adults. Thus the adult may have to do this work by 'becoming a child' and using his or her reflective skills. The assumption is that there will be some similarity between these two worlds. Discovering what children 'really' know may be almost as difficult as learning what our pet kitten really knows; we can't trust or quite understand the sounds they make. We think that we can make sense of what behaviours have just occurred, but can we be sure that we are not reading into their actions? (1988: 47)

Other researchers firmly reject this idea, arguing that participant observation is always possible and that even the youngest children have the means of communicating with adults, if only adults are prepared to see them as people who can interact and communicate.

One such researcher is Priscilla Alderson (see Chapter 5), who has spent many years working with young children, including premature and neo-natal babies. Based on close observation of these babies she and her colleagues have made radical claims about their abilities to communicate and their agency (Alderson et al. 2005a, 2006a). This work is controversial, for reasons which will be discussed later, but it is important in that it takes the possibility of participant observation seriously even with the very youngest children and suggests how it might be achieved.

Alderson's team based their study in four neonatal units during 2002–04 and focused on babies who were born prematurely. They examined how these babies were conceptualised by their carers and the impact this had on the care they were given. To do this they interviewed parents, doctors, nurses and support staff, and observed and participated in their daily lives on the ward. But their research was designed to look at more than adults' thoughts about these vulnerable babies: they also looked at how babies themselves responded to their circumstances, and whether they could become useful informants. They write:

> All babies give cues about their feelings and seek for optimal conditions. For example, we saw babies looking relaxed and contented in soft fabric 'nests' that, like the uterus, help them to maintain a foetal curved position, limbs gathered together and hands close to the face, so that they can soothe themselves such as by sucking their fingers, or

stroking their face if they have oral ventilator tubes. In some units, the babies' limbs hang over loose loops of rough towelling and they try to gather their splayed limbs together, and to wriggle into a corner of the cot that could contain them more firmly. Nurses may then move them back to the centre of the cot. The babies' subtle behaviours can be 'read' as their language to inform understanding about babies' preferences and best interests. (Alderson et al. 2005b: 72)

The authors seem to imply that these babies have a form of language through which they can express preferences and make some sort of decision about their treatment. Therefore, they argue for a rethink of what observation and non-verbal communication might mean in particular contexts. They claim that far from being passive recipients of care, babies seemed to express particular likes and dislikes. One baby, for example, did not like his feet being touched, another one seemingly expressed a preference for one nurse over others. All these actions may be forms of communication, and the authors claim that both parents and paediatricians sometimes saw these babies as independent, autonomous beings: 'Many parents and practitioners … gave examples of babies continuing to survive against all expectations, or sometimes unexpectedly "giving up" as if, in some ways, the babies had the final say in whether they lived or died' (Alderson et al. 2005b: 39).

These babies are obviously limited in terms of how they can communicate and participate and it may be meaningless to talk about children acting as informants in these contexts. There is also always a danger of adults reading into children's behaviour what they want to see and labelling children in unhelpful ways. As Alderson and her colleagues point out, while some adults saw and praised these tiny children's struggles, others labelled some of them more pejoratively as 'naughty', 'lazy' or 'greedy' (Alderson et al. 2005b). What the authors do not acknowledge, however, is that they too are looking at these babies through a particular ideological lens and attributing to them communicative intent. They do not distinguish between expression and communication, adaptation and decision-making; and, while it is undeniable that the babies are expressing something in their behaviour, it is highly questionable whether these babies are making decisions based on any form of knowledge or that adults can 'read' these behaviours as children *communicating* preferences. Interpreting these children's actions through adult eyes and with adult ideology – whether this is to see them as active agents and useful informants, as difficult and resisting care, or as helpless and uncommunicative – is always problematic and open to continual contestation and debate.

What is the point of participant observation?

Participant observation allows researchers to get close to the children they are studying and to learn about their worlds, their feelings and understandings. Yet it also has drawbacks: it is time consuming and often practically difficult – finding children willing to talk and let you become part of their lives can be hard, and the researcher may need to go through many gatekeepers. Researchers also almost never work exclusively with children, they work with them in contexts where there are other adults who also play various roles, and negotiating these various relationships is complex and sometimes ethically fraught. In a school, for example, working with children may mean 'siding' with them against teachers but this might not be in their best interests, it may exacerbate conflicts and become uncomfortable for both the researcher and the children. Working with children and young people also raises intractable ethical issues about how far children can really consent and choose to be part of research, the extent to which they can separate your role as a researcher from that of a friend, and what responsibilities a researcher has to children in the short and longer term, as well as perhaps, most importantly, what benefit is in this research for them. While these issues exist for all researchers who deal with human subjects, they become particularly acute when working with children.

All researchers have to ask themselves about the point of their research. For some the answer may be completely instrumental – they need to complete this research for their university project or because they were told to as part of their job. For others it may be intellectual curiosity, interest in other people or to make a contribution to scholarship. Increasingly, however, there is a pressure to 'do' something with social research, especially that which involves children (or other vulnerable or disadvantaged groups such as the disabled), and to try to ensure that research improves their lives in some way. Funding bodies and university ethics committees now want to know the impacts, both positive and negative, of undertaking research, and some tie research funding to guaranteed 'outputs' and usefulness to 'stakeholder groups'. Consequently, research with children often becomes a prelude to intervention, even though it is highly questionable whether this is a good recipe for producing sound knowledge. Many researchers might hope that their work will bring about improvements, but to set out with this explicit purpose in mind may well mean starting the research with preconceived notions and with the built-in potential for translating these into false conclusions.

On the ground, there are also many issues about the responsibilities of researchers to the individual children with whom they work. It is the duty of the researcher to explain that while research may help groups of children in general, it may not help the individual children taking part – an issue with which children may struggle. Researchers must try to ensure that children know the limits of their role and researchers should be wary of making friends with children if they do not envisage ongoing relationships once the project is over. Researchers must therefore negotiate their exit from the field as carefully as their entry. While many researchers are very conscientious about telling children who they are, why they are trying to do research and what its benefits might be, they are less good at leaving. For children who have become used to an adult being there on a daily basis, who have learnt to like and trust that person, it can be bewildering and upsetting for them if the researcher suddenly leaves without an explanation.

There is also the wider question of intervention during the research, and, again, in this respect working with children differs from research with most adults. Researchers must not only observe and participate, they must also intervene when necessary:

> Children's perceived vulnerability means that a further fundamental difference is that the obligations, duties and responsibilities that researchers have towards their subjects are qualitatively different when working with children and relate to adult responsibilities towards children in general ... researchers need to recognise their moral obligations as adults to protect children at risk even when this may mean losing access to, or the trust of, the children concerned if they do intervene. (Morrow and Richards 1996: 98)

This, however, is often easier in theory than in practice. What may be possible in a classroom in the UK becomes much harder when dealing with children in difficult circumstances outside the confines of a bureaucratised state, or indeed when the researcher is interested in issues such as teenage pregnancy, or underage sexual experience, or drug use. How does a researcher interested in child soldiers, street children, or child workers in an illegal factory, intervene in their lives, even when what they are doing is illegal or abusive? How can they best protect young people engaged in risky and possibly criminal behaviour? And should they even try to do this if their role is that of a participant observer? It may be possible to use research to raise awareness of the various issues and to campaign for better conditions or services, but being unable to help the particular children and young people with whom the researcher has established trusting relationships, and who might hope for some good to come out of participation in the research project, can be extremely distressing, and is likely to leave the researcher feeling impotent.

Conclusion

As a qualitative method, participant observation is inevitably open to criticisms of subjectivity and bias. Yet it has become one of the most important and popular ways of collecting data about the lives of children and young people. Data collected through participant observation is now used, in varying forms, by anthropologists, sociologists, educationalists, psychologists and others to study a wide range of issues. At its best it enables researchers to describe and analyse patterns of social interaction between children and their peers, parents, carers and teachers and allows for a full description of the character, features and consequences of these patterns. Participant observation might seem an easy and relatively straightforward means of conducting research with children – after all how difficult can 'deep hanging out' really be? Yet its simplicity is deceptive. As this chapter has shown, there are enormous differences between the ideal model and the reality, between how participant observation was conceptualised in the past and how it is used by researchers now. Participant observation raises difficult questions about how to gain access to children's worlds, when to observe, when to participate and when to intervene, what sort of role the observer should play in the setting and what kinds of relations can be developed with people there. All these issues have profound implications for the validity of research findings and also for ethics.

References

Alderson, P., Hawthorne, J. and Killen, M. (2005a) 'Are premature babies citizens with rights? Provision rights and the edges of citizenship', *Journal of Social Sciences*, 9: 71–81.

Alderson, P., Hawthorne, J. and Killen, M. (2005b) 'The participation rights of premature babies', *The International Journal of Children's Rights*, 13(1–2): 31–50.

Corsaro, W. (1981) 'Entering the child's world – research strategies for field entry and data collection in a preschool setting', in J. Green and C. Wallat (eds), *Ethnography and Language in Educational Settings*. Norwood NJ: Ablex.

Corsaro, W. (1985) *Friendship and Peer Culture in the Early Years*. Norwood: Ablex.

Fine, G. (1987) *With the Boys: Little League Baseball and Preadolescent Culture*. Chicago: University of Chicago Press.

Fine, G.A. and Sandstrom, K.L. (1988) *Knowing Children: Participant Observation with Minors*. Newbury Park, CA: Sage.

Franzese, R. (2009) *The Sociology of Deviance: Differences, Tradition, and Stigma*. Springfield, IL: Charles C. Thomas.

Geertz, C. (1998) 'Deep hanging out', *New York Review of Books*, 22 October pp. 69–70.

Hargreaves, D. (1967) *Social Relations in a Secondary School*. London: Routledge and Kegan Paul.

Hecht, T. (1998) *At Home in the Street: Street Children of Northeast Brazil*. Cambridge: Cambridge University Press.

Iantaffi A., Sinka I. and Jarvis J. (2002) *Inclusion – What Deaf Pupils Think*. London: RNID.

James, A. and Prout, A. (1997) *Constructing and Reconstructing Childhood: Contemporary Issues in the Sociological Study of Childhood*, 2nd edition. London: Falmer Press.

Kehily, M.J. (2004) 'Girls on girls: Tensions and anxieties in research with girls', *Feminism and Psychology*, 14(3): 366–70.

Laerke, A. (1998) 'By means of re-membering: Notes on a fieldwork with English children', *Anthropology Today*, 14(1): 3–7.

Laerke, A. (2008) 'Confessions of a downbeat anthropologist', in H. Armbruster and A. Laerke (eds), *Taking Sides: Ethics, Politics and Fieldwork in Anthropology*. Oxford: Berghahn. pp. 175–98.

Malinowski, B. [1922] (2002) *Argonauts of the Western Pacific: An Account of Native Enterprise and Adventure in the Archipelagos of Melanesian New Guinea*. London: Routledge.

Mandell, N. (1991) 'The least-adult role in studying children', in F. Waksler (ed.), *Studying the Social Worlds of Children*. London: Falmer Press. pp. 38–59.

Mead, M. [1928] (1971) *Coming of Age in Samoa: A Study of Adolescence and Sex in Primitive Societies*. London: Pelican.

Montgomery, H. (2009) *An Introduction to Childhood: Anthropological Perspectives on Children's Lives*. Oxford: Wiley-Blackwell.

Morrow, V. and Richards, M. (1996) 'The ethics of social research with children: An overview', *Children and Society*, 10(2): 90–105.

Richards, A. (1956) *Chisungu: A Girls' Initiation Ceremony among the Bemba of Northern Rhodesia*. London: Faber and Faber.

Waller, T. and Bitou, A. (2011) 'Research with children: Three challenges for participatory research in early childhood', *European Early Childhood Education Research Journal*, 19(1): 5–20.

Werthman, C. and Piliavin, I. (1967) 'Gang members and the police', in D.J. Bordua (ed.) *The Police*. New York: John Wiley and Sons. pp. 56–98.

8 Interviews

Rosie Flewitt

Introduction

Interviews, in one form or another, have long been used by researchers interested in understanding particular issues in their own society or the history, character and context of other cultures and other societies. For instance, they were used in nineteenth-century studies of poverty in English industrial cities, and were also often used by Western anthropologists as they sought to understand the social organisation and characteristics of 'primitive' or non-Western cultures. Throughout the twentieth century, researchers developed the use of interviews to investigate many different social issues, including in the fields of education, care and health. In the second half of the twentieth century, as research methods across the social sciences began to move away from the dominance of 'measuring' social phenomena using quantitative methods, so the use of interviews moved towards more informal approaches in qualitative research to investigate participant experiences, perceptions, identities and beliefs.

Social science researchers who are seeking to understand the lives and perceptions of others often opt to use interviews as at least one of their chosen methods for investigation. Yet the interview is not a simple 'tool' that can be selected unproblematically from a methodological 'toolkit'. It involves a relationship between two or more people, and however brief that relationship may be its nature and quality will deeply influence what can be found out through the interview process. In this chapter, I encourage readers to reflect critically upon how interviews are always social events, where an interviewer and interviewee(s) meet to exchange information face-to-face, by telephone or in a virtual environment. Although, in most interviews, the interviewer usually asks most of the questions and the interviewee responds to them, both participants express their opinions and views through what they say and the ways they say it. I review some of the many different forms that interviews can take, including structured, semi-structured and unstructured, and consider social relationships during the interview process, the different kinds of data that interviews can generate and how these might be interpreted. Although the chapter focuses on interviewing young people and children, thought will also be given to interviewing adults.

What are interviews?

The Latin prefix *inter* (meaning *between* or *among*) suggests an exchange of *view*, that is, far from being a process where 'you ask, they answer, and then you know' (Hollway 2005: 312), research interviews are a particular kind of social interaction where data are constructed in the process of exchanging questions and answers: 'a place where views may clash, deceive, seduce, enchant' (Schostak 2006: 1). Conducting interviews is sometimes referred to as collecting stories about people's lives in order to 'know' (Seidman 2006).

When people tell such stories, they select information from a stream of consciousness, drawing on their memories of experiences and making meaning of them through the process of telling. Stories that have been told and re-told over time have been one of the main ways throughout history that humans have recorded and made sense of their social and cultural lives. The stories we tell are always shaped in some way by our sense of the story audience, and, in this respect, researchers who are planning to embark on interviewing need to consider not only what questions they are going to ask in order to find answers to their research questions (or raise new questions), but also how, where and when they are going to ask these questions. As much attention should be paid to the *process* of interviewing as to the *product*. It is fundamentally important never to lose sight of the social nature of the interview, where the 'view' of the interviewee is explored through the 'view' of the interviewer, as expressed through the questions asked. Regardless of whether an interview is structured by the researcher or led by the study participants, the research agenda will always in some way shape the interview responses that are generated.

Why are interviews used as a method for collecting data?

Different researchers use interviews for different purposes, depending on the research questions they are seeking to answer, and the research approach they have chosen to adopt. However, regardless of the methodological framing, interviews can:

1   generate insights into participants' lives which would otherwise remain hidden
    to the researcher;
2   give access to individuals' understanding of the contexts they are in, to their
    opinions, aspirations, attitudes and feelings;
3   generate complex insights into others' perceptions of social phenomena and
    why they make certain choices and act in the ways they do.

To illustrate this last point, I give a brief example from research conducted by
Johanna Einarsdottir (2005) in an Icelandic pre-school. In this participatory
study with pre-school children and teachers, Einarsdottir encouraged the children to be actively involved in data gathering by drawing and taking photographs
using both digital and disposable cameras. However, when it came to interpreting the visual data with the participants, not only did the teachers' voices pre-
dominate in the analysis but they drew largely on their professional expertise,
rather than on what they had learnt through the process of research. To overcome this bias, Einarsdottir designed group interviews for the child research
participants to talk about their drawings and photographs, and in this way 'the
children's reality came into view as they explained things concerning the pictures
that were not evident without their elucidations' (2005: 538). Although one could
argue that what the children said was inevitably co-constructed with the interviewers during the process of informal interview, the results surprised both the
researcher and teachers as they learnt how important outdoor play areas were to
the children, along with 'private spaces' and their friendships. Without adapting
the methods to include the child interviews, the children's views would not have
been heard, and without the children's explanations the study findings would
have been very different.

Qualitative research such as this uses interpretive methods of data analysis,
that is, the researcher is tasked with accurately recording what is said and then
interpreting meanings for the purposes of answering specific research questions.
There is, therefore, a risk that during the process of interpretation the researcher's own values, life experiences and understandings (sometimes referred to as
the researcher's 'subjectivity') will shape the research account. If researchers are
reliant on observational data alone, then they may unwittingly draw on their own
subjective viewpoints to explain participants' behaviours, and run the risk of
falsely attributing intentions and motives. Furthermore, interviews give participants the chance to reflect on their actions and perspectives, which can open up
ways of seeing, thinking and acting that are almost always more complicated and
often very different from what might be assumed.

Interviews can also prompt participants to consider details which would otherwise be inaccessible, for instance through snippets of life histories, personal
anecdotes and social events that have occurred in times and places that the
researcher cannot personally experience or visit, and can only learn about

through the process of interviewing. Interviews are equally useful for increasing researchers' understanding of documents by exploring, for example, why national and local guidelines and policies in the areas of health, education and social care have evolved in particular ways and how they are put into practice by different people in different institutional settings.

Some researchers use interviews as the primary means of collecting data and focus on participants' subjective stories or narrated realities. Rather than seeking to verify if these correspond to others' perceptions of the same or similar events, these accounts are valued as individuals' life histories. However, there are critically important methodological issues to bear in mind about the extent to which any interview responses are true representations of interviewees' views or are influenced by the interview process and are co-constructed by the interviewer and the interviewee(s). Depending on the nature and aims of a study, it may be advisable to build complementary methods into the research design that run alongside interview data, to check the validity of what is reported.

Structured, semi-structured and unstructured interviews

Interviews can take many different forms, depending on the research aims, scope and design, and are often categorised as structured, semi-structured or unstructured. Decisions about which kind(s) of interview to use are dependent primarily on which approaches are most likely to provide answers to the research questions that are being asked, but also depend on what is practicable and achievable in the allotted timescale, on the financial (if applicable) and human resources available to carry out a study, and, last but certainly not least, on the participants. The key point to bear in mind is that depending on the approach used, the researcher(s) will end up with a different dataset. Whether you are conducting research or reading research reports, you should reflect critically on how the research approach and methods have shaped the data and the subsequent analysis and conclusions.

Structured interviews

Structured interviews sometimes resemble the format of a questionnaire, particularly in studies where geographic distance is an issue, and in large-scale studies dealing with big samples or populations. In these cases, the only feasible way to conduct interviews across the cohort might be by telephone, by post or in a virtual space, with several interviewers working from a pre-agreed and tightly adhered to schedule of questions. The questions asked usually offer a range of possible responses to choose from which are presented in an easily measurable way. Such highly structured interviews may have the advantage of allowing what can be extensive data to be gathered comparatively consistently from large groups of respondents, yet they are limited in how much they can tell us about the subtlety of respondents' individual viewpoints. They may require respondents to indicate to what extent they agree or disagree with a supplied statement, for example on a 5-point scale from 'Strongly agree' to 'Strongly disagree'. Respondents' answers can be influenced by many different factors, such as: the length of time they have to answer; how relevant they find the questions; the feeling that they should express a view even if they don't have one; a desire to appear well-balanced leading to the choice of 'middle-of-the-road' options. These factors can be countered to some extent: by only offering an even number of options, so there is no clear 'middle view'; by including open-ended questions that allow respondents to give more in-depth views; and by allowing time for respondents to reflect before giving their views. However, it is unlikely that a trusting and empathetic relationship can be built between interviewee and interviewer, and that in itself will shape the responses that interviewees feel comfortable expressing. Furthermore, however closely structured an interview might be, each interviewee has to interpret the questions asked (and the available answers), and may do so in unexpected ways.

Semi-structured interviews

For smaller research cohorts, semi-structured interviews offer a more flexible approach, where the interviewer starts with a set of questions which provide a 'backbone' for the interview, but may use this flexibly, adding in new questions where appropriate. The interviewer is therefore free to formulate new questions spontaneously in response to the answers given. This interplay more closely resembles the ebb and flow of everyday exchanges, and thus, despite the interviewer having a pre-set list of questions to which they refer, it can help both interviewee and interviewer to relax and result in more personalised responses, opening up areas of enquiry that emerge from the participants' rather than from the researcher's preconceptions.

This approach is often used in qualitative research, for example as part of a broader ethnographic study, where time is spent observing community activity with the aim of gaining understanding 'from the inside'. In this case, the planned interview questions are usually generated through a combination of the research aims and the observations made. Semi-structured interviews are often conducted in the interviewee 'space', or study site, so the interview is likely to unfold within the usual communicative norms and conventions of that site (Briggs 1986).

Unstructured interviews

Alternatively, interviews might be 'unstructured' or take the form of more naturally occurring talk, where a researcher who is also a participant in an activity spontaneously joins in a discussion amongst research participants, and later notes down what was said. There is a fuzzy boundary between unstructured interviews that occur naturally in the field, and the process of collecting data as a participant observer (see Chapter 7). During such exchanges, it is important to remain critically aware of the influence of the researcher's motivations on the direction of subsequent discussion, and to bear this in mind when interpreting research findings – whether your own or someone else's. Although an interview may be called 'unstructured', if an interviewer is present, then what the interviewee says is always co-constructed with the interviewer, depending on how questions are asked, and how the respondent has answered previous questions. Unstructured interviews can lead to original and rich insights, but the resultant data will require considerable analytic and interpretive work, rendering this approach impracticable for larger participant cohorts. When researching with young children, who are unlikely to be familiar or at ease with interview procedures, some researchers describe the process as a 'conversation' (Gollop 2000). However, 'conversation' is potentially misleading, as research 'conversations' are inevitably driven by a research agenda and bear little resemblance to the kind of undirected chatter that occurs spontaneously as part of everyday social life.

Mixed methods approach

Rather than opting for just one of the above approaches, some studies use structured interviews and primarily quantitative methods of data analysis to collect responses from large participant populations, and then complement these with qualitative analysis of semi-structured interviews with smaller sub-samples of the same participant cohort. This mixed method approach was used in a large-scale study of student and teacher perceptions of English teaching practices in Bangladesh (English in Action 2011). The project, spearheaded by a team of researchers at The Open University, used questionnaires and interviews to achieve both a broad-based and rich picture of participant perceptions. The initial structured interviews enabled fieldwork to take place in a comparatively large sample across six divisions in Bangladesh, with 1,693 secondary students completing a highly structured questionnaire, and 288 subsequently taking part in semi-structured group interviews. The data collected thus afforded both broad and deep understandings of young people's experiences and perceptions of the teaching of English in Bangladesh, such as the negative impact of noise and disturbance on their learning in large classes, and the positive impact of feeling supported by their teachers. A mixed methods approach was also used by the large-scale longitudinal qualitative study *Inventing Adulthoods* (see www.restore.ac.uk/inventingadulthoods). This ongoing project follows the lives of young people from five socially and economically contrasting areas of England and Northern Ireland as they develop throughout their teens, twenties and early thirties at the turn of the twenty-first century. The study began in 1996 and is based primarily on in-depth repeat interviews with over 100 participants, but has also involved extensive use of questionnaires and focus groups (see Chapter 13 for detailed discussion of this study).

How many people should be interviewed?

So far, I have discussed different possible approaches to conducting interviews with children, young people and adults, depending on the research aims, participants and settings. A further consideration is whether to conduct one-to-one interviews, group interviews or focus groups, and the gains and losses of each of these strategies. The size of an interview group can have an effect on what participants feel free to say or to remain silent about. Interviewees may fear they are being judged in some way by their colleagues if interviewed in a group, or that there are 'right' and 'wrong' answers to the questions they are being asked. Whether you are conducting research or reading research reports, you should bear in mind that interview data depends upon how researchers manage the interview process and the relationship between themselves and the participants, and also between the participants in group interviews.

One-to-one interviews may work well with some research participants, particularly those who wish to maintain confidentiality, but for others this may seem such a strange and intimidating procedure they are unable to relax or articulate their views. When working with children and young people, some researchers opt to conduct group interviews, as we saw in Einarsdottir's research (2005). The talk between youngsters, or indeed between adults, in a group can be richer and more relaxed than in a potentially more intimidating one-to-one situation. Many children and young people are unlikely to be familiar or at ease with a standardised interview procedure. Their views and knowledge may be implicit, that is, they may be unaware of what they know, and less familiar with the processes of critical reflection that are involved in giving their views and opinions, so informal and indirect methods are often considered preferable (see Graue and Walsh, 1998).

A focus group involves facilitating discussion of a topic among a relatively large group of participants (perhaps between 10 and 12). Rather than asking direct questions of individuals, the researcher acts as a 'moderator' or 'facilitator' to keep the group talk going and broadly 'on topic'. This can be an effective way of stimulating debate amongst participants to scope out an area of enquiry and to learn about participant experiences and perceptions (Hennessy and Heary 2005). For example, Souza, Downey and Byrne (2012) used activities and focus groups as a way of gathering 11-year-old pupils' views on the implementation of new curricula. Rather than relying on talk alone, they designed a set of activities based on creative methods and imaginative processes to help the pupils describe and give meaning to their experiences, including making a pie. The resultant talk afforded rich insights into the impact of a new curriculum on pupils' attitudes, motivation and feelings concerning their educational progress.

The data gathered in interviews is highly dependent upon the degree of mutual trust that can be established between the interviewer and interviewee(s), on the assurances that the researcher has given and on the consent obtained (see Chapter 5). Interviewees of any age may be very selective in what they want the researcher to know about, and exercise their right to remain silent and/or be selective about the information they divulge.

Power in interviews

Whatever format is chosen for interviews, they are also infused with complex relations of power: who chooses what (and what not) to discuss, who asks what questions, when, and how, who is allotted the status to answer and who is not, who determines when to end a line of questioning, and so on (Talmy 2011) – and power can shift between interviewer and interviewee, depending on the particular circumstances of each interview. Power is also enacted beyond the immediate context of the interview, for example, in the researcher's selection of particular extracts that are written up and included in research reports, where it is lifted from its original context and could be misrepresented by a researcher and/or misinterpreted by readers. As Briggs (2007: 562) notes:

> power lies not just in controlling how discourse unfolds in the context of its production but [in] gaining control over its recontextualization – shaping how it draws on other discourses and contexts and when, where, how, and by whom it will be subsequently used.

Furthermore, an interviewee's previous life experiences of power relations in interviews may also influence how they respond in the context of a research interview. For example, an adult may wittingly or unwittingly associate the process of being interviewed with a potentially life-changing outcome, such as a job interview, a medical consultation or being questioned by police. Or power could swing the other way: if researching their place of work, interviewers might avoid asking questions which risk suggesting they are critical of the workplace or that they lack respect for those above them in the hierarchy. Similarly, respondents in this circumstance might consider it ill-advised to give full and frank answers to all the questions they are asked.

Beyond these issues of power are concerns about exploiting research participants for one's own scholastic gain. Although research may be conducted in the interests of improving conditions for participants and wider populations, there is almost always an aspect of personal gain which researchers should endeavour to balance out with benefit for participants, for example by giving participants the chance to reflect on and talk about their experiences, and to identify the need for and to bring about change in their practices, environment or understanding as a result of the research process.

Participatory approaches to interviewing

Researchers sometimes attempt to diffuse some of the potential tensions discussed above by engaging participants in some form of activity during interviews (Parkinson 2001; Cappello 2005) such as using props, paper and pen(cils), sand, clay, pictures, photographs, dolls and puppets when interviewing children (Brooker 2001). In their interviews with twin children about their friendships in pre-school education, Danby et al. (2011) used a sticker task where young participants were asked to create a pictorial representation of their friendships and relationships with their twin siblings. These tasks enabled the children to express their views in non-verbal modes, which then provided a focus for discussion and led to the children talking about unexpected details of their friendships.

Having something to share which is of interest to the interviewer and interviewee(s) can also create reciprocity and a bond of communication which encourages common engagement. In their investigation of older children with Acquired Brain Injury (ABI), Boylan, Linden and Alderdice (2009) overcame the participants' attention difficulties by encouraging them to draw pictures of whatever they chose during the interview. They found that the act of being physically engaged in an activity led the children to speak more freely, and using photographs as a basis for talk helped children with ABI who found verbal comprehension difficult.

Photographs can elicit a high level of interest during interview, particularly if they feature and/or are taken by the participants, and can enable researchers to ground an interview in participants' own experience. To explore the lives of child Buddhist monks in Sri Lanka, Samuels (2004) compared data collected from word-only interviews with data collected using photographs taken by the participants as a basis for photo-elicited interviews. Samuels found that not only did the latter method evoke greater descriptions from the research participants, but those descriptions were more emotionally charged than word-only descriptions. He also found that this approach was an effective means of bridging the culturally distinct worlds of the researcher and the researched, and enabled the research to step outside the narrow frame of his own thinking.

In a recent study with much younger participants using drama to enhance their story-telling in East London early years settings, my colleagues and I used a freely downloadable picture-based story-telling App called 'Our Story', developed by researchers at The Open University (see www.youtube. com/watch?v=Z76jcP-np60). Using this picture-based App encouraged the young children to talk about their experiences of telling and acting out their own stories.

An innovatory approach to participatory methods which push the boundaries of what constitutes an interview was used by Clarke, Boorman and Nind (2011) in their study of teenage girls who had been excluded from mainstream provision. Clarke and colleagues argue that sometimes 'voices are missing because people have been silenced' (2011: 769), and after years of negative school experiences the girls needed to be convinced that their voice was 'worth listening to and, moreover, that people will hear their voice and that it will make a difference' (Lewis and Porter 2007: 226). Rather than relying on conventional interview approaches, the researchers sought to value the communication styles preferred by the girls, and to enable the girls' excluded voices to be heard in an education system where their identity was constructed in terms of behavioural, emotional and social difficulties. A particularly effective approach was a video diary, where a camera was placed in a quiet room at school. This was soon named the Diary Room, reflecting the girls' interest in the UK television series *Celebrity Big Brother*. Rather than talking to an interviewer, the girls talked to the inanimate camera, but in the full knowledge that the researchers would watch and listen to what they had said. This approach drew on the girls' strengths and interests, and led to very deep insights into their perspectives which might not have been shared during a more standard interview procedure. Furthermore, the researchers found working positively with the girls an empowering personal, educational and political process for the participants and for themselves.

Depending on the research participants, participatory methods may or may not work well. Some children and young people may find certain approaches patronising or strange, whilst others might respond positively to them. Researchers have to be sensitive, responsive and creative in their approach, and readers of research have to adopt a critical stance towards how the methods used have shaped the data collected.

Reflecting critically on what questions to ask and how to ask them

How can researchers devise 'good' questions that will get to the heart of the topics they are exploring and which will lead to innovative and well-grounded conclusions? Particularly when conducting exploratory research, it is difficult to plan for an unknown outcome. Dewey (1938: 105) referred to indeterminate situations as 'disturbed, troublesome, ambiguous, confused, full of conflicting tendencies [and] obscure'. So, if you find planning or evaluating interview questions problematic, then you can be comforted by the fact that you are not alone! Ultimately, 'good' questions are ones which lead to the kind of data needed to inform the overarching research question(s). Some questions may turn out to be redundant or to diverge from the main research focus, yet they may unexpectedly unearth rich and relevant findings.

What must always be borne in mind is that participant responses are shaped as much by the way questions are asked as by what respondents feel or believe. Linguistic analyses of interview data have shown the extent to which respondents display conscious awareness of the interviewer's perspective and interests, and hedge their responses accordingly, often hesitating in order to assess the interviewer's likely response before speaking, and mimicking the phraseology used by the interviewer (Talmy, 2011). This applies to interviewees of any age, but may be more marked with youngsters who may feel they are expected to give an answer whether they have one or not. Young respondents may also blur the role of the interviewer with the authoritative role of a teacher, and this can result in them trying to give 'right' answers, rather than answers which truly reflect their standpoints. It is therefore essential when interviewing to build a rapport with research participants, to earn and to merit their trust so they feel confident to voice personal responses. This means balancing the human concern of putting respondents at their ease with the precision needed to probe for information, and listening actively and responsively to what is said.

There are also different types of questions to consider. Interviews often move from the factual (name, age, etc.) and the everyday (e.g. questions about who, when, where and how much/often) to the more abstract and reflective (e.g. questions about how, why, what is your view of ... ?). Many interviews begin with questions that are comparatively easy to answer, and gradually lead into more demanding questions which require reflection. However, asking even comparatively straightforward 'who/when/where/how much ... ?' questions can elicit rich descriptions from participants and may raise issues that can be returned to at a later stage. In this way, data gained through interviews can shape the future development of data collection. It is essential to remember that participants may not always be able or willing to provide answers to research questions, however straightforward the questions may seem to be, and their right not to respond must always be respected sensitively.

The art of interviewing

Once all the planning and preparation have been completed, the actual task of conducting interviews can seem daunting, coloured perhaps by a lurking fear that you may not gather the insights you hope to prompt. Interviews, like all social situations, require practice, and interviewers need to have a clear understanding of:

- What the research aims are
- When to speak
- When to be silent
- When to prompt
- When to be passive
- When to offer or refrain from comment.

Some researchers conduct 'pilot interviews' to test out questions, and this process can help novice researchers get a feel for the interview process. The initial moments of an interview can be crucial, as each meeting of two people is unique, so thought should be given to opening statements and how to put respondents at ease. Particularly when working with children, making one or two visits prior to the interview maximises opportunities to enter into the children's 'cultures of communication' (Christensen 2004) and can help to develop a rapport with children, parents, and staff.

Interviewers should think about their own communication style, for example, by curbing any tendencies to interrupt people or to 'think out loud'. It can help to write brief notes during an interview, even if it is being recorded, as interviewees may feel less intimidated if they are not being stared at. This can also help the interviewer, for example, if an interviewee expresses a point of view with which they do not agree – even if researchers remain silent, flickers of their opinions can often be read in their faces, and any such interpretation by interviewees would shape their subsequent responses. I personally have worn many a pencil down to its stub by pressing hard on paper as I make notes about viewpoints which I find difficult to comprehend in the moment they are uttered. We are all human, after all.

Most respondents, whether adults or children, need time to reflect on their ideas before speaking, so silences are often a feature of interviews. There are different kinds of silences: silence to think; silence to refuse to answer; silence that reflects the fact that an interview is not going well. Interviewers also need to pay close attention to participants' body language to gauge when it might be appropriate to prompt or not (see Chapter 4 for discussion of this). Respondents are far more likely to feel at ease if an interviewer is patient, calm, attentive and responsive.

Choosing who to interview

Identifying a set of people to interview can be one of the most challenging aspects of conducting research, as participants must be carefully selected to ensure the study aims can be achieved. A range of respondents may be needed to get a sense of different perspectives and experiences, but finding participants can be problematic. Whether you are planning or evaluating research, it is vital to reflect critically on who the participants are, and why they have been chosen. Some researchers select sites where they already know people, such as their place of work, or a place where they socialise. Whilst this arrangement may be practically convenient, serious thought should be given to the role of a researcher in a familiar setting – how will the previous relationships with familiar participants shape the outcomes of the interviews? Will participants feel comfortable about giving their honest opinions? Might they temper what they say because they know the interviewer? On the other hand, for novice and even experienced researchers, contacting unfamiliar people can require overcoming shyness and a sense of social awkwardness – being an interviewer is an unusual thing to find yourself doing if you are not familiar with the process. Yet overcoming these potential obstacles and successfully completing an interview can be a very satisfying experience.

Participants of any age, whether known personally to the researcher or not, all need reassurance that the information they give will be treated as confidential, and issues of confidentiality should be clarified at the outset of the research process when participant consent is first sought, along with clarifying participants' rights to withdraw from an interview at any time (see Chapter 5).

Recording interviews

I have already discussed the importance of considering the location of where interviews are held, and the advantages of choosing a site where respondents feel at ease. The site of the interviews in turn may dictate how the interviews are recorded. For example, sound recordings can be problematic in a noisy environment, and in this case taking detailed notes may be the best option. However, note taking inevitably means that the interviewer can only write down a selection or summary of what is said, and responses gathered in this way are more likely to be skewed by the interviewer's perspective. Audio recordings are often preferable, particularly given the compact size and discrete appearance of recording devices, along with the affordability of directional microphones. In some instances, video recordings may be preferable, such as when using artefacts or creative activities as a basis for interviews, or when interviewing participants who may express their views through body movements and facial expressions.

Whatever method is used for recording an interview, the data will need to be transcribed and checked, and this is an extremely time-consuming process. One hour of audio-recorded data can take four hours or more to transcribe, and video data can easily take twice or three times as long. The length of time transcription takes is of course dependent upon the transcription techniques and conventions that are used. Whilst there is not space in this chapter to discuss transcription styles in detail, it is important to choose a transcription method that will accurately represent the data in a form that is most useful to answer the research questions (also see Flewitt 2006; Plowman and Stephen 2008). This should also be borne in mind when reading research reports. It may sometimes be appropriate to return interview transcripts to respondents, so they can check there have been no misunderstandings. This process takes time and needs to be built into the overall research timetable.

How many interviews are enough?

This is a particular issue for qualitative researchers where the boundaries of a study may be more flexible than in quantitative research. The answer of course depends on the overall aims and approach of a study, along with practical considerations such as time and money (if the research is funded). If the intention is to conduct a small number of case studies, then 'enough' would be when the information sought has been obtained. If the intention is to contribute to or build on theory, then 'enough' would be when a point of 'saturation' is reached, that is, when new data are only adding in a minor way to the patterns that have already been identified. 'Enough' could be when sufficient data has been gathered to provide a strong and tightly woven evidence base for the research findings. Analysing interviews soon after they are conducted can therefore help researchers to recognise when to stop.

A further consideration is how many times to meet with each interviewee. If interviewers adopt a 'one shot' approach to interviewing a participant who they have not met before, then they are skating on very thin contextual ice (see Locke et al. 2004: 209–26). In my research, I have found that for in-depth studies, three interviews with each participant or group of participants can work well, although this is not always possible. For example, the first interview can be used to establish the interviewee's 'context' by asking them to talk about themselves, focusing on whatever information is needed for the study. The second can follow up on this, and include points that have arisen during observation or as a result of analysing the first interview. During a third interview participants can be encouraged to reflect on what their experiences mean to them. This final interview can also be used for the interviewer and interviewee to discuss their different perspectives, if appropriate. Longer-term studies are rare, but as with *Inventing Adulthoods*, data collected from interviews over extended periods of time often reap richly rewarding findings.

One final consideration is how long interviews should take. This is rather like asking how long is a piece of string, yet there are limits to be borne in mind. An interview should be no longer than it needs to be. Informal or impromptu interviews may last only a few minutes if they occur naturally during the course of observation, for example. The timing of structured interviews can be gauged fairly accurately, but semi-structured interviews can vary in length depending on the respondents' enthusiasm. However, it is good practice to allot a specific time and attempt not to overrun that time. It is also important to read interviewees' silent signals that they are ready to stop: if an adult starts to check her or his watch, or if a child appears tired, then whether the planned questions have been asked or not, the interviewer must respect participant preferences. Participants also need to plan their lives so that keeping to schedule, or finishing early if needs be, ultimately reaps benefits for all.

Interpreting interviews

We have seen how interviews are particularly valuable tools for gaining insights into participants' perspectives on particular issues. However, as previously mentioned, researchers must be wary of interpreting participants' verbal accounts as a substitute for the observation of actual behaviours, as there is an inevitable gap between what people say and what they do. Equally, the reality that participants are talking about may not be stable and there may be marked differences between different participants' perceptions of the same event or issue. Furthermore, as discussed, researchers must acknowledge that accounts gathered through interview are co-constructions between interviewee and interviewer.

For these reasons, it is essential for any research study to be clear about the particular contribution interviews have made to research findings. Rich insights can be gained by making cross-case comparisons and by observing what happens in practice. Whatever approach to interviewing is used, researchers must be wary of making grandiose claims, and must be clear that interviews are only one of many different data collection techniques, all of which give particular insights into social phenomena.

Some concluding thoughts

Interviewing people can be a fascinating and enjoyable experience. It can help us to understand the world from other people's perspectives, and, in the process, it can change our own views. It can also offer innovative insights into new or familiar behaviours, and, as such, contribute to theoretical and practical understanding and knowledge. There is little doubt that if we want to observe and comment on issues related to the social organisation of life, whether in a culture we know well or in unfamiliar spaces and places, and whether in schools, hospitals, homes, in the street or elsewhere, then our understanding will be more complete if we seek the views of the people whose lives we are studying.

However, conducting interviews is no walk in the park. It takes up a great deal of time: first to plan the study, to prepare structured or outline questions, identify and enlist participants, gain written consent, plan visits at times that are convenient to participants, rearrange them if necessary, conduct the interviews, reassure participants if they talk about sensitive issues, reflect and decide on a transcription technique, transcribe the interviews, check them, share them with the participants (if appropriate), then work with the data to see whether and how it informs the research questions. Interviewing can also be expensive if it involves travel, and if recording equipment needs to be purchased. A central focus for researchers is to design interview techniques that suit the research questions and to develop flexible techniques that enable the active engagement of diverse research cohorts. Despite these trials, interviewing can be a deeply satisfying process, where friendships are forged, where power imbalances can be levelled and where deep insights can be gained into the experiences of those who walk alongside us in life.

Bibliography

Boylan, A-M., Linden, M. and Alderdice, F. (2009) 'Interviewing children with Acquired Brain Injury (ABI)', *Journal of Early Childhood Research*, 7(3): 264–82.
Briggs, C.L. (1986) *Learning How to Ask: A Sociolinguistic Appraisal of the Role of the Interview in Social Science Research*. Cambridge: Cambridge University Press.

Briggs, C. (2007) 'Anthropology, interviewing, and communicability in contemporary society', *Current Anthropology*, 48: 551–67.

Brooker, L. (2001) 'Interviewing children. Doing early childhood research: international perspectives on theory and practice', in G. McNaughton, S.A. Rolfe and I. Siraj-Blatchford (eds) *Doing Early Childhood Research: International Perspectives on Theory and Practice*. Buckingham: Open University Press.

Cappello, M. (2005) 'Photo interviews: Eliciting data through conversations with children', *Field Methods*, 17: 170–82.

Christensen, P. (2004) 'Children's participation in ethnographic research: Issues of power and representation', *Children & Society* 18: 165–76.

Clarke, G., Boorman, G. and Nind, M. (2011) '"If they don't listen I shout, and when I shout they listen": Hearing the voices of girls with behavioural, emotional and social difficulties', *British Educational Research Journal*, 37(5): 765–80.

Danby, S., Ewing, L. and Thorpe, K. (2011) 'The novice researcher: Interviewing young children', *Qualitative Inquiry*, 17(1): 74–84.

Dewey, J. (1938) *Logic: The Theory of Inquiry*. New York: Holt, Rhinehart & Winston.

Einarsdottir, J. (2005) 'Playschool in pictures: Children's photographs as a research method', *Early Childhood Development and Care*, 175(6): 523–41.

English in Action (EiA) (2011) *Research Report: Perceptions of English Language Learning and Teaching Among Primary and Secondary School Teachers and Students Participating in English in Action (study 2b3b)*. Dhaka, Bangladesh: EiA. Available at: www.eiabd.com/eia/index.php/pilot-phase-reports (accessed 24 September 2013).

Flewitt, R.S. (2006) 'Using video to investigate preschool classroom interaction: Education research assumptions and methodological practices', *Visual Communication*, 5(1): 25–50.

Gollop, M.M. (2000) 'Interviewing children: A research perspective', in A.B. Smith, N.J. Taylor and M.M. Gollop (eds) *Children's Voices: Research, Policy and Practice*. New Zealand, Pearson Education. pp. 18–37.

Graue, E.M. and Walsh, D.J. (1998) *Studying Children in Context: Theories, Methods and Ethics*. Thousand Oaks, CA: Sage.

Hennessy, E. and Heary C. (2005) 'Exploring children's views through focus groups', in S. Greene and D. Hogan (eds), *Researching Children's Experience: Approaches and Methods*. London: Sage. pp. 236–52.

Hollway, W. (2005) 'Commentary', *Qualitative Research in Psychology*, 2: 312–14.

Lewis, A. and Porter, J. (2007) 'Research and pupil voice', in L. Florian (ed.), *The Sage Handbook of Special Education*. London: Sage.

Locke, L., Silverman, S.J. and Spirduso, W.W. (2004) *Reading and Understanding Research*, 2nd edition. Thousand Oaks, CA: Sage.

Parkinson, D.D. (2001) 'Securing trustworthy data from an interview situation with young children: Six integrated interview strategies', *Child Study Journal*, 31(3): 137–56.

Plowman, L. and Stephen, C. (2008) 'The big picture? Video and the representation of interaction', *British Educational Research Journal*, 34(4): 541–65.

Samuels, J. (2004) 'Breaking the ethnographer's frames: Reflections on the use of photo-elicitation in understanding Sri Lankan monastic culture', *American Behavioral Scientist*, 47(12): 1528–50.

Schostak, J. (2006) *Interviewing and Representation in Qualitative Research*. Maidenhead: Open University Press.

Seidman, I. (2006) *Interviewing as Qualitative Research: A Guide for Researchers in Education and the Social Sciences*, 3rd edition. New York: Teachers College Press.

Souza, A., Downey, C. and Byrne, J. (2012) '"Making pies" – a way of exploring pupils' views on curriculum innovation' *Children and Society*. DOI:10.1111/j.1099-0860.2011.00418.x.

Talmy, S. (2011) 'The interview as collaborative achievement: Interaction, identity, and ideology in a speech event', *Applied Linguistics*, 32(1): 25–42.

van Lier, L. (1988) *The Classroom and the Language Learner*. London: Longman.

9 Working with Texts, Images and Artefacts

Helen Hearn and Pat Thomson

Children and young people use various forms of media to make and keep connections with their friends, families and beyond, and for making sense of their lives and experiences (Carrington and Robinson 2009; Sefton Green 1998). These media exist beyond the moment as texts, images, and artefacts. We can think of them as a partial record of social relationships, interactions and networks. Researchers who are concerned that research about children and young people is generally conducted from adult perspectives often seek to redress the imbalance by focusing on these kinds of data (Bragg 2007; Thomson 2011). Many of these researchers also believe that using texts, images, and artefacts will not only engage young people, but also make visible youthful 'voices', views, cultures and relationships (Anning 1997; Christensen and James 2000; Moss et al. 2007; Veale 2005; Wagner 1999). In addition, the organisations and adults with whom children and young people are involved also produce material of this kind, and this too can be useful research data.

Using texts, images, and artefacts for the purposes of research may sound deceptively simple. It might be thought that children just need to be given permission to take pictures with their mobile phones, or that a school will provide copies of information about their pupil population, and that these can then be analysed. If only things were that simple and straightforward. In this chapter, we discuss a range of issues that researchers need to consider in using texts, images, and artefacts, and that need to be taken into account in reading research reports that employ these sorts of data. We will begin by defining key terms, then explore how such material can be used, illustrating this by reference to an actual research project. We then conclude with some questions that readers of research might ask about the use of texts, images, and artefacts.

But first of all, who are 'we'? We are a doctoral researcher, Helen, and her supervisor, Pat. Helen is researching bullying among primary school girls and how it might differ from bullying among boys, and from bullying among secondary school girls. She decided to work with children as co-researchers, and the project involved the co-production of images and artefacts, as well as the analysis of documents produced by schools related to policies on bullying. Pat has also conducted research with pupils (Thomson and Gunter 2006, 2008) in which she has used images, artefacts, and texts (Thomson 2008). We don't claim to know everything there is about this topic, but we do want to share our experiences.

Defining our terms

It is important to begin by defining the ways in which we will use the three key terms – (1) 'text', (2) 'image' and (3) 'artefact'. We will also introduce the term 'documents'.

(1) Text

While it is not uncommon to see almost everything referred to as a text, we will use this word to mean written or spoken language put together to communicate a message to a reader. There is always a reader for texts, even if that reader is only the writer, as is the case with private diaries. Once written, a text does not have any meaning in itself, it is in the reading that meaning is produced (Holub 1984). We understand words as belonging to a language. Numbers can also be thought of as language-like in that, like words, they are ways that we use to make sense of the world. Neither words nor numbers correspond exactly to a material reality – they are socially agreed ways of describing things which we then use to make sense of what we see, think, feel, believe and do (Bruner 1991; Lather 2007; Rosaldo 1989). Because words and numbers are cultural constructions (Connell 2007; Said 1983; Smith 1993), researchers must never take them at face value, but always look at them as unnatural, and in need of careful scrutiny (Riessman 2008; Tierney and Lincoln 1997).

(2) Image

Images can take a variety of forms, for example they may be paintings or drawings, photographs, films or screens, diagrams, maps or graphs. Images can be produced in different media (on paper, electronically, on glass or canvas) and can be still or moving, presented as collage or montage, and can be realistic or abstract. However, images are also language-like, and do not correspond in any simple way to material reality (Rose 2001; Schirato and Webb 2004). This may seem counter-intuitive, because we are used to hearing sayings such as 'A picture never lies'. However, someone somewhere has made the image, has decided what to include and exclude, what to put in the foreground, and what to cast in shadow. And, just like words and numbers, images often go through several editing stages where there is interpretation and choice at every point. There are also often conventions about the use of images that most of the time we are not aware of. However, if we think about why it is that black and white films and photographs are sometimes thought to be more 'real' than colour ones, then we can begin to see that, just as with words and numbers, we cannot take pictures at face value. We must think about their production, and also how they can be variously understood (Emmison and Smith 2001).

The use of images may be combined with other forms of data collection, for example they are sometimes used in interviews as a way of stimulating conversation (Hurworth 2003; see Chapter 8). On other occasions they may be used as stand-alone data (Banks 2007; Prosser 1999). Indeed, images can sometimes be the main means of presenting research findings, accompanied by a minimal set of carefully selected words (see, e.g., the photo-essays in Ward 1978; Thomson 2002).

In her research, Helen used images about bullying that she found on the internet to stimulate conversations with primary school girls; she also showed them examples of anti-bullying images to encourage them to think about what images they could make for themselves

(3) Artefact

An artefact is simply an object that is developed or made. Artefacts are diverse in nature – they might be a board or computer game, a map or a toy, something more complex like an exhibition or a wiki, or even a performance complete with a recording. As some of these examples make clear, artefacts may also contain textual material and images. Like texts and images, artefacts are made by someone somewhere, for a particular purpose, and are framed by social conventions, and involve taken for granted ways of doing things.

Texts, images, and artefacts as cultural constructions

Texts, images, and artefacts, along with people, can be understood to form networks of activity (Engestrom et al. 1999; Latour 1987). For example, these kinds of material may constitute 'tools' that offer particular opportunities for action. They are all cultural constructions (Pahl and Rowsell 2010), but we can distinguish between those that have been produced independently of any research

Table 9.1   A matrix of types of text, image, and artefact

	Existing prior to the research ('found')	Generated through the research process
Produced by children and young people	Displays on a school wall School assignments Facebook pages YouTube clips	Photographs or films Drawings Maps
Produced by adults	Demographic data Case notes and school reports Newsletter articles Inspection reports	Photos or films of activities Reports of meetings Biographies

project, sometimes referred to as 'found' materials, and those that researchers have asked people to produce. For example, some of the girls in Helen's study manufactured board games and z-folds (a sheet of paper folded like a fan); and these artefacts stayed in the schools after Helen left. We can also distinguish between texts, images, and artefacts that have been developed by children and young people, and those that have been produced by adults. Putting these two dimensions together in Table 9.1, we can get a sense of the variety of forms that these materials can take.

Any of these sorts of text, image, and artefact might be used in a research project, depending on what we want to find out.

Most researchers routinely begin their project by collecting a range of texts. This is a way to find out about the location and/or context of their study. 'Insider' researchers – those who work in their research site – may have access to documents which will not be made available to 'outsiders' – those who come into a site from elsewhere. However, sometimes the reverse is true – visiting researchers are given access to texts which are not widely available to 'insiders' (Kara 2012).

Working with texts, images, and artefacts

We have suggested that texts, images, and artefacts are cultural constructions. We now want to suggest that we can also think of them as *representations* (Hall 1997). It is perhaps easiest to explain the idea of representation through the use of a hypothetical example. Let us imagine a piece of participatory research, that is, one where the researcher and young people work together in deciding what is to be studied and how. We have chosen a participatory example because it helps to set the scene for Helen's case study, which will be discussed later, and it shows some of the kinds of decisions that researchers need to consider when doing research 'with', rather than 'on', participants. However, the example should not be taken as a suggestion that this is the only or even the best way to do research with children and young people.

Hypothetical research project

We are probably all familiar with the way in which news media sometimes portray young people as hoodies, as feral and dangerous, as reckless (Davies 1997; MacDonald 1997). These kinds of representation usually make at least some young people upset. They may very well produce their own counter-representations as a result – in text, image and as artefact – showing that they cannot be equated to the clothes that they wear and the music that they listen to.

Imagine now that we wanted to research young people's responses to these media portrayals. We decide to work with a carefully selected group of young people to research their peers' responses. We begin by collectively accumulating 'found' media materials which show these stereotyped representations and some counter-representations, which present young people in very different ways. Some of the images are highly sexist, but the research team collectively makes a decision that they should be included despite the risk that some young people might share these views. The young researchers work with their peers to produce a set of alternative images which are to be mounted as an exhibition to which journalists will be invited.

The manufactured images tackle the sexism of the found images. However they also reproduce some racist stereotypes and this alarms us. Should we censor the views of the young researchers, or should we accept that they have a right to express them? After a protracted and inconclusive period of negotiation within the team about whether this is acceptable, we, as the designated adult responsible researcher, assert our authority and remove the potentially offending images. It falls to us to write something for publication about the research. The young people are not interested in this, beyond wanting to see what we have had to say. We do the writing, but now feel uneasy about claiming this as co-research.

At the end of the project, the research data consists of images taken from the media, manufactured images as well as various kinds of texts, including the minutes of meetings and records of conversations among the research team. The final exhibition is a manufactured artefact. We can work with this corpus further, but is it 'ours' to do so?

There are a number of important issues that arise from this hypothetical story, but we want to highlight three. The first issue is that it is not sufficient to simply produce the story of the exhibition as the final research 'findings'. As researchers, we need also to consider the various representations that are produced before and during the project. Despite wanting to make visible young people's voices and views, we must, if we are interested in 'truth' (however we understand this) (Hammersley 2011), analyse what the young people were saying about themselves in particular, and about young people in general. And we need to see this analysis as both particular – about this group of young people – as well as situated – that is, as coming from their life experiences of living as gendered, raced and classed people in particular places at particular times. We must therefore report on what the young people said, but also signal what emerged in the process. To generalise from the point we are making, no text, image, or artefact – regardless of whether it is found or produced for the research – can be taken simply at face value and be seen as somehow being an 'authentic truth'. This includes our own representations, as well as those of participants.

The second issue that we want draw attention to is related to ethics. Quite difficult ethical issues can arise when working with texts, images, and artefacts (Hall 1997). If we have 'found' them, do we have permission to use them? Whose permission do we need? How might we obtain this? In the hypothetical example above, the found images were published and in the public domain, and we might assume that the journalists had obtained permission for them to be used. However, this may not be the case, since many 'reality' and 'paparazzi' shots are taken without the permission of the people involved. There are also ethical issues when asking participants to make texts, images, and artefacts for the research. For example, these will often include representations of people other than those who are making them. As researchers, we do need to get formal permission to make images of people, and sometimes places too. This can be time-consuming, but is essential. However, we generally do not ask permission for any captioning or interpretation we might make. Do those about whom we are making comments have the right to be consulted about captions and interpretations? We also have to consider here the potential harm that the research might produce. This could be to the people whose images we have used, but it might also be harm to potential audiences. In the case of the racist images in our hypothetical exhibition, the adult researcher decided that there would be more harm done by showing the images than by denying the rights of the young researchers to 'voice' them in public.

The third issue relates to the question of ownership. This is often very difficult in participatory research (McIntyre 2008). If the images manufactured for the hypothetical exhibition in our example have been a collective effort, who can be said to own them? The adult researcher? The adult researcher and the young researchers as a team, or only those involved in the specific image? The adult researcher, the young researchers and their peers? And who decides where the exhibition can be shown after its initial viewing? The list goes on: does the researcher have the right to then publish the work under her own name? What to do if the young researchers lose interest in the research 'product'? While these questions are difficult, they are not irresolvable. However, they must be formally negotiated before the project ends in order to avoid nasty after-research dealings and recriminations.

Holding these dilemmas and issue in mind, we now turn to Helen's real research story. This raises additional questions and issues.

Helen's story: Researching bullying with primary school girls

This section of the chapter is written by Helen and thus talks of 'I' not 'we'.

The research project

My research was an intervention study with three primary school 'cases'. Four 'lunch club' groups were set up in the schools and each was held once a week during the academic year 2011–12. The anti-bullying lunch club groups consisted of 7–11-year-old girls who had volunteered to take part. The role of the girls in my research was as co-researchers, and together we designed a survey, conducted group interviews and produced anti-bullying resources. These data were used to address the following research questions:

1   What are the similarities and differences in the prevalence and severity of bullying experienced or witnessed, and what are the coping strategies favoured by tweenage girls (7–12 year olds)?
2   How does the gender of the bully impact on tweenage girls?[1]

Recruitment of the schools started with the secondary school followed by an invitation to all the feeder primary schools. The three primary schools, Briston, Contor, and St Beth's (school names chosen by the co-researchers) were the 'feeder' schools that volunteered to be involved. The schools are all located in rural village settings in the East Midlands. The main difference between the schools is their size, with Briston being more than four times bigger than the smallest school, St Beth's. Contor had two lunch-club groups with same-aged pupils, while the other two schools had one mixed-age group each.

For each stage of the research – the survey, the interviews, and production of anti-bullying resources – different research tools were needed. Possible layouts for the survey were developed, along with a checklist for how to write interview questions and be an interviewer. All the groups were shown examples

---

[1]There was also a comparison with teenage girls in the secondary school to which children from the three primary schools went when they were older, but this aspect of the project is not discussed here.

of anti-bullying resources such as posters, z-fold leaflets and booklets. Examples of board game layouts and spinners were also found, along with pictures from the internet for use in webpage design and as board game counters. Some of the groups chose to base their resources on these, while others used their own ideas. Briston chose posters; Contor produced board games, plans for a webpage design and z-fold leaflets; St Beth's made z-fold leaflets and performed an assembly on bullying. The production of resources for the school may have been a key to my being given permission to work with the girls for a protracted period of time.

Researching with primary school girls

Working with co-researchers from three research sites produced a variety of problems and these affected the number of sessions required to complete the research:

1. **Size and composition of the groups.** I found that the larger the lunch-club group the more difficult they were to control in terms of behaviour. The youngest group, consisting of 7–8 year olds, struggled the most in staying motivated on tasks and often asked to go out early or miss sessions so that they could play outside when it was warm and sunny in the spring and summer, or when it had snowed in the winter. I had to learn to be flexible, balancing the number of activities to be completed and keeping the girls' interest in wanting to continue to attend the lunch club.
2. **Competing school agendas.** During the research I had to adapt some sessions because other school activities took precedence. At the start of the research I had a rigid timetable with a number of tasks that needed to be completed each week. By the end of the research I was more flexible, adapting activities and extending the number of sessions, with the only restriction being that the research was completed by the end of the academic year.

I had to adapt continually, and consciously engage in reflection after every session to consider what might need to change. I had to make decisions about how involved the girls were at each stage of the research. For example, I decided that the co-researchers and I would work together to design the surveys and the interview questions. When I showed them some examples of surveys their automatic reaction was to fill them in. It took a while for the girls to understand that I was asking for their opinions on the design. Time constraints limited how much involvement the girls had in some activities, such as the analysis. I did not want to exclude them from the analysis but also was concerned that they might find it boring. I chose to work with them on thematic analysis of some of the interview questions but I did all of the analysis of the surveys myself.

Despite these challenges, I found that the girls were competent co-researchers and were generally more than capable of most of the tasks I set them. They had very definite views about the design of their surveys, wanting tick boxes and text boxes with space for answers to be written or drawn in. They were confident interviewers and were able to follow the interview schedule we had collectively designed, and they added their own appropriate questions to encourage the interviewees to give longer responses. The girls were able to use their ICT skills independently to produce some of the anti-bullying resources. The girls all reported that they enjoyed making these resources, tasks that involved drawing and activities where they asked other girls for their opinions.

Working with texts, images and artefacts: Choosing, designing and making the anti-bullying resources

During the process of the co-researchers choosing, designing and making the anti-bullying resources, I had to make two key decisions which could have adversely affected the project outcomes.

1 **Ownership.** I had to balance the amount of support given to the girls so they could make resources that reflected our findings, without taking away their creative input and ownership of the product. After the co-researchers were shown and had an understanding of what an anti-bullying resource was, they had definite ideas of what theirs should be. I found that I had to overrule some of their ideas, as they were just not feasible because of our collective limited skills and time constraints. There were also ethical issues to consider – such as whether an anti-bullying resource could compromise the co-researchers' anonymity and put them at potential risk of harm. One example of this was an idea to have a public website about our research findings. This raised questions of how we could develop the website, who would be able to access it, whether the girls could be identified and who would moderate and manage it once the research had finished. After consultation with the head teacher, it was decided it would be more appropriate to have a webpage on the school's own website.
2 **Practicality and appropriateness.** I had to judge if the resources could be made in the time we had available. I also had to weigh up the cost of producing the resources (I was paying for them from my studentship allowance), versus the number and quality needed for the resources to be as effective and accessible as possible.

During the production of the anti-bullying resources I had to provide different amounts of support depending on the type of resource being made and the age of the girls. The groups who chose to design a webpage and produce z-fold leaflets were able to work independently once I had provided a summary of the survey results. For the assembly, the girls worked independently, writing scripts for their role plays and speeches on the findings they had chosen to present. Together we adapted their scripts.

The groups who produced the posters and the board games needed most support from me. Briston girls struggled to put the findings of the research into their posters and were more interested in selecting and producing the pictures on the poster than the writing. Initially they copied examples of posters I had showed them rather than basing them on our results. In order to deal with this, I designed frameworks for the girls to follow, choosing key findings from our research. Some of the girls chose to follow these as a guide, whereas others chose to produce their posters without this support.

The youngest group at Contor had definite ideas about their board game, but did not know how to include the findings of our research in the design. There was disagreement about whether the board game should be based on Snakes and Ladders or on Monopoly. They struggled with how we could make a game that was like both. I offered the girls three designs to choose from. By giving the girls the choice of three designs and asking them to decorate the boards, make the counters and decide on the rules, they still had ownership of the resource despite my assistance.

I decided to make the resources of good quality so they were durable and the school would be able to use them. Six posters were printed professionally and laminated to allow a collection of different styles to be presented to the school. As the posters were produced individually, this allowed a number of girls to see their work being used. The board games were professionally mounted and laminated and the z-fold leaflets were professionally printed on thin card.

Helen's data and its analysis

Helen's research did not use 'found' texts extensively, but she did collect school bullying policies and she also looked for the kinds of anti-bullying images (posters) that were on display around the school. Most of the documents in this project were purpose-made for the research, as shown in Table 9.2. But these, of course, were not all the data used in the whole project. Accompanying these documents are the survey results, interviews with the student researchers, student researcher interviews with each other and peers, and audio recordings and field notes covering all lunch time sessions.

While analysing the survey results was relatively straightforward (Helen used the software programme SPSS for this task), dealing with the wide range of material was less so. Texts can be examined to ascertain their themes, narratives, metaphors and/or symbolic content. Images can be counted and categorised but can also can be seen as discourse and narrative (Pink 2001). The

Table 9.2 Helen's data

	Existing prior to the research ('found')	Generated through the research process
Produced by children and young people		Questionnaires (n = 3) Cue cards for interviews (n = 20) Board games (n = 2) Z-fold leaflets (n = 3) Play scripts (n = 1) Song lyrics (n = 1) Video of assembly performances (n = 2) Posters (n = 6) Plans of webpage design (n = 5) Pictures for webpage (n = 8) Quiz for webpage (n = 1)
Produced by adults	School bullying policies School anti-bullying materials	Helen's reports of the research for the schools

design – placement of images, use of colour, and so on – can be examined (Kress and Van Leeuwin 2006). Artefacts are usually highly complex, and combinations of analytic methods are usually used (Plowright 2011). In this case Helen's time limitations and the questions she was asking dictated what could be done.

Because she was interested in what the girls regarded as bullying, how they experienced it, and what they thought were mechanisms for coping and prevention, it was these interests that dictated Helen's analysis. She was primarily concerned with content rather than design – looking to see what kinds of bullying incident were represented, among whom, in what circumstances, and who was not involved; what was said and not said to whom; who was shown as being powerful and powerless; and what kinds of terms were used to describe this range of events and interactions (see Figure 9.1). All of the texts, images, and artefacts were analysed in relation to these issues, which are drawn from her two research questions outlined earlier. It was also possible to analyse cultural and school influences in the images and text. Helen conducted a straightforward content analysis: hand-coding interview and group discussion transcripts, and going through the visual material manually, looking for themes, and inclusions and exclusions. For example, most of the materials referred to cyberbullying, whereas Helen's survey suggested that very little cyberbullying actually happened. Helen therefore had to consider why the girls thought this was significant enough to put on their posters and to see whether there were any clues in her extensive recordings of group discussions.

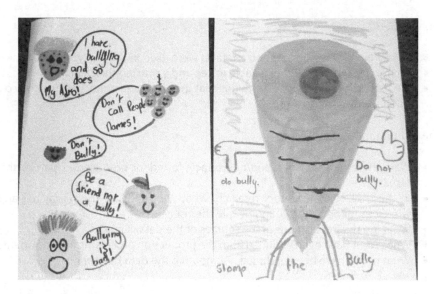

Figure 9.1 Anti-bullying poster

It is helpful to consider what Helen can and cannot say as a result of this research. For example, it is not possible to know what effects the anti-bullying materials will have in the schools, or how they will be interpreted by individuals or groups of pupils and teachers – there simply wasn't enough time to build that into the timeline she was working with. This limitation draws attention to the ambiguity of documents – they are not only produced but also must be interpreted. While the intentions of document producers are important, texts and images also exist as material objects which readers/viewers make their own sense of. It is important not to confuse makers' intentions with assumptions about the meaning-making activities of those who 'read' the documents; finding out about 'reception' requires further specifically designed activities, such as audience surveys, interviews with document users, and the like.

Conclusion: Some principles for reading about research with texts, images, and artefacts

We have not been able to discuss all of the issues that arise when working with texts, images, and artefacts, but we have raised some questions that are important. In conclusion, and arising directly from the hypothetical example and Helen's real research, we want to offer a set of questions that might be used to interrogate reports of research with children and young people using material of these kinds:

The dataset:

- What kind of texts, images and artefacts were used in the study?
- What might the researcher be able to see and say using this dataset?
- What are the blind spots – the things that they can't see or say because they do not have the data to do so?

The manufacture of the data:

- Were these texts, images, and/or artefacts found, or produced as part of this research?
- In the case of participatory research, what was made by the researcher and what was made by the young people themselves?
- What are the implications of the sources of the data, if any?
- Who might have been excluded from the production process? Is this important?
- What might have been excluded or ignored if the data has been 'found'?

Power and ethics:

- Who made the key decisions about research texts, images, and artefacts – the topic, the approach, the analysis, their use to report findings?
- What questions of ownership might arise in relation to these texts, images and artefacts? How were these accounted for?

Analysis and interpretation:

- How were the texts, images, and artefacts analysed, and by whom?
- What alternatives were there to this approach, if any?
- Were they understood as representations, and if so how?

Helen's story can be re-read using these questions and we encourage you to do so.

References

Anning, A. (1997) 'Drawing out ideas: Graphicacy and young children', *International Journal of Design and Technology Education*, 7: 219–39.

Banks, M. (2007) *Using Visual Data in Qualitative Research*. Thousand Oaks, CA: Sage.

Bragg, S. (2007) *Consulting Young People: A Review of the Literature. A Report for Creative Partnerships*. London: Arts Council England.

Bruner, J. (1991) 'The narrative construction of reality', *Critical Inquiry*, 18(1): 1–21.

Carrington, V. and Robinson, M. (2009) *Digital Literacies: Social Learning and Classroom Practice*. London: Sage.

Christensen, P. and James, A. (eds) (2000) *Research with Children*. London and New York: Falmer.

Connell, R. (2007) *Southern Theory: The Global Dynamics of Knowledge in Social Science*. Cambridge: Polity.

Davies, S. (1997) 'A sight to behold: Media and the visualisation of youth, evil and innocence', in J. Bessant and R. Hil (eds), *Youth, Crime and the Media: Media Representation of and Reaction to Young People in Relation to Law and Order*. Hobart: National Clearinghouse for Youth Studies. pp. 55–63.

Emmison, M. and Smith, P. (2001) *Researching the Visual*. Thousand Oaks, CA: Sage.

Engestrom, Y., Miettinen, R. and Punamaki, R. (eds) (1999) *Perspectives on Activity Theory*. Cambridge: Cambridge University Press.

Hall, S. (ed.) (1997) *Representation: Cultural Representations and Signifying Practices*. London: Sage.

Hammersley, M. (2011) *Methodology. Who Needs It?* Thousand Oaks, CA: Sage.

Holub, R. (1984) *Reception Theory: A Critical Introduction*. London: Methuen.

Hurworth, R. (2003) 'Photo-interviewing for research', *Social Research Update*, 40. Available at: http://sru.soc.surrey.ac.uk/SRU40.html (accessed 18 July 2004).

Kara, H. (2012) *Research and Evaluation for Busy Practitioners: A Time-Saving Guide*. Bristol: Policy Press.

Kress, G. and Van Leeuwin, T. (2006) *Reading Images: The Grammar of Visual Design*, 2nd edition. London and New York: Routledge.

Lather, P. (2007) *Getting Lost: Feminist Efforts Toward a Double(d) Science*. New York: State University of New York Press.

Latour, B. (1987) *Science in Action: How to Follow Scientists and Engineers through Society*. Cambridge, MA: Harvard University Press.

MacDonald, R. (ed.) (1997) *Youth, the 'Underclass' and Social Exclusion*. London and New York: Routledge.

McIntyre, A. (2008) *Participatory Action Research*. Thousand Oaks, CA: Sage.

Moss, J., Deppeler, J., Astley, L. and Pattison, K. (2007) 'Student researchers in the middle: Using visual images to make sense of inclusive education', *Journal of Research in Special Educational Needs*, 7(1): 46–54.

Pahl, K. and Rowsell, J. (2010) *Artifactual Literacies: Every Object Tells a Story*. New York: Teachers College Press.

Pink, S. (2001) *Doing Visual Ethnography: Images, Media, Representation*. London: Sage.

Plowright, D. (2011) *Using Mixed Methods. Frameworks for an Integrated Methodology*. Thousand Oaks, CA: Sage.

Prosser, J. (1999) 'Visual sociology and school culture', in J. Prosser (ed.) *School Culture*. London: Paul Chapman Publishing. pp. 82–97.

Riessman, C.K. (2008) *Narrative Methods for the Human Sciences*. Thousand Oaks, CA: Sage.

Rosaldo, R. (1989) *Culture and Truth: The Remaking of Social Analysis*, 1993 edn. Beacon Press: Boston.

Rose, G. (2001) *Visual Methodologies*. London: Sage.

Said, E. (1983) *The World, the Text and the Critic*. Cambridge, MA: Harvard University Press.

Schirato, T. and Webb, J. (2004) *Reading the Visual*. Crows Nest, Sydney: Allen & Unwin.

Sefton Green, J. (ed.) (1998) *Digital Diversions: Youth Culture in the Age of Multimedia*. London: UCL Press.

Smith, D. (1993) *Texts, Facts and Femininity: Exploring the Relations of Ruling*. London: Routledge.

Thomson, P. (2002) *Schooling the Rustbelt Kids: Making the Difference in Changing Times*. Sydney: Allen & Unwin (Trentham Books UK).

Thomson, P. (ed.) (2008) *Doing Visual Research with Children and Young People*. London: Routledge.

Thomson, P. (2011) 'Coming to terms with "voice"', in G. Czerniawski and W. Kidd (eds), *The International Handbook of Student Voice*. London: Emerald.

Thomson, P. and Gunter, H. (2006) 'From "consulting pupils" to "pupils as researchers": a situated case narrative', *British Educational Research Journal*, 32(6): 839–56.

Thomson, P and Gunter, H. (2008) 'Researching bullying with students: A lens on everyday life in a reforming high school', *International Journal of Inclusive Education*, 12(2): 185–200.

Tierney, W.G. and Lincoln, Y.S. (1997) *Representation and the Text: Reframing the Narrative Voice*. Albany, NY: State University of New York Press.

Veale, A. (2005) 'Creative methodologies in participatory research with children', in S. Greene and D. Hogan (eds) *Researching Children's Experiences: Approaches and Methods*. London: Sage. pp. 253–72.

Wagner, J. (1999) 'Visual studies and seeing kids' worlds', *Visual Sociology*, 14: 3–6.

Ward, C. (1978) *The Child in the City*. Harmondsworth: Penguin.

10 Methodological Ideas

Martyn Hammersley

Research is a very practical activity in which pressing decisions must be made –
for example, about what it would be fruitful and feasible to investigate, what data
to use, how to go about gaining access to these data, how to analyse them, what
conclusions can be drawn from the analysis, and how to disseminate the findings
to audiences that have an interest in them. Moreover, these practical decisions
arise in situations that involve a variety of constraints, including material ones to
do with what funding is available, what access to the necessary data can be
achieved, and so on.

At the same time, however, it is important to recognise that research is not
simply a matter of doing what is possible or necessary in the circumstances. It
relies upon ideas of various kinds:

1   About the nature of the phenomena being studied. These are often referred to
    as ontological assumptions – 'ontology' is a philosophical term referring to
    study of what types of thing exist in the world and their character.
2   About how these phenomena can best be understood. These are epistemologi-
    cal assumptions, epistemology being concerned with the nature of knowledge.
3   About what the purpose of research, or of a particular research study, ought to
    be: is the task solely to contribute to a developing body of academic knowl-
    edge, to inform public policy, to directly transform the lives of the people being
    studied, or what? These might be thought of as political issues.
4   About how the people involved in the research process should be treated, or
    what human values it ought to exemplify. These are ethical concerns.

These ideas form part of the rationales that researchers use to explain and justify
what they do: to themselves, to colleagues, to funders, to gatekeepers, and to
other audiences. Equally important, such ideas are also incorporated as assumptions into the very methods researchers employ, and this is true whether or not
they are aware of them. One of the ways in which research dealing with children
and young people has changed over the past few decades is that many researchers
have given increased attention to the assumptions on which their work is based,

and have come to reject some of the key ideas on which much research in this field previously relied.

This reflects broader changes within the field of psychological and social research, including in areas like education and health, where researchers now adopt many different sorts of methodological approach. Perhaps the most obvious contrast is between work that employs quantitative data and that which uses qualitative methods, though this by no means captures all of the relevant variation. The divisions within this field have sometimes been described as representing conflicting 'paradigms', or methodological philosophies. What the word 'paradigm' refers to in this context is a set of ontological, epistemological, political, and ethical assumptions, plus a tendency to use particular methods of data collection and analysis that are assumed to follow from those assumptions. In the course of this chapter a number of such 'paradigms' will be introduced – positivism, interpretivism, constructionism, and 'critical' research. However, each of these labels covers a range of ideas and practices – rather than one single set – and there is also some overlap amongst these four categories in what they include. While these are by no means the only labels that are used to distinguish different approaches in the field, they do give a good sense of the main sets of ideas influencing research concerned with children and young people today.

Before discussing these four approaches, in the next section I want to examine a particular study, one that can be seen as strongly influenced by one of these paradigms: positivism. This will enable us to get a sense not only of what this type of research involves in concrete terms, but also to explore the assumptions on which it relies, and how questioning these can lead us towards other modes of research influenced by rather different sets of ideas.

An example

The study I am going to discuss here represents an approach to research on children and young people that was dominant in the past and is still influential today in some fields. The specific aim of this study was to determine whether an intervention designed to increase the physical activity of young children (4 year olds) would reduce their levels of body mass, thereby reducing the chances of their becoming obese. The intervention consisted of an 'enhanced physical activity programme in nursery (three 30-minute sessions a week over 24 weeks) plus home-based health education aimed at increasing physical activity through play and reducing sedentary behaviour' (Reilly et al. 2006: 1). The children were fitted with devices called accelerometers, which measure their levels of physical activity and changes in these. We can think of this study as a piece of experimental research, albeit one that took place 'in the world' rather than in a laboratory. The label often given to the particular method used is 'randomised controlled trial', and this is indeed the name that the researchers themselves employ.

124 nurseries in the Glasgow area had been invited to participate, and, of the 104 nurseries who agreed, 36 were randomly selected to be involved in the intervention, these involving 545 children. Data collection took place over a 12-month period, with children's body mass index being calculated at the start, again after six months, and then finally after 12 months. The measurements for children in the nurseries selected for inclusion in the intervention (the 'treatment group') were then compared with those that had not experienced the intervention (the 'control group'), with a view to deciding what impact the intervention or treatment had had. The conclusion from the research was that 'Physical activity can significantly improve motor skills but did not reduce body mass … in young children in this trial' (Reilly et al. 2006: 1). The authors add that: 'Our intervention probably provided an inadequate "dose" of physical activity to have any net impact on overall physical activity … or [on] body mass' (Reilly et al. 2006: 4). As the language used here implies, the randomised controlled trial method was initially developed in the field of medicine, notably in testing drugs.

The researchers were aware that children would vary in their initial levels of body mass: this was measured at the beginning, so that the focus could be on *changes* in body mass. The researchers also recognised that there were probably other factors that affect levels of body mass. It was in order to control for these that they used a random procedure for allocating nurseries to treatment and control groups (those involved in the intervention, and those not involved). Random allocation is a commonly employed device in experimental research – it is designed to minimise variation in background factors between treatment and control groups, so that if any outcome difference is found between the two groups we can be reasonably confident that it was a product of the intervention, not of those background factors.[1]

If we examine this research we can find a range of assumptions built into it that will repay some attention. I am not suggesting that these assumptions are necessarily false, or are all equally contentious, but some of them mark important points of difference from other research paradigms.

---

[1]In fact, the researchers used a rather more complex random allocation procedure than I have indicated here, one that operated within bands set by variables that they believed were likely to be closely associated with background differences in physical activity and body mass: type of nursery (school, class, extended day, private sector); size of nursery (number of children); and socio-economic status of the area.

Ontological and epistemological assumptions

Starting with ontological assumptions (those concerning the nature of the phenomena being investigated), the researchers assumed that:

1　'Level of physical activity' varies along a single dimension, and can be significantly changed by the sort of intervention involved in this research.
2　Body mass is a separate feature of children that also varies on a single dimension, and one where some normal level can be identified for children in a particular age range. By implication, 'normal' here refers to a medical standard, in terms of which evaluations can be made regarding who is 'overweight' and who 'underweight' – it is not simply a statistical norm indicating the typical level of body mass in children in a particular population.
3　There is a fairly direct causal relationship between being 'overweight' at age 4 and being obese in later childhood and as an adult.
4　Any relationship between level of physical activity and level of body mass will take the form of an empirical law, involving a determinable relationship that holds across all circumstances, rather than varying according to the particular children involved, or between localities. Moreover, these variables are assumed to exist within the same domain; in the way that, say, the volume and temperature of a gas do. In short, both the variables measured in this study are treated as physical in character, and as capable of being measured and controlled in similar ways to many other physical properties.

We can also identify some epistemological assumptions underpinning this study, in other words assumptions about how to gain knowledge about the phenomena investigated. The researchers assumed that:

1　The variables studied need to be measured in a standardised way, by means of explicit procedures.
2　The relationship between the two variables (level of physical activity and body mass) can be inferred from any change in the body mass index of children receiving the treatment, by comparison with those not receiving it.
3　The children studied are representative, in relevant respects, of children of this age more generally.

These ontological and epistemological assumptions may seem relatively uncontentious in the context of this particular study, but the same kind of methodological approach has been applied to other phenomena where serious questions have been raised about their validity. For example, there have been randomised controlled trials focused on the question of which method of teaching is most effective in improving children's literacy (see Torgerson et al. 2006). Here we need to ask whether 'method of teaching' is a variable that can be handled in the same way as something like 'level of physical activity'. One difference between the two is that mode of teaching is generally formulated as a categorical attribute rather than a continuous variable, in other words in terms of a set of categories (for example, methods relying upon phonics versus those employing a 'whole language' method) rather than different positions on a scale, as in the case of 'number of minutes spent on physical exercise'. This has implications for the kind of statistical analysis that can be carried out. More fundamentally, we might ask whether, in practice, teaching falls into discrete and stable types in this way. If it does not, if teachers combine elements of different approaches, and/or change their strategy somewhat over time, perhaps according to the nature of the children or students they are dealing with, this renders the phenomenon being studied much less determinate and more complex, making the conclusions of the research, and the inferences that can be drawn from these, more uncertain.

It could also be questioned whether literacy is a variable whose ontological character is similar to that of body mass in relevant respects, or one that is open to measurement in the same manner. While ability to sound letters and words in a way that is recognisably correct to a native speaker may be close in character to body mass, in respects relevant to choice of research strategy, what we mean by 'literacy' or 'reading' usually goes beyond this. It would normally include comprehension, of some kind; and comprehension of the meaning of a text is, arguably, in a different domain from physical features like level of physical activity and body mass. We could say that it lies within the socio-cultural rather than the physical realm. And, in fact, much of the dispute over competing approaches to reading arises from divergences in view about what counts as literacy and, more generally, what counts as education. Moreover, if we move away from basic literacy to other issues, for example educating children to appreciate Shakespeare, or a programme designed to foster citizenship in young people, even more serious questions may arise, in both ontological and epistemological terms, about the appropriateness of the kind of approach we have been examining here.

Moreover, it is important to emphasise that there is not a simple and sharp contrast between the study of physical phenomena and of socio-cultural phenomena. Turning back to the original study that we examined, it is worth remembering that obesity is socio-culturally defined: it relates to ideas about body image and well-being, ones that may vary according to gender, and about which very different judgements are often made. Furthermore, the physical activity in which the 4 year olds were required to engage will have had some meaning for them – as fun, exciting, enjoyable, boring, painful, etc. And this will have affected how they engaged in it, so that if it had taken a different form they might have engaged in it more vigorously, or less vigorously. This could also have affected whether the intervention increased or reduced the amount of physical activity the children engaged in at other times; which may have influenced the results of the study.

We can see, then, that the ontological and epistemological assumptions built into this form of research are often contentious. At the very least, their appropriateness may be judged to vary according to what is being studied. It is equally important to recognise that there are also political and ethical assumptions involved in this type of research that may need attention.

Political and ethical assumptions

We should notice, first of all, that the starting point for Reilly et al's research was the existence of a social problem judged to require intervention – obesity in young children that has effects on their health as adults. The authors declare right at the beginning of their article: 'Obesity in children has increased dramatically in recent years. It has adverse health consequences, and there is an urgent need for population-based interventions aimed at prevention' (Reilly et al. 2006: 1). And they add that: 'In 2001 in Scotland at least 10% of children aged 4–5 and 20% of children aged 11–12 were obese. ... Children in Scotland establish a physically inactive lifestyle before school entry'.

While many of us would agree that there is a genuine problem here – though there are some who question whether obesity is a serious problem, or how serious it is – there is still scope for disagreement about whether interventions concerned with reducing obesity in children are desirable. For instance, it could be argued that they increase the risk of anorexia for some children, perhaps especially for girls. Instead, it might be argued that what is required is public education, or the reduction of portion sizes in food products. The key point is that assumptions are being made about what is good for young children and for their later adult selves; or at least about what would be bad for them and must be prevented. Furthermore, it might be argued that these are not matters about which science can legitimately claim to legislate.

There could also be questions about whether the sort of treatment involved in the intervention is legitimate in ethical terms. Within the nurseries selected, the programme was a compulsory one – while the nurseries responded voluntarily to the invitation to be involved, it does not seem that informed consent was gained from the children, though there was parental consent, at least for participation in the home-based element. Meanwhile, children within the control group were also affected to a degree, one suspects without any informed consent from parents or children: 'In the control group, nurseries continued with their usual curriculum and headteachers agreed not to enhance their physical development and movement curriculum' (Reilly et al. 2006: 2). In other words, there was a commitment not to increase the level of physical activity of these children, in terms of the school curriculum, during the year.

These features of the research raise issues not just about how researchers should treat children – a matter of research ethics – but also about how social agencies, in this case nurseries – with the state as the main agent lying beyond them – should treat client populations. We can note that, generally speaking, what is done in nurseries is not decided jointly by children, staff, and parents – it is largely determined by the staff, on a professional basis and under guidelines laid down by the state. So, the intervention involved in this research is very much in line with a model of governance that some would insist infringes children's rights, or at least does not respect their autonomy. Similarly, the intervention might be seen as colluding with a 'nanny state' that is intent upon enforcing a 'healthy lifestyle', instead of allowing people to decide for themselves, and for their children, what is best on the basis of whatever evidence they judge to be relevant.

The point of all this is not to debate these issues here, but rather to note that the study we have examined, and others like it, are implicated in a particular set of ethical and political assumptions. And, like the ontological and epistemological assumptions we discussed earlier, these touch on fundamental disagreements that can be found among researchers about the form that inquiry dealing with children and young people ought to take, and about the proper function of this research. The study we have discussed is typical in its general approach of a great deal of work – especially in the health field – though similar studies can be found in education and elsewhere. The assumptions on which this type of work is based are, as we noted, characteristic in many respects of what is often referred to as 'positivism'. In the next section I want to highlight the main contours of this methodological philosophy.

Positivism

'Positivist' is a label that few researchers today would apply to themselves or to their own work: it is almost entirely used as a means of critically dismissing others' views and work. One consequence of this is that what this term now means has come to be uncertain and variable. However, in the past there were researchers who adopted this label, and the philosophical assumptions to which they were committed are coherent and understandable, though they are rejected by many people working within the field of Childhood Studies today.

The key feature of positivism, in these terms, is that it treats the kind of knowledge produced by the natural sciences, especially physics and chemistry (but we might also include medical research), and the methods typical of those disciplines, as the proper model for all knowledge and inquiry. Indeed, according to many positivists we must not believe anything that has not been well-established by scientific means (see Clifford 1947). Furthermore, positivism dismisses questions that cannot be addressed by these methods as 'metaphysical' or 'speculative', and therefore as meaningless (because they are beyond the realm of what is knowable). Positivists in the nineteenth and twentieth centuries argued that the great advances that had been made in physical science since the seventeenth century arose from the application of scientific method – in particular, from the measurement and control of variables – and that applying this to other fields would lead to similar progress, thereby eliminating ignorance, myth and ideology.

Generally speaking, positivism portrays scientific knowledge as abstract in form: as consisting of laws that capture relations operating across all times and places. An example commonly cited by early positivists was Newton's physics, with its identification of a small set of principles that govern the behaviour of all physical objects, whether in the heavens or on earth. The emphasis, then, is upon the need for research to abstract from the study of particular cases to produce this kind of general knowledge.

For positivists, the experiment is the exemplar of scientific method. This is because they believe that it can produce conclusions whose validity is to a great extent certain. It can do this, they claim, for at least three reasons. First, because it involves clear identification of the outcome to be explained, and measurement of variation in this, so that the effects on it of any proposed explanatory factor can be detected. Secondly, rather than assuming that we can see causal relations directly, or that we intuitively know 'what causes what', science involves systematic testing of causal hypotheses, and this is done by manipulating the level of the hypothesised causal factor and controlling the impact of other factors. Finally, this is carried out by procedures that are explicitly stated and that others can replicate, so as to check the validity of the results. In this way, it is believed, any bias coming from the preferences or characteristics of particular researchers is minimised.

However, much social research influenced by positivism does not employ experimental methods, either in laboratories or 'in the field'. While it uses quantitative data, it is non-experimental in design, for example relying upon questionnaire surveys or large-scale structured observation studies. In such research there are attempts to control variables 'statistically' by comparing cases in which the treatment variable has different values while those background variables judged likely to affect the outcome are at roughly the same level. Such comparison is used to try to detect whether there is any stable relationship between the hypothesised cause and the effect or outcome of interest. For example, as part of the *Young Lives Project*, Glewwe, Qihui and Katare (2012) used survey data to investigate factors affecting educational achievement among ethnic minority students in Vietnam. Using test data, they document the gap in average achievement to be explained, and they then explore the role of various factors, including level of family income, time spent in school, and level of nutrition, in accounting for this gap, using the kind of statistical comparison just outlined. This enables tentative conclusions to be drawn about the causal factors involved.

As we saw earlier in discussing the research of Reilly et al., positivism involves not just ontological and epistemological assumptions but also political and ethical ones. The central idea underpinning it is that through science human beings can at last exercise collective control over their lives. Moreover, frequently the nation-state was seen by early positivists as having the responsibility for exercising this control on behalf of its population, and for the benefit of all. We saw earlier that this political philosophy has not gone unchallenged. It stands in contrast, for instance, to libertarian strands of thinking which argue that individual people should be free to determine their own lives, as far as possible; an idea that is sometimes underpinned by the assumption that such freedom will generate wealth and happiness for all.

In the second half of the twentieth century, across many fields of social research, there were increasing challenges to the dominance of experimental and quantitative research and to associated positivist ideas. It was shown that, in some important respects, positivist philosophy of science had not accurately represented how natural scientists actually go about their work, underplaying the role of hunches and judgment for example, and exaggerating the level of likely validity of scientific findings. Furthermore, the results of quantitative research in psychology and social science, and in applied areas like health and education, were often conflicting, inconclusive, or open to serious question. And it came increasingly to be questioned whether methods modelled on those used in the physical sciences were appropriate in this field.

Partly as a consequence of this, alternative sets of ideas to positivism developed, ones that involved rather different ontological, epistemological, political, and ethical assumptions. In the next section we will look briefly at three of these alternative philosophies: interpretivism, constructionism, and 'critical' theory.

Interpretivism, constructionism, and 'critical' research

During the second half of the twentieth century, quantitative social science came to be challenged on a number of grounds, including:

1   The importance of studying what happens in the 'real' world, rather than what happens under experimental conditions, or in other circumstances heavily controlled by the researcher such as formal, highly structured interviews or the administration of questionnaires.

2   The need to *observe* what happens rather than to rely solely upon respondents' accounts in interview or questionnaire responses.
3   The requirement that people be allowed to speak in their own terms rather than being required to conform to those of researchers for example through answering relatively closed questions. This can be seen as essential if we are to be able to understand their perspectives and how these relate to their actions.
4   The danger that quantification results in the meaning of central concepts being lost, through their being reduced to the results of measurement procedures, these necessarily relating to appearances rather than to underlying processes. This was an issue that arose in our discussion of literacy earlier.
5   The concern that the kind of 'variable analysis' employed by quantitative researchers ignores the complex, contingent, and context-sensitive character of social life, and the extent to which actions and outcomes are produced by people interpreting situations in diverse ways, and acting on the basis of these interpretations, rather than passively responding to external causes.

There were also political and ethical criticisms of quantitative research, and of positivism, along the lines we noted earlier: that it colludes with forms of governance that should be opposed, because they dehumanise people or are unethical in other respects. Partly at issue here are questions about the image of human beings, and especially of children, built into the very procedures employed by quantitative research: as mere units of statistical aggregates, as passively responding to causal processes, and so on. Equally important, there were challenges to the ways in which people are treated in research of this kind: we illustrated some of the grounds for this concern in discussing the study by Reilly et al. As we saw, this relates to broader political issues about the role of the state and individual freedom.

Over and above these criticisms, many came to argue that, rather than having an apparently neutral concern with establishing 'the facts', for example about whether an intervention 'works', research should be explicitly directed at political goals, and/or should exemplify the sorts of social relations that ought to operate in society. This has been a central theme in much feminist writing about research methodology and in arguments for participatory methods more generally. Along these lines, it was insisted that researchers have an ethical duty to treat children and young people in ways that match ideals of freedom and democracy, even though, or in fact precisely because, they are not treated in this way in the wider society.

On these grounds, many researchers shifted to using qualitative methods of various kinds. As noted earlier, in this they were influenced by ideas that challenged the positivist conception of science, offering rather different models, sometimes even questioning whether a scientific approach is what is needed. Each of these alternative paradigms challenges key elements of positivism, but they do so in different ways, and in a manner that generates conflicts among them.

Interpretivism

The starting point for interpretivism is the argument that human social actions, relationships, and institutions are fundamentally different in kind from physical phenomena. Whereas the latter may be subject to universal causal laws, patterns of human action vary across cultures, and furthermore people exercise agency in conforming to or deviating from the cultural rules involved in particular social institutions.

This first (ontological) argument immediately led to a second (epistemological) one: that we cannot study human social life using more or less the same methods as had been developed for studying physical phenomena. Studying people is seen by interpretivists as carrying both advantages and disadvantages in comparison with the study of physical objects. A disadvantage is that simply describing the patterns of physical behaviour in which people engage, however carefully, does not provide us with a basis for understanding their actions, and the reasons for these. A child raising her hand, in exactly the same way in physical terms on different occasions, could be produced by a variety of intentions and motives. In other words, human actions are much more complex than the behaviour of physical objects, or indeed than that of other animals. At the same time, it was argued that we have an advantage in studying human beings that the physicist does not have in studying physical objects: we share with other people a capacity to learn cultures, and thereby to interpret their actions and make sense of them. So the argument is that we must necessarily draw upon this capacity if we are to be able to study the social world; we cannot simply rely upon the sort of physical description of external behaviour that is characteristic of natural science.

An implication of this is that, rather than it being possible for just anyone to study human behaviour in a particular context, using a standard method, the researcher must have the cultural knowledge and capacities that are required to make sense of what is going on. For example, we might come to be convinced that the child who raised her arm was offering to answer a teacher's question because we notice that the teacher asked a question immediately before the girl put up her hand and that the teacher nominated her after she had done this and she answered his question. Yet, in order to come to this conclusion, we need cultural knowledge to recognise that a particular form of schooling is operating here, and the ability to identify what the teacher said as a question, and what the child provided as an answer to that question. On another occasion these features may be absent and we would have to make sense of the girl's raising her arm in a different way, for example as trying to draw the teacher's attention to the fact that there was smoke coming from under the door of the science lab, or that the headteacher had entered the room.

Whether or not we have the necessary cultural knowledge and capacities is always an important question to ask, from an interpretivist point of view, even when we are carrying out research in our own society; indeed, even in locations with which we have everyday familiarity. For instance, it is all too easy for adults to assume that they understand how children or young people view the world and feel about it. Adults may seek to justify this by pointing to the fact that they have been children themselves and can draw on memories of this. However, there are questions to be asked here: Are our memories of childhood not shaped by our subsequent adult lives? Can we really access how we felt about things as children? Furthermore, like adults, children are differentiated in terms of the socio-cultural conditions in which they live, not least by generational changes, and these will affect their experience. From the point of view of interpretivism, then, considerable effort is required if we are to be able to understand the activities of children and young people, and even of other adults: to grasp why they do what they do, and how this reflects how they see and feel about the world. So, there must be resistance to the strong temptation immediately to apply adult models, especially models that ascribe to children a deficit of one kind or another. Equally important there must be a commitment to learn to understand the perspectives of others, rather than seeking to explain their behaviour in terms of external appearances or prior theories.

An illustration of how interpretivism shapes research on children and young people is provided by a study that was concerned with 10–12-year-old Greek Cypriot children's experiences of crossing to the northern, Turkish-occupied part of Cyprus. The researchers report that:

> during these highly emotional visits, the parents and grandparents of children who come from refugee families usually go back to the family home and community that they were forced to abandon in 1974. Children become witnesses in this memory journey and encounter, usually for the first time, the 'enemy' that they have been hearing about at school or at home.

Given this, in their research, the authors sought 'to unravel the ways in which children's narratives reveal the mechanisms through which ethnic difference is constructed', drawing on observations and interviews, but also on 'innovative visual methodologies (drawings and mapping exercises) that add different layers of information …' (Christou and Spyrou 2012: 303). In short, they recognised that in order to understand how Greek Cypriot children come to understand their relationship to Turkish Cypriots it was necessary to explore how their perspectives were formed through their experiences, and to use a range of interpretive methods to do this.

Partially overlapping with interpretivism is a second alternative philosophy to positivism, what is often called constructionism (though this term is used in a variety of ways). We will now examine this.

Constructionism

What is central here, first of all, is rejection of any idea that cognition, or even perception, is a process whereby objects that already exist in the world impress their character upon our understanding. Instead, it is argued that perception and cognition are active processes, in which anything apparently 'given' is actually a product of processes of selection and construction. Another key theme is that these processes are socio-cultural in character, with different cultures generating divergent experiential worlds and stocks of 'knowledge'.

All this is similar in many ways to interpretivism, but there remain important differences. Where interpretivism tends to assume that people's behaviour is governed by stable perspectives built up to make sense of and deal with their circumstances, constructionists view people as constructing particular understandings on particular occasions in a much more fluid way, drawing upon a range of conflicting discourses available to them. Similarly, interpretivism assumes that it is possible for researchers to grasp the modes of experience and ideas of others, even those who belong to quite different cultures, whereas constructionists raise questions about whether such understanding is possible. Indeed, constructionists often question whether understanding other people and perhaps even understanding oneself, is ever fully possible. They argue that the 'understandings' we produce of others' intentions and motives reflect our own cultural or personal assumptions and practices. In other words, cultural worlds are brought into existence and sustained in and through the practices in which people engage in particular local contexts, and there is no escape from these (for the researcher, or for anyone else), and certainly no access to some 'real' world beyond them. This suggests that the focus of research should be on those practices themselves, and perhaps even on how socio-cultural processes position and constitute people as individuals with particular identities in particular contexts. In other words, even who we are is itself socio-culturally constituted, rather than simply given.

For some constructionists, these processes of socio-cultural construction are all that exists or that can be studied. This idea has important implications for how inquiry should be pursued. The task can no longer be to document the characteristics of various types of object (children, adults, schools, teachers, hospitals, doctors, etc.) existing in the world – their actions and relationships, the causes and consequences these have, etc. It is insisted that we must not be misled by appearances into forgetting that such 'objects' (including people's beliefs, identities, actions, etc.) owe their very existence and character to the constitutive processes involved in generating them as perceivable and conceivable phenomena.

Shifting the focus of study to these processes involves a major re-specification of the goal of inquiry. For example, we would have to treat children's personal and social characteristics not as intrinsic to them but rather as the product of discursive practices, including for example those operating in schools, through which they are characterised (say) as intelligent/stupid, motivated/lazy, 'gifted'/ having 'special needs', and so on. Furthermore, much the same argument would have to be applied to their sense of who they are and their lived experiences – these could no longer be treated as simply belonging to them, or as existing independently of the accounts that they produce.

An example of a constructionist approach is provided by Davies' analysis of Sylvia Fraser's autobiographical story *My Father's House* (Fraser 1989; Davies 1995). Davies shows, in detail, how Fraser's account of abuse by her father, and her subsequent coping with the resulting trauma, is constructed in terms of two main discourses: a 'socialist feminist' narrative and a 'therapeutic' narrative. She argues that:

> each of these narratives constructs very different sequences and relationships between events, resulting in different 'plots' with radical implications for the construction of causality, morality and individual agency. … For instance, the 'socialist feminist' narrative creates a version of events which serves to connect the 'personal' victimization suffered by Fraser as a child to the more 'political' question of treatment of women more generally within a patriarchal society. By contrast, the alternative … therapeutic narrative is based on the typical pattern of psychoanalytic procedure set out by Freud. … This psychoanalytic model provides the basic structure of *My Father's House* and serves to connect the incidence of incestuous abuse to themes of inheritance and a dysfunctional family history. (Crossley 2000: 77)

Davies shows how in Fraser's book the therapeutic narrative comes to dominate and to suppress the socialist feminist narrative. One effect of this is that Fraser's mother is portrayed as responsible for failing to protect her child, while her father is presented as a passive victim of his own childhood and thereby largely excused of blame.

In practice, the constructionist perspective is rarely fully applied (Foster et al. 1996), since this would require researchers to treat the phenomena they study as constructed through their own research practices, rather than as existing independently of these. Nevertheless, in recent years it has become very influential.

The fourth and final methodological philosophy I will discuss is what is often referred to as 'critical' theory and research. (I have put 'critical' in quote marks because the meaning here goes beyond the sense in which all researchers adopt a critical orientation in assessing knowledge claims.)

The 'critical' tradition

One way in which a 'critical' orientation contrasts with positivism, interpretivism, and constructionism is that whereas they may be concerned solely with describing and/or explaining the perspectives and/or practices of children and young people, and of relevant adults, 'critical' researchers also evaluate the phenomena they study. They do this either in terms of some set of ideals built into their own political and ethical positions or against standards that they identify as inherent within the socio-cultural contexts they are examining (this second approach is sometimes referred to as 'immanent' or 'internal' critique).

So, 'critical' research involves evaluative as well as factual concepts – for example those using this approach are concerned with the 'exploitation' or 'oppression' of one group by another, or with the denial of 'rights'. And research is seen as properly directed towards achieving particular kinds of political goal: reducing or eliminating exploitation and oppression, bringing about emancipation, and/or ensuring that rights are respected.

Equally important, whereas interpretivism and constructionism aim to a large extent at understanding other cultures 'in their own terms', 'critical' research usually insists that they can only be properly understood within the framework of a comprehensive theory that locates them in the wider social system and/or within a larger process of historical development that has been properly theorised. In this way, like some positivists but unlike many interpretivists and constructionists, 'critical' researchers insist that people's behaviour will often need to be explained by factors that are beyond their awareness. Indeed, 'critical' researchers argue that in many cases this awareness will have been systematically distorted by social processes, in other words it will be 'ideological'.

The original source of many of the ideas underpinning 'critical' research was Marxism. However, there are important divergences from this approach in how this kind of research is pursued today. One change is that the focus is no longer solely on social class inequalities and conflicts, which were central for Marxism, but on other kinds of social division: gender, race and ethnicity, and also those of age and generation.

Despite these changes in the 'critical' tradition, what is usually retained is the idea that research should operate within an explicit framework of political assumptions, and should be geared to serving political goals. Thus, some of those committed to children's rights believe that their research must be primarily directed towards bringing about recognition of these rights across the fields in which they work. Indeed, almost all 'critical' researchers insist that researchers have a responsibility to resist dominant ideologies and to challenge inequitable social relations through their work.

An example of research strongly influenced by the 'critical' paradigm is the study by Nancy Scheper-Hughes and Daniel Hoffman (1994) on 'street children' in Brazil. They draw the following evaluative conclusion from their analysis:

The outcome of the struggle for childhood in Brazil will weigh heavily on the success of activists in the MNMMR [The National Movement of Street Children] and other organizations that share its vision of a new society in which all children are valued. For all its power, however, the Brazilian street children's movement has been unable to strike at the source of the problem. Until the chaotic economic and social conditions that cause desperately poor parents to 'lose' their children to the streets are reversed, childhood for the vast majority in Brazil will continue to signify a period of adversity to be survived and gotten over as quickly as possible, rather than a time of nurturance to be extended and savored.

Conclusion

We can find the influence of all of the methodological philosophies discussed in this chapter evidenced in research concerned with children and young people today, though their relative influence has changed somewhat over time. Moreover, elements from these different paradigms are frequently combined by particular researchers in their work.

While the last few decades of the twentieth century witnessed the growing influence of interpretivism, constructionism, and 'critical' research in recent years, in some quarters, there has been a resurgence of positivism. Thus, there have been increased calls for research to serve policymaking and practice by demonstrating 'what works' and what does not 'work'; in other words, what is and is not effective in some sense (McNeish et al., 2002). This has led to calls for more randomised controlled trials to be carried out, along the lines of the study by Reilly et al. that we discussed at the beginning of this chapter. More broadly, there has been increased emphasis on the value of quantitative research in many areas of social research, including some that deal with children and young people. Alongside this, there have also been growing calls for 'mixing' quantitative and qualitative methods. However, the methodological philosophies discussed in this chapter have generated conflicting paradigms even *within* mixed methods research (see Tashakkori and Teddlie 2010).

References

Christou, M. and Spyrou, S. (2012) 'Border encounters: How children navigate space and otherness in an ethnically divided society', *Childhood*, 19 (3): 302–16.

Clifford, W.K. (1947) *The Ethics of Belief*. London: Watts.

Crossley, M. (2000) 'Deconstructing autobiographical accounts of childhood sexual abuse: Some critical reflections', *Feminism & Psychology*, 10(1): 73–90.

Davies, M. (1995) *Healing Sylvia: Childhood Sexual Abuse and the Construction of Identity*. London: Taylor and Francis.

Foster, P., Gomm, R. and Hammersley, M. (1996) *The Construction of Educational Inequality*. London: Falmer Press.

Fraser, S. (1989) *My Father's House: A Memoir of Incest and Healing*. London: Virago.

Glewwe, P., Qihui, C. and Katare, B. (2012) 'What determines learning among Kinh and ethnic minority students in Vietnam? An analysis of the Round 2 Young Lives data'. Available at: www.younglives.org.uk/files/working-papers/wp80-what-determines-learning-among-kinh-and-ethnic-minority-students-in-vietnam (accessed 13 October 2012).

McNeish, D., Newman, T. and Roberts, H. (eds) (2002) *What Works for Children?* Buckingham: Open University Press.

Reilly, J., Kelly, L., Montgomery, C., Williamson, A., Fisher, A., McColl, J., Lo Conte, R., Paton, J. and Grant, S. (2006) 'Physical activity to prevent obesity in young children: Cluster randomised controlled trial', *British Medical Journal*, 333(7577): 1041. Available at: www.ncbi.nlm.nih.gov/pmc/articles/PMC1647320/ (accessed 14 October 2012).

Scheper-Hughes, N. and Hoffman, D. (1994) 'Kids out of place'. Available at: http://pangaea.org/street_children/latin/sheper.htm (accessed 8 November 2012).

Tashakkori, A. and Teddlie, C. (eds) (2010) *Handbook of Mixed Methods in Social and Behavioral Research*, 2nd edition. Thousand Oaks, CA: Sage.

Torgerson, C., Brooks, G. and Hall, J. (2006) *A Systematic Review of the Research Literature on the Use of Phonics in the Teaching of Reading and Spelling*. London: Department for Education and Skills. Available at: http://collection.europarchive.org/tna/20060731065549/www.dcsf.gov.uk/research/data/uploadfiles/RR711_.pdf (accessed 3 April 2012).

SECTION 3

THE REALITY OF RESEARCH WITH CHILDREN AND YOUNG PEOPLE

Introduction

Discussions about research methodology can provide broad principles for carrying out research as we discussed in the Introduction, but not a specific guaranteed toolkit for applying in any context. We are Interested in how researchers adapt a range of methods to the contexts in which they carry out research. This requires close attention to decisions made throughout the research process, from identifying research interests and research questions to deciding on a methodology and engaging with research participants in the field through analysis and writing up. We have explored some of the central issues faced by researchers carrying out research with children and young people in Section 1 and discussed specific research methods and approaches to research design and methodological ideas in Section 2. Here we move on to focus on four researchers' reflective commentaries of research they have been involved in. The aim is to peel back the research process to reveal some of the research stories behind these studies. This is not an attempt to provide a step-by-step guide to individual methodological approaches. The intention is to bring to life the reality of carrying out research, including considering the kinds of questions researchers often face and challenges they may need to overcome. Our aim in this section is to support others as they seek to understand research accounts and to consider what is possible in research with children and young people.

There is not space within four chapters to represent examples of every approach to childhood research or examples of every experience of childhood. Instead these first-hand researcher accounts have been chosen to indicate contemporary examples of the breadth of research with children and young people. This breadth includes research on a local and global scale, across age groups from children under 5 to young adulthood, from a doctoral study to a large-scale international study, and covering topics including partnerships with parents, poverty, transitions and children's experiences of learning environments. The range of methodologies covered includes practitioner, participatory and longitudinal research with discussion of qualitative, quantitative and mixed method approaches.

Nicola Smith in Chapter 11 discusses her doctoral study of parental involvement in pre-school education from the perspectives of 'British Asian' parents, nursery practitioners and children. Smith discusses the catalyst for this study emerging from her professional role as a nursery practitioner. Reflecting on the research process, Smith illustrates how the theoretical and methodological thinking that she encountered during the early stages of her doctorate equipped her to conduct the study and to re-examine her own practice as well as dominant school cultures.

The focus continues on young children in Chapter 12 where Alison Clark reflects on developing and adapting the Mosaic approach (see Chapter 2) as an example of participatory research where children are included in the design process for new buildings they will inhabit. This commentary provides a reflection on a multi-method research approach developed since 1999 in three research studies carried out by the author. Clark indicates the organic nature of this process, including the methodological challenges of working within the constraints of real building projects. Different ethical considerations have continued to emerge as the studies have developed and are discussed here in relation to visual research and the ethics of social inclusion.

The research commentary in Chapter 13 by Sheila Henderson and Rachel Thomson is also able to provide a 'long view' reflecting on the large-scale qualitative longitudinal study, *Inventing Adulthoods*, which was first begun in 1996 and follows the transition to adulthood of over 100 young people. The authors explain the evolutionary process through which four separate studies merged over time into one longitudinal study. The theoretical and methodological emphases changed over the lifetime of the study. However, the overall focus on young people's personal biographies in social contexts continued. The challenges they faced included deciding on from what point in time to tell the stories, how to manage the volume and depth of data and how to integrate the wider social and historical pictures with the individual lives.

The final research commentary in this section, Chapter 14 by Caine Rolleston, offers one researcher's reflections on particular aspects of another large scale longitudinal study, *Young Lives*, an international study of childhood poverty based in Peru, Vietnam, Ethiopia and India (On Young Lives, see also Chapter 3). This commentary is a personal reflection on one particular aspect of this multi-layered study, the gathering of quantitative data about education across the four countries. Here Rolleston demonstrates how this aspect of the *Young Lives* study added a further dimension to the overall research purpose of understanding childhood poverty by examining the relationship between poverty and education in the four countries studied. His account indicates some of the methodological challenges faced by setting out to measure school quality across such diverse social, cultural and linguistic settings.

Thus these four commentaries offer researchers' perspectives on different stages of the research process across a range of topics, age groups, methodologies and scales. Their inclusion in this book is a reminder of the importance of on-going reflection for those engaged in carrying out and understanding research with children and young people.

11 Perspectives on Parental Involvement: A Discussion of Practitioner Research

Nicola Smith

Summary of the research

My PhD research study examined perceptions of parental involvement from the points of view of nursery practitioners, 'British Asian' parents and their children. It was created as a result of my own experiences as an early years practitioner and as a parent. Bhabha's notion of 'third space' (1994: 53) was examined in relation to developing more effective relationships between parents, children and practitioners. Case studies were developed in two nursery classes, using interviews, group work and documentation from the settings. Data was analysed using elements of a 'grounded theory' approach as well as using concepts from the work of Bourdieu (1977) and Bhabha (1994), as discussed in the next section of this commentary. The research findings demonstrated that whilst practitioner participants are well-intentioned in their work with parents and children, existing structures and power relationships make the construction of meaningful partnerships extremely difficult. The research also indicated that of all participants, the children had the most positive attitude regarding parental involvement. The findings suggested that practitioners need to move away from efforts to 'involve' parents towards more democratic notions of participation which involve children, parents and teachers in ongoing dialogue.

Starting points

The research was carried out in two nursery classes in a primary and a first school, named Orchard Road and Forest Hill in this commentary. I had previously been employed as a teacher in each of the schools. I was interested in examining whether perceptions of the parental involvement of British Asian parents were similar or different in the two settings. For example, did white, monolingual practitioners approach building relationships with British Asian bilingual parents in a different way when they were working with just one family who was bilingual?

Orchard Road School is a large primary school in a city centre in the West Midlands. The vast majority of children attending Orchard Road Primary are of Pakistani or Bangladeshi origin, with Mirpuri and Sylheti being the main languages spoken. Forest Hill School is situated in the middle of a housing estate in a West Midlands town and most of the children attending the school live on the estate. All but a few of the pupils are of white, British heritage. There was one child of South Asian origin attending the nursery class at Forest Hill School when my research was carried out.

The seed of the idea for my PhD research project was a result of my work with Fahima, a child in my nursery class when I was teaching at Orchard Road. Fahima found the transition from home to school extremely difficult and as I did not share a language with her mother, I struggled to support them both throughout the process. I became very aware that my ethnic origin, language and style of dressing may be alienating and even worrying for children and for their parents. I also felt that the ways in which we were working in the nursery at the time were not always appropriate for helping individual children to settle in. Parents were not encouraged to stay with their children and this way of working was not questioned by staff or by parents, it was accepted as the way things were. It was reflecting on these experiences which led me to begin my research project.

At the beginning of the research, I was interested in the ideas of the French sociologist, Pierre Bourdieu. In particular, I wanted to explore his notions of 'symbolic violence' and 'méconnaissance' (Bourdieu 1977) in my own research. 'Symbolic violence' is a term used by Bourdieu to define how one individual or group of individuals maintains dominance over another in a particular context, or 'field' as Bourdieu calls it. This dominance is achieved because one social group conforms to the values of a particular field more closely than the other group and expects others to do the same. So, in the context or field of school, teachers conform more closely to 'school values' since they are trained to work in schools and have first hand experiences of the school culture. Parents may also have their own experiences of school life, but these will probably be from their own childhoods, when they were expected to conform to teacher expectations.

Since teachers are dominant in the field of school, the teachers' ways of doing things become accepted as the 'right' way. As this happens mostly at a subconscious level, individuals or groups of individuals do not challenge this accepted way of doing things but continue to conform to expectations. This is what Bourdieu calls 'méconnaissance' (1977: 5).

I was interested in exploring how parents', teachers' and children's ethnicities and home languages may or may not contribute to the phenomenon of 'symbolic violence'. As Blackledge (2001) points out, 'school values' can include the notion of English as the language of success. I wanted to know if research participants' monolingualism or multilingualism impacted on their relationships with each other and how this related to the idea of English speaking being more desirable in the school context. Moreover, if the notion of English as the language of success was visible in the settings, was this idea challenged or did it form part of the accepted ways of doing things (méconnaissance)?

I had also studied the work of researchers such as Fumoto et al. (2007), Cummins (2000) and Robinson and Jones-Diaz (2006), who all highlighted the emotional experiences of children who were learning English in order to be successful in the field of school. Drury (2007) highlights the importance of relationships between parents and teachers in supporting bilingual children's transitions from home to school, including support for children building relationships with their teachers. I wondered how better relationships between parents and teachers might be developed to support bilingual and multilingual children as they made the transition from home to school.

Bhabha (1994) looks at how individuals and groups of individuals move between cultures and how cultures are at different stages in a process of 'hybridisation'. There is no such thing as a 'pure' culture, rather cultures are in an ongoing process of partially blending with each other.

Bhabha is interested in looking at the margins of this blending process. Through the process of hybridisation, a 'third space' emerges which allows new cultural identities to be formed, independently of previous structures. In my research, I wanted to examine whether, in the blending of home and school cultures, a 'third space' could emerge where parents, children and teachers could build new, more equally balanced relationships.

The research questions

In carrying out this research study, my interest was not in determining the importance of parental involvement in nursery education. Previous research already pointed to the importance of parental involvement in schools in relation to the educational success of their children (e.g. Bennett 2006; DCSF 2008;

Wheeler and Connor 2009). Other research also indicated that where parents have higher levels of self-confidence and feel involved by practitioners, then this has a positive effect on their children's well-being (e.g. Wheeler and Connor 2009; Roberts 2010). As such, I began the research from an assumption that it is better for children and their parents if parents and teachers work together to build on intellectual, social, physical and emotional development. I was interested in how parents, teachers and children perceive parental involvement. Do they have the same ideas about what positive parental involvement should mean? Do they think that parental involvement is effective as it exists presently? If not, how would they change it and what might be the barriers to parental involvement? I was also interested in the benefits to practitioners of parental involvement. How does working effectively with parents support practitioners in their role? How does it make them feel about themselves as practitioners? Reflection on these ideas supported the development of the research questions:

- How do British Asian parents and children and their teachers perceive parental involvement?
- What influences these perceptions of parental involvement?
- How are these perceptions similar and how are they different?
- What might be the reasons for similarities in and differences of perception?
- Having investigated the first four research questions, what are the implications for future practice?

As a practitioner researcher (Doyle 2007; McNiff 2007) I was determined that my research should be firmly rooted in practice and that part of my analysis and writing up should include implications for how practitioners might do things differently. When I began the PhD research, I was studying on a part-time basis and working part time as a nursery practitioner, mostly with families of British Asian origin. I was concerned with the 'real-life' experiences of participants in my study (see Guba and Lincoln 1985; Yin 1994). So in examining participants' perceptions I was interested in capturing the realities of their day-to-day lives in the two nursery settings. My main motivation as a researcher was, as already indicated, to open up a space in which participants' voices could be heard (Haw 1996), as this was something I felt that as a practitioner I had not done in the past.

Choice of research methodology

From the beginning of the research project, I was interested in the power dynamics between parents, children and teachers and how these might affect parental involvement. It was clear that I had to think carefully about my own role as a practitioner researcher (see Clark 2005; McNiff 2007) and how this might impact

not only on the research project itself, but also on the child and parent participants in the research. I carried out a pilot study for the research in the setting
where I was employed as a part-time nursery teacher. However, it would not have
been appropriate to carry out any more fieldwork with the parents and children
I worked with on a daily basis. Part of my research involved examining existing
power imbalances between parents, children and teachers. Research in my own
setting might have exerted pressure on parents and children to participate and to
give what they perceived as the 'right' answers to any questions I might ask.

Throughout the research, I could see the relevance of the Bourdieuian concept of 'symbolic violence' (1977) discussed above, whereby one group of individuals might unconsciously wield power over another individual or group of
individuals in a particular social context. My research was rooted in ideas of
social justice (Griffiths 1998) and I was concerned that the research methodology itself should not reinforce the phenomenon of symbolic violence between
practitioners and children and their parents in the settings. It was important
that participant voices were heard truthfully in this research. I did not wish the
participants to feel that the research was something which was being done to
them, rather it was being shaped with them. At the same time, I needed to select
methods of collecting robust data which could be analysed in a meaningful and
coherent way.

I felt strongly that children's voices should be given space to be heard in the
research. Although my research study was focused on perceptions of parental
involvement and therefore examined the relationships between parents and
teachers, analysis of these relationships would be meaningless without including
the children in the settings. As Pascal and Bertram (2009) point out, it is often
the case that children from minority ethnic groups are not really listened to in
their nursery settings. It is the children who are the reason for the settings' existence and who should be at the heart of any research in the field of early childhood. I needed to make sure that I listened carefully to the children so that their
views could be truthfully represented in the research. I needed to select methods
which allowed these views to come straight from the children and minimise the
possibility of data including my inferences or interpretations of their words.

The children in both nurseries knew me as a teacher; several of them had
older siblings who had previously been members of my class. I was aware that my
position as a teacher might mean that interviewing children would not provide
me with reliable, trustworthy data for my research. I needed to make sure that
children felt comfortable enough to talk to me openly, rather than feeling that
there was a 'right' answer to any question I might pose. I was aware that some
children might feel more comfortable speaking with someone in their home
language but that this would need to be carefully planned, since I would then be
analysing someone else's translation of the children's words.

One of the things which I did to help the children and their parents build relationships with me before beginning the research was to spend time in the nursery settings working and playing alongside them. For half a term, I visited the settings each week and joined in with the nursery children in their play. I also spent time with the teachers, helping to prepare a new role play area and putting up displays, for example. I joined the children, teachers and parents from Orchard Road School on a coach trip to a local adventure play park, taking my own young daughter along with me. I hoped that in doing so, I would be able to build up relationships of trust with all the participants in the study. During these visits, I talked with the children about my PhD study, explaining to them that I was 'trying to find out about children, their mums and dads and teachers and write about it all in a book'.

During this time, I noticed that children in both the settings enjoyed book-making and were used to making books independently and with their teachers. I had been reading about Paulo Freire's (1996) use of codifications in his research, where a familiar situation was represented to participants in a drawing to stimulate discussion. I had decided to use photographs to start discussions in my focus group work with parents. This led me to plan a bookmaking activity with the children using photographs of parents and children in the Nursery and at parent workshops (see Clark and Moss 2011). As this was a familiar activity to the children, it would mean that we could talk about parental involvement in a more spontaneous manner than through interviews. Children's ownership of the books should also mean that the likelihood of a child feeling they should give a 'right' answer could be minimised.

The bookmaking activity was offered to all children in the settings, as part of the available activities over a number of days. Some children chose to take part in the activity with me and some children preferred to work with another member of staff using home languages. This meant that I had to prepare the activity carefully together with the two nursery nurses at Orchard Road who would be working in home languages with the children.

Making sense of the data

In terms of the volume of data, the bookmaking activity provided me with lots of conversations which needed careful listening to, and in some cases translation. I organised the data into clips which I logged on a spreadsheet, using direct quotations from the children – for example, 'Daddy brings me to nursery and then goes to work'. A significant amount of this conversation involved talk about the practical aspects of making the book and these clips were taken out in the final stage of analysis. The data was organised according to themes emerging from the data collected from all participants, rather than according to themes imposed by me. So, my first step in the analysis of the case studies was to make a list of everything which parents, teachers and children talked about in each setting. I made a list of topics of discussion using speech bubbles. The process of going through each clip log, document or set of field notes and listing topics of discussion in this manner allowed me to spend more time familiarising myself with the data. I chose to make a list using a speech bubble graphic rather than a table, for example, for two reasons. Firstly, I needed a way of listing the topics which had a strong visual impact for me, to support my memory of the interviews and group work sessions, etc. Secondly, it meant that I was able to print out the list and physically cut out the speech bubbles. I was able to do this away from the computer which enabled me to look at the topics of conversation all together in a way which is difficult on screen. It also meant that I could physically handle the data, which again supported me in remembering in detail what participants had talked about. By recording topics of conversation in this way, I was able to physically move them around, sorting them and seeing where topics of conversation might belong together, in considering themes emerging from the data. It also meant that I could make more than one copy of some of the speech bubbles, since some topics of conversation belonged with a range of others. At the end of this process, I had identified eight categories of data, indicating the influences of perceptions of parental involvement, namely experiences, representations, knowledge, feelings, opinions, values and beliefs, interactions and time. I was then able to analyse each category in relation to my literature review and conceptual framework.

The children's voices were pivotal in helping me to overcome a sticky point in my analysis of the data from this study. I was concerned that in writing up my study, I was identifying a number of significant concerns about relationships between practitioners and parents in both settings. As a practitioner researcher, I knew that practitioners in both nurseries had good intentions towards parents, but, despite this, my analysis showed that British Asian parents were marginalised in terms of parental involvement. I was concerned that my research might seem overly critical of practitioners, but at the same time I needed to give voice to the concerns of parent participants. Analysis of the data from the children showed that they amongst all the participants had the most positive 'can do' approach to parental involvement. For the children, it was clear that parents wanted to be involved in their nursery life and that teachers also wanted this involvement. It was the children's voices which led me to reflect that it was the structures of the school settings which constrained practitioners and not the motivations of the practitioners themselves.

The key finding of my research was that as practitioners we need to move away from attempts to involve parents (on our terms) in their children's education towards more participatory approaches to working together. The 'third space' where dialogue can begin will look different in different settings and when working with different groups and individuals. When working with bilingual children we need to find ways of understanding each others' identities and cultures before we can begin to work together. For practitioners, this means being ready to listen to children and their parents. For schools, this means allowing teachers time to listen to children and their parents and not encouraging the reproduction of existing relationships by presenting teachers as the 'experts' on children's education.

References

Bennett, J. (2006) *Starting Strong II: Early Childhood Education and Care*. Paris: OECD publications.

Bhabha, H.K. (1994) *The Location of Culture*. London: Routledge.

Blackledge, A. (2001) 'Literacy, schooling and ideology in a multilingual state', *Curriculum Journal*, 12(3): 291–312.

Bourdieu, P. (1977) *Outline of a Theory of Practice*. Cambridge: Polity Press.

Clark, A. (2005) 'Ways of seeing: Using the Mosaic approach to listen to young children's perspectives', in A. Clark, A.T. Kjørholt and P. Moss (eds), *Beyond Listening: Children's Perspectives on Early Childhood Services*. Bristol: Policy Press. pp. 29–49.

Clark, A. and Moss, P. (2011) *Listening to Young Children: The Mosaic Approach*, 2nd edition. London: National Children's Bureau for the Joseph Rowntree Foundation.

Cummins, J. (2000) *Language, Power and Pedagogy: Bilingual Children in the Crossfire*. Clevedon: Multilingual Matters.

DCSF (2008) *The Impact of Parental Involvement on Children's Education*. Nottingham: DCSF Publications.

Doyle, D. (2007) 'Transdisciplinary enquiry: Researching with rather than on', in A. Campbell and S. Groundwater-Smith (eds), *An Ethical Approach to Practitioner Research: Dealing with Issues and Dilemmas in Action Research*. London: Routledge.

Drury, R. (2007) *Young Bilingual Learners at Home and School: Researching Multilingual Voices*. Stoke-on-Trent: Trentham Books.

Freire, P. (1996) *Pedagogy of the Oppressed*, new revised edition. Harmondsworth: Penguin.

Fumoto, H., Hargreaves, D. and Maxwell, S. (2007) 'Teachers' perceptions of their relationships with children who speak English as an additional language in early childhood settings', *Journal of Early Childhood Research*, 5(2): 135–53.

Griffiths, M. (1998) *Educational Research for Social Justice: Getting off the Fence*. Buckingham: Open University Press.

Guba, E.G. and Lincoln, Y.S. (1985) *Naturalistic Inquiry*. London: Sage.

Haw, K.F. (1996) 'Exploring the educational experiences of Muslim girls: Tales told to tourists – should the white researcher stay at home?', *British Educational Research Journal*, 22(3): 319–29.

McNiff, J. (2007) 'The significance of "I" in educational research and the responsibility of intellectuals' [Online] July 2007. Available at: www.jeanmcniff.com/items.asp?id=20 (accessed 26 February 2013).

Pascal, C. and Bertram, T. (2009) 'Listening to young citizens: The struggle to make real a participatory paradigm in research with young children', *European Early Childhood Education Research Journal*, 17(2): 249–62.

Roberts, R. (2010) *Wellbeing from Birth*. London: Sage.

Robinson, K. and Jones-Diaz, C. (2006) *Diversity and Difference in Early Childhood Education: Issues for Theory and Practice*. Maidenhead: Open University Press.

Wheeler, H. and Connor, J. (2009) *Parents, Early Years and Learning*. London: National Children's Bureau.

Yin, R.K. (1994) *Case Study Research: Design and Methods*. London: Sage.

12 Developing and Adapting the Mosaic Approach

Alison Clark

Starting points

The original study that led to the development of the Mosaic approach began in 1999. This study, *Listening to Young Children* (Clark and Moss 2011 [2001]), was part of an evaluation of Coram Community Campus, an experiment in multi-agency working which included early years provision, a parents' centre and a homeless families' project. The aim of the study was to explore ways of including the views and experiences of young children, under 5 years old, in the evaluation and included a development stage to allow new methods to be explored.

The initial research questions focused on how could young children's perspectives be gathered? The terminology 'views and experiences' was deliberately broad. 'Views' alone suggested we were only interested in opinions that could be stated. My colleague Peter Moss and I felt that the methods needed to move beyond the spoken word if we were going to be able to capture the complexities of the everyday experiences of young children.

The development of the Mosaic approach was an organic process. I began with an initial review of the literature, which involved looking beyond early childhood research to raise possibilities for new ways in which young children could be active participants in research. This included drawing on the emerging sociology of childhood (for example Mayall 2002; Christensen and James 2008) and on Participatory Action Research (e.g. Fals-Borda 2006). This reading was followed by days spent in the nursery observing the children, interspersed with more reading and discussions with early years practitioners and my academic colleagues. All three elements – observing, reading and discussing – were essential for the methodology to develop. It wasn't a question of locking myself away for six months and then, as in *Chitty Chitty Bang Bang*, opening the door and revealing the final product. The methodology developed as a reflexive and discursive process, adapted and amended as the study progressed.

Purpose

This chapter focuses on the *Living Spaces* study (Clark, 2010), the third study carried out by the authors of the Mosaic approach. The aim of the *Living Spaces* study was to investigate how young children's views and experiences could inform the planning, design and development of early years provision. The focus was on changes to the learning environment. There were three objectives:

1 To explore how young children's views and experiences can inform the planning and designing of new provision;
2 To explore how young children's views and experiences can inform changes to established provision;
3 To contribute to cross-national and cross-disciplinary/professional exchange and dialogue about young children's involvement in change in the indoor and outdoor environment.

The objectives indicated the applied nature of the study. This was not intended as a hypothetical exploration of young children's capacities to contribute to change, but as the opportunity to actively engage their perspectives in the midst of real design projects:

> I reserve the term *applied research* for inquiry that is intentionally developed within the context of decision-making and that is directed towards the interests of one or more clients ... (Chambers 2003: 390)

There was a deliberate intention to promote dialogue across academic and practice communities both during and after the completion of the study. It was not therefore a question of thinking about dissemination as a final stage of the study but more a question of articulating ongoing dialogue as an intended objective from the onset.

Adapting the methods

The *Living Spaces* study involved two case studies based on actual design projects. The first case study was based in a primary school where a free-standing nursery class was to be demolished and the nursery integrated into the main body of the school. The second case study focused on a review of a recently completed Children's Centre. There were particular methodological challenges in working within the constraints of real building projects with all the uncertainties of delays and problems that these entailed. These challenges were magnified by the complexities of involving young children in a longitudinal project with inevitable long periods between research visits due to slow progress on the building work.

I was keen to find ways of supporting the young children involved in the first case study to think about their present environment before considering possible future changes. This involved considering how the Mosaic approach could provide a 'thinking space' for young children and adults to consider what their existing environment was like to be in. My implicit research question here was 'what does it mean to be in this place?' It was important to provide several different modes of communication for enabling the children to explore their thoughts and feelings about their learning environment. These included child-led tours of the site in which the children were in charge of the route and the way in which the tour was recorded using a digital audio recorder and camera. Children then chose from their own images to make individual or group maps of the school that were shared with other children and displayed for practitioners and parents to see.

Digital technology provided a means for children and adults to revisit their ideas about their current learning environment. After a child-led tour, for example, children gathered to review and discuss their images on a laptop computer (see Figure 12.1). This revisiting became an important methodological feature that had particular resonance in a longitudinal study with young children where the images became a way of re-engaging with research participants after pauses in the research process. The length of these pauses was directed by the speed of progress in the building progress.

There was also a future-orientated dimension to this study as the purpose was to engage young children in the process of designing the new environment. The intention here was not to turn young children into architects but to see if new designs could benefit from a deeper understanding of how young children experience and think about space. Methodologically this presented a number of challenges. What modes of communication could support young children to think about future spaces? This included introducing a short interview to ask the children about what their new nursery should be like, and demonstrated the importance of including both verbal as well as visual and kinesthetic modes of communication.

Making sense of the research material

There are challenges involved in working with a multi-method, poly-vocal and participatory approach. Firstly, in terms of multi-methods there was a need to

Figure 12.1 Children review their own photographs on a laptop computer, taken on a tour of the school (*Living Spaces* study, Clark 2010)

look closely for emerging themes from each of the research tools adopted, such as observation, child interviews and child-led tours as well as to the research outputs such as the group or individually-made maps. These different tools and outputs included a range of modes of expression with an emphasis on visual material (see Clark 2011).

Secondly, the *Living Spaces* study set out to engage the perspectives of a range of stakeholders who were in some way involved in or affected by the design and review of learning environments. Thus making sense of the research material included distinguishing between the perspectives expressed by young children, early childhood practitioners, parents and architects.

Thirdly, working within a participatory paradigm raised the important question of how and to what extent the research participants of different ages and professional backgrounds could be involved in the review of the research material. Here the longitudinal nature of the study added to the difficulties of keeping the group of young participants involved.

I found it helpful to think about making sense of the research material in terms of levels. Young children were involved in the initial analysis of the research material

Figure 12.2 Members of the school council discuss maps produced by the youngest children in the school (*Living Spaces* study, Clark 2010)

as they commented on their photographs and constructed their maps. This initial analysis at an individual and small-group level was then opened out to the whole class and whole-school level as their maps were displayed and discussed in class and in an exhibition held in the school hall attended by the architect. These maps made by the youngest children in the school were also reviewed by members of the school council (composed of two members from each class in the school) (see Figure 12.2). This provided an unusual opportunity for older children to take seriously the perspectives of younger members of the school community (Clark 2010: 182).

There were ethical considerations to take into account at the point at which research material was to be shared beyond the individual or group level. There were occasions when the views and experience shared were not appropriate to bring to a whole-school level, for example when children expressed negative opinions about another child.

The next level involved architects making sense of the research material. A workshop was organised in the architects' offices after the first phase of the fieldwork had been completed. Research material was drawn together to bring to this meeting, including children's maps and photographs from the child-led tours, individual photo books compiled by the children and extracts from interviews (see Clark 2010: 157–60). The purpose of this workshop was to explain the research process, to discuss emerging themes and to listen to the architects' reactions to the research material.

A further level of analysis took place with the advisory group. It was a requirement of the funding body, the Bernard van Leer Foundation, that research studies were supported by an advisory group. This interdisciplinary and cross-national group of academics and practitioners provided an important sounding board for exploring emerging themes. Advisory group members brought professional and disciplinary perspectives from education, childhood studies and architecture that raised new questions to think about in relation to the research material. My role as researcher involved engaging in these debates alongside reflecting on the literature and reviewing my fieldwork to develop the themes. My research journal became an important element in maintaining my 'voice' within this participatory research process (see Clark 2010: 189–92).

Writing up, dissemination and impact

One of the tasks of the writing-up process was how to bring together a complex range of materials, including visual and verbal elements. I saw my role as co-interpreter rather than sole interpreter. The Mosaic approach was designed to provide a framework for discussion and interpretation led by the children, in conjunction with myself as researcher and the adults who knew the children well. Creating the opportunities for the children to 'revisit' the research material they had produced during the course of the study was an important part of this process. This is in keeping with the use of documentation in the pre-schools of Reggio Emilia where the negotiation of meanings is a central part of the learning process (e.g. Project Zero/Reggio Children 2001; Rinaldi 2006). However, this was a research project and I had the responsibility to make judgements and to draw conclusions. The final writing-up involved a presentation of some of the key themes to the practitioners in the nursery, in order to share my interpretations and to hear their responses. This emphasises the iterative process that was involved throughout the research and has continued during subsequent presentations about the study.

The dissemination process was a challenge. This exploratory project did not lend itself to a condensed executive summary, particularly in view of the visual data. This raises a general point: what are the best ways of bringing the results of qualitative research to the attention of policymakers, in such a way that the richness of the original research is not lost? The development of visual, participatory methods also challenges expected modes of dissemination, as research, for example, using participatory video demonstrates (Lomax et al. 2011).

Reflections on ethics

Developing the Mosaic approach has been underpinned by ethical consider-ations that have featured throughout the research process. I draw attention here to three of the many issues that have featured in the development of this research: an ethics of engagement, of representation and of social inclusion.

Researching with young children has raised complex questions about consent, assent and dissent, which can be seen as an ethics of engagement. As the partici-pants were under 5 years old and therefore of minority status, informed consent was firstly gained from the children's parents or guardians, in keeping with ethi-cal research guidelines at the time (BERA 1992). However, in these participatory studies I was anxious to find ways of gaining informed and on-going assent from the children involved, at each stage of the research process (Harcourt and Conroy 2005; Kellett 2010). This included focusing on the language I used to explain the studies to the children and to remain alert to moments when my silence was required to enable children to communicate. I also needed to pay close attention to my own body language and posture, for example sitting on small chairs to be at eye-level with the children. I considered how I could show respect and exercise sensitivity to how the children might express their willingness to continue to take part or to exercise 'informed dissent':

> It is not only a question of seeing the world from children's perspectives but of acknowl-edging their rights to express their point of view or to remain silent. We are keen that a participatory approach to listening is respectful of children's views and also of their silences. (Clark and Moss 2011 [2001]: 9)

Some of the children involved in these studies were able to verbally articulate their wishes, for example John in the *Listening to Young Children* study who told me part way through an interview: 'I've done enough talking now' (Clark and Moss, 2011: 64) and subsequently left the interview. Other children signalled their wish to withdraw by non-verbal communication, for example displaying signs of boredom or greater interest in a class activity.

Giving status to young children's views and experiences has raised ethical questions about representation. One aspect of these considerations has focused on how to actively engage children in reviewing the research material gathered – to involve them in the act of re-presenting their own ideas and experiences. This has included making individual photo books with the chil-dren of their images and captions and making time to review these with indi-viduals and groups on subsequent visits to the settings. A second strategy has involved making a collective book of photographs and interview comments in the *Spaces to Play* study to review with children and adults (Clark and Moss 2005: 56–8).

As my research has developed I have become increasingly aware of new discourses of ethics in visual research (e.g. Lomax et al. 2011; Prosser et al. 2008). One dimension of these ethical considerations in participatory research focuses on the balance between a desire to protect participants' confidentiality and anonymity versus a desire to recognise their authorship and give status to their images. Sweetman has made the case for an ethics of recognition (2009), and this debate has resonance with my own research. I had to consider when recognition of individual children may be a more ethical response than anonymity. I chose to preserve the children's own names on data shared within the research setting but to use pseudonyms in wider publications and to explain to the children involved why this is thought necessary, sometimes to their incredulity.

The Mosaic approach is based on an inclusive view of the child. The ethical assumption is that all children regardless of race, ethnicity, gender, (dis)ability, or class are holders of unique perspectives about their own lives. This strength-based view of children is therefore not designed to be limited to only the most articulate, advantaged children, but to be extended to all children. The intention has been for this approach to be socially and culturally inclusive and to respect diversity of background, ability and experience. One example of my attempts to articulate this position arose with regard to refugee children involved in the *Listening to Children* study:

> This competent model of the child may have particular relevance where children are seen as being the victim of difficult circumstances. While not seeking to deny the trauma these children may have experienced, this approach starts from the position of recognising their skills in being themselves. (Clark and Moss 2011 [2001]: 53)

Part of my ethical considerations about social inclusion has focused on how to engage young children with a range of communication skills, including those, for example, on the autistic spectrum. This applied to one boy, Charlie, in the *Listening to Young Children* study (see discussion, Clark and Moss 2011 [2001]: 69). I developed a strategy whereby after Charlie had taken a photo of himself and returned the camera, his key worker took a series of photographs of Charlie engaged in his favourite activities so these images could be part of the discussion about children's experiences of being in the nursery. This is an illustration of how adaptation of a specific method may be necessary to play to the strengths of particular children. Such adaptation is based on the understanding that conceptually the Mosaic approach is inclusive. This does not mean that exactly the same communication tools will be used with every child but that the underlying assumption is that every child has views and experiences that are of value.

References

British Educational Research Association (BERA) (1992) *Ethical Guidelines for Educational Research*. London: BERA.

Chambers, E. (2003) 'Applied ethnography', in N. Denzin and Y. Lincoln (eds), *Collecting and Interpreting Qualitative Materials*, 2nd edition. London: Sage. pp. 389–418.

Christensen, P. and James, A. (2008) 'Childhood diversity and commonality: Some methodological insights', in P. Christensen and A. James (eds), *Research with Children: Perspectives and Practices*, 2nd edition. London: Routledge Falmer. pp. 156–72.

Clark, A. (2010) *Transforming Children's Spaces: Children's and Adults' Participation in Designing Learning Environment*. London: Routledge.

Clark, A. (2011) 'Multimodal map making with young children: Exploring ethnographic and participatory methods', *Qualitative Research*, 11(3): 311–30.

Clark, A. and Moss, P. (2005) *Spaces to Play: More Listening to Young Children Using the Mosaic Approach*. London: National Children's Bureau.

Clark, A. and Moss, P. (2011 [2001]) *Listening to Young Children: The Mosaic Approach*, 2nd edition. London: National Children's Bureau.

Fals-Borda, O. (2006) 'Participatory (action) research in social theory: Origins and challenges', in P. Reason and H. Bradbury (eds), *Handbook of Action Research: Concise Paperback Edition*. London: Sage. pp. 27–37.

Harcourt, D. and Conroy, H. (2005) 'Informed assent, ethics and processes when researching with young children', *Early Child Development and Care*, 175(6): 567–77.

Kellett, M. (2010) *Rethinking Children and Research: Attitudes in Contemporary Society*. London: Continuum.

Lomax H., Fink J., Singh N. and High, C. (2011) 'The politics of performance: Methodological challenges of researching children's experiences of childhood through the lens of participatory video', *International Journal of Social Research Methodology*, 14(3): 231–43.

Mayall, B. (2002) *Towards a Sociology for Childhood: Thinking from Children's Lives*. Maidenhead: Open University Press.

Project Zero/Reggio Children (2001) *Making Learning Visible: Children as Individual and Group Learners*. Reggio Emilia: Reggio Children.

Prosser, J., Clark, J. and Wiles, R. (2008) *Visual Research Ethics at the Crossroads*. NCRM Working Paper, Manchester, National Centre for Research Methods.

Rinaldi, C. (2006) *In Dialogue with Reggio Emilia*. London: Routledge.

Sweetman, P. (2009) 'Revealing habitus, illuminating practice: Bourdieu, photography and visual methods', *The Sociological Review*, 57(3): 491–511.

13 Inventing Adulthoods: A Qualitative Longitudinal Study of Growing Up

Sheila Henderson and Rachel Thomson

The study

Inventing Adulthoods is a large-scale qualitative longitudinal study which has involved a team of researchers working together since 1996. The research follows over 100 young people from five socially and economically contrasting areas of England and Northern Ireland as they move through their teens, twenties and early thirties at the turn of the twenty-first century. A bit like the popular TV documentary series *Seven Up!*,[1] the rich biographical material resulting from up to seven in-depth interviews with each person offers fascinating insights into how experiences of education, family, leisure, work and local community help to shape young lives. Unlike a majority of qualitative studies that provide just one retrospective snapshot of life pathways, *Inventing Adulthoods* provides a sense of 'growing' with young people in real time (between 1996 and 2006 in England and 1996 and 2010 in Northern Ireland). We follow each person as they reflect on life as it is 'now', how it was in the past and how they would like it to be in the future – at up to seven points in time. The resulting time-layered picture of the twists and turns in a life evolving is, therefore, more complex, rich and immediate than a 'one-off' account. Arguably,

---

[1]The *Seven Up!* World in Action documentary series first filmed in 1964 a group of 7 year olds from a diverse range of backgrounds in England and has made subsequent documentaries of the group at 7-year intervals.

this also more closely reflects life as it is lived and experienced, as each person's collection of life stories entails recurring themes and a return to the same significant events and experiences but viewed from new and contradictory perspectives.

This exploration of the evolution of young lives was conducted at a particular historical moment and provides an important historical archive[2] of what growing up was like for young people at the turn of the 21st century. The landscapes of everyday life and the big historical events and developments of the period all come alive in these unfolding biographies, among them: the Millennium, the digital revolution, the collapse of the youth job market, the evolution of a thriving night-time economy, the credit bubble boom before a world recession and the Northern Ireland Peace Process.

This is a generation facing a very different landscape from their parents and grandparents. Where in the past transitions were intensive – the majority of people left school, found work, left home and settled down with marriage and children in fast succession – this generation faces extended dependence on parents and life pathways with no clear sequence or inevitability (Jones 2009). So, although the study participants generally aspire to traditional transitions to adulthood (education to job-for-life to marriage to kids) when in their early teens, the adulthoods they are actually able to build vary enormously. Their stories richly illuminate how shaping one's life can vary according to differences in chance and opportunity, particularly as they relate to the places one grows up in.

Methodology

Like the young people's lives it follows, the *Inventing Adulthoods* study (www.restore.ac.uk/inventingadulthoods/) evolved over time with an unknown end point (see Table 13.1). It was not planned as a qualitative longitudinal study but adapted according to funding resources and the theoretical imperatives of the day. The first of the four studies that comprise *Inventing Adulthoods* was a mixed-method exploration of children's moral landscapes. Participants (aged 11–17 years) were recruited from nine secondary schools in five sites (an isolated rural area, an inner city area, a leafy suburb and a disadvantaged estate in England; and a city in Northern Ireland) and involved questionnaires (1,800), focus groups (62) and individual interviews (57). In the studies that followed, the individual interview became the primary method of a biographical approach but others included further focus groups and memory books (a flexible diary/scrapbook). The dataset now comprises over 500 individual interviews, 66 focus groups and 49 memory books, as well as other data.

---

[2]Some of which is available on application to Qualidata at the UK Data Archive.

Table 13.1 The composite studies known collectively as *Inventing Adulthoods*

Inventing Adulthoods	Age	Interview	Focus group	Lifeline	Memory book	Questionnaire	Research assignment
Youth Values 1996–1999	11–17	Int. 1 57	356 62 groups			1800	272
Inventing Adulthoods 1999–2001	14–23	Int. 2 121		104			
		Int. 3 98			49		
		Int. 4 83		Revisited at this round			
			4 groups				
Youth Transitions 2002–2006	17–28	Int. 5 70					
		Int. 6 64					
Growing Up in Northern Ireland		Int. 7 18					

A typical dataset for a single participant (e.g. Keith) might include:

- **Questionnaire:** collecting baseline data and view of a range of values issues and completed by the participant aged 13 years
- **Focus group data:** taped and transcribed focus group in which the young person participated aged 14 years
- **Interview 1:** exploring the evolution of moral identity aged 15 years
- **Interview 2:** exploring continuities and change since last interview and predicting their planned future through a lifeline aged 16 years
- **Interview 3:** exploring continuities and changes since last meeting through a discussion of a memory book created for the project aged 16 years
- **Interview 4:** exploring continuities and changes since last meeting and revisiting the lifelines conducted in Interview 2, aged 18 years
- **Interview 5:** exploring continuities and changes since last meeting aged 19 years
- **Interview 6:** exploring continuities and changes since last meeting aged 20 years.

Inventing Adulthoods actually began life in 1996 as 'Youth Values', a three-year study of young people's moral values funded by the Economic and Social

Research Council (ESRC). At a time when 'social exclusion' among young people was high on the public agenda, it explored how young people's identities and moral world views were formed and how these differed according to age, gender, ethnicity, faith, social class, family formation and location. What were the sources of moral authority for young people (aged 11–17 years) and had they changed? How did young people develop morally and what strategies did they employ to cope with moral dilemmas? The research team wanted to find out and make practical contributions to youth policy.

This work led on to another three-year study in 1999. Funded under the ESRC Youth Citizenship and Social Change programme, *Inventing Adulthoods* extended the focus by addressing the proposition that traditional transitions to adulthood had been eroded in a post-modern, globalised world. We wanted to document the process of becoming adult, adding qualitative 'flesh' to the 'bones' of large-scale quantitative studies of youth transitions. We also hoped to advance theory on the degree to and ways in which (young) people are able to act on their lives, the role of values in the construction of adult identity and the impact of globalisation on the individual (Beck 1992; Giddens 1991). As *Inventing Adulthoods* evolved and matured, we became convinced of the importance of capturing the processes through which people 'make' and 'remake' themselves over time – in theoretical terms, the 'habitus-in-process' (McLeod 2003) or 'continued becomings' (Stanley 2007).

By now we had come to know our participants well and were eager to continue 'walking alongside' them (Neale and Flowerdew, 2003). Funding for the next study – *Youth Transitions* – between summer 2002 and 2006 (part of the Families & Social Capital ESRC Research Group [www.lsbu.ac.uk/ahs/research/families. shtml]) allowed us to do this as well as to engage in debates about the role of social capital in mediating inequalities. A further two-year study – *Growing Up in Northern Ireland* –was funded by the Joseph Rowntree Foundation between 2008 and 2010 and allowed us to focus on our participants in Northern Ireland, exploring their biographical journeys against the backdrop of the political, economic and social policy landscape in Northern Ireland from 1996 to 2010.

Our methodological approach was incremental and participatory throughout, engaging young people at each stage, and feeding their input into the design of the next. We have managed to maintain a sample over time (with an attrition rate of 30 per cent over the length of the study). We ran competitions and sent birthday and Christmas cards as strategies for maintaining contact with participants. Continuity of the research relationship was established early on via a de-centralised team structure whereby three team members took responsibility for one or more research site, interviewing and maintaining contact in their site(s). Regular phone calls were later complemented by texts, emails and social media messaging. Data management and study administration were centralised, with quarterly team meetings providing an important physical structure for collective working.

Starting points

The five female researchers who came together and became the enduring core team[3] were from different disciplines: sociology, psychology, art history and cultural studies. We were born in different eras and had different personal and professional histories, yet we shared a vision of passionate social research. For us, the researcher was always in 'the mix' of the research encounter and of its interpretation, unavoidably bringing her/his own personal and professional concerns of the moment to a dynamic research relationship. Influenced by the feminism and cultural politics of the 1980s, we were committed to the project of 'giving voice' to those whose lives we researched and involving them as active participants in the research as far as possible (Holland et al. 2001). We also valued collective working and tried to challenge some of the established hierarchical nature of academic work, awarding recognition to all involved in the research process. A basis for this kind of team work had already been laid by some team members (Holland et al. 1998).

Our shared interest and experience in research with young people was also an important team 'glue'. Fresh from studies that responded to concerns about young people's sexuality in the light of HIV/AIDS and their illicit drug use, our collective starting point was to look beyond the picture of young people as social problems perennially painted in the media and public debate. What we wanted to explore were young people's actual experiences, views and opinions and to get them heard in the corridors of power.

A key theoretical starting point for the research was Anthony Giddens' idea of 'the reflexive project of self' (Giddens 1991) in which self-identity is seen to be formed through the processes of self narration and of (re-)ordering these stories of self. For Giddens, the 'self' is made up of stories about our past, which are re-evaluated at key turning points ('fateful moments') when we rework our accounts of the past in response to the demands of a changing present. In basing the research in five very different parts of the UK, we aimed not only to capture changing individual projects of self as they evolved over time but also the role of different contexts in shaping them. Our interest in exploring social change was, therefore, at both the micro-level of the individual forging the story of their life and the macro-level of the historical conditions shaping the emergence of a new generation.

---

[3]Sheila Henderson, Janet Holland, Sheena McGrellis, Sue Sharpe and Rachel Thomson, assisted by numerous others at various stages of the research.

Research questions

Although our overall concern with personal biography in social context remained central, the focus for investigation shifted across the four studies. This, to some degree, reflected changing funding opportunities. Questions from the first study included: 'What or who do young people recognise as sources of moral authority and what factors contribute to the legitimacy of moral authority?' and 'How do young people understand the processes of their own moral development and how does this contribute to adult identity?' The following studies addressed questions such as: 'What are the material, social and cultural resources available to young men and women growing up in different environments and how do they affect their life trajectories?', 'Can "critical moments" in the construction of adulthood be identified and if so what part do they play in processes of social inclusion and exclusion?', and 'What is the relationship between socially structured opportunities, the contingencies of individual biographies and broader social processes of individualisation and globalisation?'

Analysing, writing and representing young people's stories over time

In the first mixed-method study, we focused on the big picture of young people's values arising from the different data sources in much the same way as for any 'one-off' qualitative study. However, as the study progressed, we found our evolving biographical approach required a shift to storing and analysing the data by case. Up to this point, we had written accounts based on analysis across the dataset as a whole (cross-sectional or synchronic analysis), pulling out the big themes and illustrating these with brief case studies. Now we began to find that the volume and density of data held for an individual demanded a focus on the case history as our primary means of analysis, representation and meaning-making (longitudinal or diachronic analysis). Before the big historical picture was illustrated by small tastes of individual lives, now rich accounts of individual lives brought the big historical picture to life.

Our approach to case history writing began life as a form of intermediate analysis ('narrative analysis') completed by the interviewer soon after each interview in order to capture changes in individual narratives and researchers' reflections over time. Later, the narrative analyses for an individual were condensed into a 'case profile' that provided an 'at a glance' overview of their changing circumstances and life events, as well as preliminary analyses and interpretations. Later still, these case profiles formed a basis for developing case histories: a method for condensing and synthesising an individual's data, reflexive accounts of the research process and theory into an analytic narrative (Thomson 2007, 2009, 2010).

Essentially, the case histories we have written weave together all the material from a person's interviews to tell an abbreviated story of their lives, drawing out central themes – or biographical motifs – of the life as it unfolds over the years. Each interview is condensed and re-told in its present, maintaining the chronological order of the person's interviews and of their life, but the story is also told from different points in time and in a variety of voices (Henderson et al. 2012).

The full case histories are far too lengthy and compromise participants' confidentiality and privacy too much to be published as they stand. Long-term research relationships pose even more difficult challenges to honouring promises of confidentiality, privacy and anonymity in the representational process than usual – as the fine details of lives told over time become clearer markers and identifiers. In our case, place has been given a prominent role in understanding the shaping of young lives, and cumulative stories told within specific communities pose a particular threat – especially in the tight-knit communities of Northern Ireland. Nonetheless, in condensed and anonymised form, the case histories have brought numerous publications and presentations to life and proved powerful tools for firing the imaginations of policymakers in Northern Ireland and engaging them in developing policy based on holistic and dynamic accounts of unfolding young lives. Unedited, they remain as data for our own use in a wide range of writing and as yet unknown contexts.

How to write up and represent qualitative longitudinal research (QLR) is a question central to qualitative longitudinal methodology but one that is little debated. Gathering biographical data at intervals over time introduces considerable complexities:

- Its sheer volume and detail can be overwhelming (in our case, up to 840 hours of audio per participant);
- Its resistance to analytical closure can be confusing (we often gained new information on a participant whilst analysing and writing up their previous interviews);
- Its multiple time perspectives are hard to represent in words (as the present and future of one interview serially became the past for both researched and researcher).

The following extract from the field notes written by one researcher after her interviews with one young woman (Maisie) between 1999 and 2005, gives a taste of the analytic roller coaster that the research involved for both the researcher and the researched:

Interview 1: Felt that she genuinely wanted to do the things she talked about and that she had a great deal of determination – but that she also didn't have the resources to draw on. Also, with ill-health and teen pregnancy hanging around her in the ether, that it was going to take a lot to pursue her dreams. Hoping she would, fearing she would not be able to.

Interview 2:   Showing determination, hanging on in college and no signs of further pregnancies. The sense of agency that came across in the interview felt limited – by her poverty (underlies much of what she says and does, it feels), her health, her compliance with her boyfriend. I felt I was wrong and hoped so.

Interview 3:   I'm seriously in awe of this determined young woman who seems to achieve against all the odds. Although she is not finding university exactly easy. Holds down two jobs and funds and runs her family home and cares for her ailing mother and siblings. It all feels so shaky but she just seems quietly determined to make it happen. Definitely got it wrong on the agency front – this girl is made of steel!

Interview 4:   Interim contact had left me seriously concerned. Did not feel that there was sufficient support to see her through. However, she has, with the support of uni staff and her friends, turned things around, it seems, at the moment. She is more confident that she will complete this time around. I so hope she does and feel confident that if there is a way, she will – such is her fortitude. However, there are [some] many chaotic factors to consider and, although she is desperate to get away from the locality, she also clearly feels a strong sense of duty towards her family.

Over the course of our long study our perspectives on the biographical material and strategies for analysis and representation shifted in order to rise to the challenges they presented (Henderson et al. 2012). The mounting number of 'presents', 'pasts' and 'futures' written into each person's growing collection of interviews and into each analysis and representation begged the question of how to 'show' the volume, depth, detail, longevity and power of the data. This demands that we choose what is significant to tell and what to leave out of a person's life story told in up to seven instalments. We have to decide at what point in time to tell the story from, and whether to tell the story from the perspective of the participant, the interviewer or the analyst. Most importantly, we seek to find ways of meshing the 'big' social and historical 'picture' painted by our data as a whole with the fascinating detail of an individual life.

Dissemination and impact

The study has generated a wealth of publications and presentations for policy and academic audiences over the years and continues to do so. The nature and extent of their impact has been wide-ranging: from training materials for young people, created with and distributed by the National Children's Bureau, and policymakers' briefings on many aspects of young people's lives to scholarly contributions to social research methods and theory. The long-term reach of the study was secured via three key strategies: collaboration with The Open

University; funding to archive the dataset and by making a contribution to the development of qualitative longitudinal research in the UK. The DVD, 'Young Lives' based on the study and produced as part of The Open University course 'Youth: Perspectives and Practice'[4] has not only proved a popular learning tool in student feedback but is also now used more widely by the research team for purposes of bringing the study instantly alive to a range of audiences. ESRC funding between 2005 and 2011 to archive the study resulted in an important legacy: the anonymised digital interview transcripts for 50 participants are now available on application to Qualidata at the UK Data Archive or the Timescapes Repository at Leeds University, along with non-digital copies of questionnaires and other written assignments that formed part of the study. Unanonymised audio versions of the archived data will be released by Qualidata in 2058. An important part of our archiving process involved building a website that functions as the public face of the archive, documenting all aspects of the research (www.restore.ac.uk/ inventingadulthoods/). Meanwhile, our on-going contribution to the development of qualitative longitudinal methods in the UK has also moved beyond the *Inventing Adulthoods* study to wider collaborations including 'Timescapes',[5] the first qualitative longitudinal study to be funded as such in the UK. Long-term involvement in research has obviously had an impact on our participants – and we have documented their reflections on this at different stages of the research.

One of the young people whose in-depth case history formed part of *Unfolding Lives* (Thomson 2009) was offered and took up the opportunity to read it and feed back. This experience was somewhat overwhelming but she remained in the study – unlike another young woman who, upon identifying her story in *Inventing Adulthoods* (all study participants were given a copy of this book), dropped out. Most young people have spoken positively about being involved, conscious of the contribution they make and of having an opportunity to discuss aspects of life they are unable to talk about elsewhere.

Hindsight

It is instructive to reflect on some of the landmarks of the study from this point in time. One of them has to be the transformative experience of asking young people to consider *all* aspects of their lives at each interview. As part of our participatory approach, we asked the same questions of our (childhood or teen) selves prior to developing and conducting the interviews – a process of memory work (Thomson and Holland 2012). This was an enjoyable part of our work

---

[4]The book *Inventing Adulthoods* is also the set text and research team members contributed directly to the course.
[5]www.timescapes.leeds.ac.uk/

together and a great team builder, as well as sound preparation. However, it did little to alleviate the power and emotional difficulty we could experience in the context of the interview – and a sense of ethical responsibility only increased with the intimacy of long-term research relationships. This despite considerable previous experience in encouraging young people to share some of the most intimate details of their lives with us (e.g. sexuality, sexual identity and drug use).

Another noteworthy landmark came in the transformation of our approach to maintaining consent and confidentiality. Previously, consent was gained and negotiated verbally at each interview on the basis of confidentiality and anonymity. When it came to making a film based on the study for an Open University course on Youth and preparing some of the *Inventing Adulthoods* dataset for archiving, we came face to face with some very practical limits (Henderson et al. 2006). Firstly, participating in the film meant abandoning anonymity and giving away a lot of extra details on-screen for the young people involved. Consent had to be re-negotiated on this basis and in terms of the possibility that, although we did everything we could to guarantee continued confidentiality, an absolutely watertight guarantee was and is always unrealistic. Secondly, over the 10 years since it was first given verbally, written consent became essential for archiving purposes and, once given, could not be revoked. This, together with a commitment to involving the relevant young people in the anonymisation process, made for a lot of soul-searching as well as people-chasing.

Much has changed in the qualitative research landscape over the study period. Just as the technological revolution changed the young lives in the study, it has transformed research technologies and methods. So, for example, almost all interviews in the study were recorded on cassette tapes, making digitisation for preservation purposes essential, and contact with young people became more direct with the advent of the widespread use of, first, mobile phones and email and then social media. Similarly with the official ethical requirements of the researcher: today CRB checks and approval from ethics committees are the required norm. Similarly, consent from parents of under-age children – whilst applicable at the start of the study – could legitimately be gained indirectly by failure to object to a general notification, as in our case.

Like so much else in this study, hindsight was a perspective revisited over time – as this year's hindsight became last year's, transformed by new perspectives. We made a virtue of this, and prioritised recording these changing 'hindsights' as part of the research process. The lessons from reflecting back on the study sometimes seem limitless but, from the distance at the time of writing (November 2012), the commitment of the core research team to sustaining the research over a long time period (in the context of changing personal and professional life situations) is clearly crucial. We will never know if that long-term commitment could have been achieved had we known in 1996 how long we would all be involved, but the unplanned nature of the study has perhaps been instrumental in securing its longevity. Our career and life pathways have certainly been shaped by this undertaking and involvement has been a privilege: not only have we been allowed to 'walk alongside' so many young people as their lives unfolded, but we have also contributed to a unique body of knowledge – social, cultural, political, biographical and historical – spanning two decades. One that is archived and hopefully available for use for decades to come.

Bibliography

Beck, U. (1992) *Risk Society: Towards a New Modernity*. London: Sage.

Giddens, A. (1991) *Modernity and Self-Identity: Self and Society in the Late Modern Age*. Cambridge: Polity Press.

Henderson, S., Holland, J. and Thomson, R. (2006) 'Making the long view: Perspectives on context from a qualitative longitudinal (QL) study', *Methodological Innovations Online* [Special Issue: Defining Context for Qualitative Data], 1(2): 47–63. DOI: 10.4256/mio.2006.0011. Available at: www.esds.ac.uk/news/publications/MIOHenderson-pp47-63.pdf (accessed 31 July 2012)

Henderson, S., Holland, J., McGrellis, S., Sharpe, S. and Thomson, R. (2012) 'Storying qualitative longitudinal research: Sequence, voice and motif', *Qualitative Research*, 12(1): 6–34.

Holland. J., Caroline Ramazanoglu, C., Sue Sharpe, S. and Thomson, R. (1998) *The Male in the Head: Young People, Heterosexuality and Power*. London: Tufnell Press.

Holland, J., Bell, R., Henderson, S., McGrellis, S., Sharpe, S. and Thomson, R. (2001) 'Youth values and transitions: Young people's participation in the research process', in J. Clark, A. Dyson, N. Meagher, E. Robson and M. Wooten (eds), *Young People as Researchers: Possibilities, Problems and Politics*. Leicester: Youth Work Press.

Jones, G. (2009) *Youth*. Cambridge: Polity.

McLeod, J. (2003) 'Why we interview now – reflexivity and perspective in a longitudinal study', *International Journal of Social Research Methodology*, 6(3): 201–12.

Neale, B. and Flowerdew, J. (2003) 'Time, texture and childhood: The contours of longitudinal qualitative research', *International Journal of Social Research Methodology*, 6(3): 189–99.

Stanley, L. (2007) 'Epistolarity, seriality and the social: Letters – between "biography" and "history"', paper presented at Constructing Lives: Biographical

Methodologies in Social and Historical Research, 4 December, The Open University.

Thomson, R. (2007) 'The qualitative longitudinal case history: Practical, methodological and ethical reflections', *Social Policy and Society*, 6(4): 571–82.

Thomson, R. (2009) *Unfolding Lives: Youth, Gender, Change.* Bristol: Policy Press.

Thomson, R. (2010) 'Creating family case histories: Subjects, selves and family dynamics', in R. Thomson (ed.) *Intensity and Insight: Qualitative Longitudinal Research as a Route into the Psychosocial*, Timescapes Working Paper 3.

Thomson, R. and Holland, J. (2012) 'Memory books as a methodological resource in biographical research', in S. Delamont (ed.), *Handbook of Qualitative Research in Education.* London: Edward Elgar Publishing.

14 Young Lives: Reflections on Quantitative Research in Education within a Longitudinal International Study

Caine Rolleston

Summary of the study

Young Lives is an international study of childhood poverty in four countries – Peru, Vietnam, Ethiopia and India (Andhra Pradesh State). The project's focus is on understanding the causes and consequences of childhood poverty and on developing policy-relevant analysis for poverty mitigation. The study collects data through both large-scale surveys and in-depth interviews across a 'pro-poor'[1] sample of households in each country and employs both quantitative and qualitative method of analysis in an observational approach which does not involve intervention in the lives of the index children or their families. The survey sample comprises 3,000 'index' (or sample) children in two age cohorts in each country – born in 1995/6 and 2001/2 and aged around 18 and 12 in 2013. The duration of *Young Lives* covers the period set out for the achievement of the Millennium Development Goals (MDGs), that is 2000–2015; these goals include

---

[1]This term means that the sample is not nationally representative as it excludes the wealthiest portion of the population in order to focus on poorer groups.

Figure 14.1 Classroom scene at a school in Vietnam with children engaged in a paper-based task

the reduction of the number of people in absolute poverty by half and the universalisation of access to good quality primary education at the global level.

Following three rounds of household-level data collection – in 2002, 2006 and 2009, *Young Lives* extended its research remit to collect data at the index children's schools. It had become apparent from research carried out earlier in the study that schooling is not only an increasingly central feature of children's lives in all the study countries, but it is also an institution in which families invest considerable resources and upon which aspirations for the future substantially depend. At the same time, school quality is a major concern in the study countries among children and parents, as well as among policymakers and donors. All four countries have seen substantial economic growth since the Millennium, as well as large increases in primary school enrolment, and all but Ethiopia had graduated to middle-income status by 2011. While it remains one of the world's poorest countries, Ethiopia is, however, among the fastest growing economies in the world; and accordingly the four study countries represent a diverse and dynamic set of contexts ideally suited to the understanding of change in the lives and circumstances of young people in the global South.

The key analytic advantages of the *Young Lives* study design lie in: (i) measuring change over time, both within and across sites in the study countries; (ii) identifying the causes of change; (iii) providing 'thick description' and depth of explanation through the integration of qualitative and quantitative data (mixed methods), including data at the community-level; and (iv) providing data suited for international comparison. A particular advantage from the point of view of education research is that *Young Lives* is able to link data collected at schools to data from households; since while linkages between educational experience and poverty depend on child, household, school and community-level factors over time, these are only very rarely observed simultaneously in developing countries.

Starting points

Education is often the most significant route through which the state and its policies influence children's lives, especially in countries where public health provision and other social services remain relatively limited. It consumes up to 20 per cent of all government expenditure in developing countries and impacts directly upon the vast majority of families and communities, meaning that education policy formulation is of particular importance socially, economically and politically. School quality improvements therefore have potentially extensive benefits, while being in some senses relatively straightforward to implement by comparison with interventions at the household level.

Young Lives secured additional funding for school-based research from the Dutch Foreign Ministry in 2010 and after school studies had been conducted in Ethiopia and India, I was appointed as Education Research Officer with responsibility for school-based data collection and analysis in 2011. Previously I had been working at the Consortium for Research on Educational Access, Transitions and Equity (CREATE) (www.create-rpc.org/) while studying for a PhD focused on the relationships between education and its economic benefits in Ghana. My interest in education and development research stemmed originally from having worked as a teacher of philosophy and economics in the UK and of English in Romania, and was developed during a Masters degree at the Institute of Education, University of London which included research on Cambodia, Uganda and Ghana. Through CREATE and other projects I had also been involved in education research in East Africa, India and Sri Lanka. My PhD employed methods from economics and statistics in micro-level quantitative analysis using national datasets, while I was also able to undertake two small-scale qualitative studies to shed further light on the importance of culture and context in mediating the relationships between education and poverty. These focused on fostered children in Northern Ghana and migrant youth labourers (most often early school drop-outs and predominantly girls) in the Southern urban centres of the country who had migrated from disadvantaged districts in the north.

Since joining *Young Lives*, I have expanded the education-focused work to include school surveys in all countries, as well as qualitative sub-studies focused on selected key issues in educational development, including, for example, the expansion of private education in India. The major focus of my work has been on the design and development of two large-scale school surveys – firstly in Vietnam and secondly in Ethiopia. These surveys aim to gather data suited to policy-relevant analysis of the key determinants of educational achievement and progression, addressing school-quality issues both in terms of the impact on the individual child and in terms of the functioning of education systems. Previous surveys had focused on the educational experience of the *Young Lives* index children, in line with the research objectives of the household-based component of the study. Given the considerable and growing interest in the processes of schooling and its improvement, however, I felt it was also important to be able to comment more directly on education systems and their impacts, as had been a focus of CREATE, while also drawing on the unique longitudinal and comparative dimensions of *Young Lives*. The development of school-based work nonetheless presents complex challenges for research design and analysis, not least because the nature and purpose of education is rooted in history, culture and context so that 'ready-made solutions' to problems of educational quality may have different impacts and different degrees of relevance and applicability across diverse settings. Understanding context and institutional and policy environment is central to the approach to educational research I have adopted, and the strong empirical focus of *Young Lives* alongside the local networks within the study countries have been crucial to the contextualisation of research questions and methodological approaches.

Research questions

The core research questions that guide the education research at *Young Lives* may be divided into two types, longitudinal child-focused and education-system focused. The first type of question links closely to the wider aim of *Young Lives* as a whole – understanding childhood poverty. These questions emphasise the potential role played by education in reducing poverty and in breaking cycles of poverty. Analysis of these questions requires the linking of household and school data over time:

1   How do the relationships between poverty and child development manifest themselves in and impact upon children's educational experiences and outcomes?
2   To what extent does educational experience reinforce or compensate for disadvantage in terms of child development and multidimensional poverty?

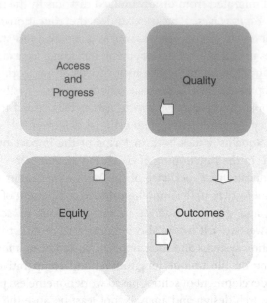

Figure 14.2 Key concepts for evaluating education–poverty relationships

These questions can be thought of as addressing four key dimensions of the relationship between education and poverty – access and progression, quality, outcomes and equity (see Figure 14.2). Because the focus of research in *Young Lives* tends naturally to change as the index children grow up, earlier research has more often focused on issues of access, and later work on outcomes; while issues of equity and quality tend to cut across questions of access and outcomes.

Illustrating the education–poverty relationship in sequence (see Figure 14.3), we see that quality lies at the centre of the system of factors which link children's 'life chances' at birth and their adult outcomes.

The second type of question focuses more directly on this key factor in the education-poverty relationship, expressed in general terms as:

1   What are the features of high-quality, efficient and effective education systems in *Young Lives* study countries and how do these features enable schools to 'add value' to children's educational outcomes and life chances?

Choice of methodology

In order to identify the factors and policies we might expect to be linked with school quality and effectiveness, we undertook a review of the literature on

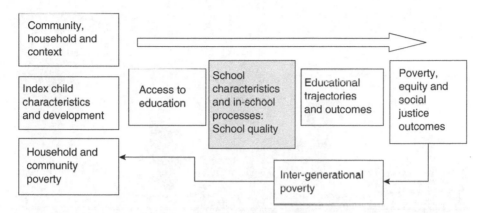

Figure 14.3 The role of school quality in the intergenerational transmission of poverty

education in Vietnam and Ethiopia and held consultations with experts in each country. In Vietnam, for example, we met with staff from the Ministry of Education and Training as well as with NGOs and international organisations, including the World Bank. Having identified a long list of potential influences on school quality, including, for example, the length of the school day and the uptake of 'extra classes' which vary widely between schools in Vietnam, we distilled these as far as possible into a series of 'indicators' which would then be 'operationalised' into research instruments, comprising tests, observation schedules and questionnaires.

In setting out to measure school quality, perhaps the most significant design development related to sampling. Examining school-, class- and teacher-level influences on achievement typically requires a fairly large sample of children, balanced at the class and school levels. To provide this, the school surveys in Peru, Vietnam and Ethiopia sampled the *Young Lives* children's class peers as well as the index child. A second requirement was having good measures of children's learning outcomes in key subject domains, plus measures of their 'softer skills', including their motivation and 'self-concept', which we might expect to impact upon their learning. However, children's home backgrounds, abilities, preferences and prior experience have an important impact on learning and, as a consequence, if efforts are not made to separate these influences from those of schooling then the effects of schooling may be misunderstood. To address this problem, we adopted a 'value-added' design whereby achievement data are collected both at the beginning and end of the school year. This was completed in Vietnam in June 2012 and comprised assessments in mathematics, Vietnamese and 'soft skills'. The two measures over time allow the researcher to identify the effects of schooling on educational progress, giving a more reliable estimate of

Figure 14.4   Three girls in school uniform carrying school books (Ethiopia)

the importance of schools and teachers, since for the period in question we know these factors to be largely fixed. Vietnamese teachers were also assessed in maths knowledge and pedagogy as well as in their 'soft skills' related to teaching, in order to extend our understanding of which teachers' characteristics are associated with better pupil progress. Pupils, teachers and principals were asked to complete background questionnaires, and both classroom and school facilities were observed in all of the school surveys, providing datasets with a hierarchical structure with a balanced sample of pupils nested within classes and schools suited to a variety of analytic methods used in economics and applied statistics.

The same basic design was also used in the Ethiopia school survey, but one important complicating factor was that in Ethiopia eight or more languages of instruction are used in the sample schools, following the mother-tongue education policies implemented by the federal states of the country in the early years of schooling. This presented a considerable challenge for measuring reading skills on a common scale. Further, a number of languages are primarily spoken languages so that few written materials are available. We engaged native speaker consultants in each language to develop comparable test items avoiding translation of items where possible because of differences in the contexts in which languages are spoken. We set out to equate difficulty levels on similar items across languages first through consultation and second by running a pilot exercise gathering data from a small sample of children in each language and applying psychometric techniques to analyse the responses and adjust the tests. In addition, we decided in Ethiopia to extend the school survey sample beyond the core *Young Lives* sites since these do not include the pastoralist regions of Somali and Afar, where education is least developed and where there is particular concern regarding educational access and quality from government, and also from Save the Children, *Young Lives*' policy and communications partner. Historically, few children in these regions attended formal schools (although some attended Koranic schools), but in recent years enrolments have grown notably as a result of government school-building programmes and improved communications and also shifting livelihood patterns which have led to growth of the 'settled' population. A third innovation in the Ethiopia survey was the inclusion of private schools, to allow comparisons of quality between state and private education providers, taking into account the somewhat different intakes of these two types of school.

Making sense of research material and writing-up

Data from the *Young Lives* surveys continue to be collected and processed, while we already have a large archive available to researchers. A part of the project's remit is explicitly to make data publicly available, which involves an intensive phase of data preparation and document writing in order to facilitate both our own internal analysis, and the use of data by external researchers whose questions vary widely, including many which were not anticipated at the design stage. Data entry and cleaning is undertaken by our country partners, after which we are able to link the data from previous rounds of data collection, enabling longitudinal analyses. Data entry consists of inputting written responses from individual paper questionnaires into a database, while 'cleaning' refers to the correction of errors of data entry and the re-coding of data to make it convenient for researchers to use in analysis. Such analysis relies upon the accurate identification of index children in each survey round at household and school, and on the linking of data through unique child identifiers (numeric codes). Once linked in this way the data form a 'panel' of observations on the index children which allow measurement and analysis of change over time and the factors associated with that change, including individual child factors such as gender and wider influences such as school quality. Data is transferred from the database software to standard statistical software packages which we use to produce both descriptive analyses of patterns and trends and inferential analyses of causal pathways and potential policy levers. For example, current work includes: (i) examination of the 'learning premium' in private schools in India which estimates the difference in progress made by pupils in these schools after controlling for their backgrounds and their selection into such schools; (ii) the gaps between high and low 'value-added' in Vietnamese primary schooling; (iii) the benefits of full-day schooling in Vietnam; and (iv) the effects of class and peer groupings on learning and 'soft-skills' in Vietnam. This work relies on collaboration between those involved in the design of the surveys and analysts experienced in particular quantitative techniques in economics and statistics. Challenges in this work often centre on the separation of correlations and causal effects as well as on how to present what can be complex findings to a variety of audiences, including to policymakers in each country. *Young Lives* is a multi-disciplinary project so that my work involves collaborating with demographers, statisticians, economists, psychologists and anthropologists, each of whom brings a somewhat different analytical lens to issues in education. This cross-fertilisation enables a holistic perspective on the issues we address and encourages self-reflection and the challenging of disciplinary boundaries.

Dissemination and impact

Our approach to engaging stakeholders and the policy community in *Young Lives*' education research has been to avoid separation between the processes of research and the 'uptake' of research by integrating the networks ultimately used for dissemination into the design process as far as possible. The strategy centres on the idea that engagement from beginning to end in the research process and investment in the development of the survey by stakeholders will provide for better understanding of both data and research outputs, plus increased benefits from collaboration in analysis and in communication of the findings in the forums where the impact is likely to be greatest. The mechanisms which link research and practice differ somewhat between contexts, depending especially on political and administrative organisation and culture, so our strategies were developed to reflect the situation in each of the study countries. In Vietnam, for example, education planning is relatively centralised and school quality improvement is organised through a number of large-scale government programmes which are led by technical experts from the national ministry with limited support from donors, international consultants and NGOs. In order to reflect this structure in our dissemination strategy, we engaged consultants from the National Institute for Educational Sciences (VNIES) in the development of curriculum-based achievement tests and in the analysis of pilot data, as well as working with a key academic educationalist on questionnaire design and with the Belgian Development Agency, DFID and the World Bank, some of the largest donors to education in Vietnam. Drawing upon their expertise and reflecting their interests in educational development allowed us to form a network of influential parties with a stake in the survey from the outset. We conducted consultation meetings and technical seminars as part of the instrument development phase of the survey and are now planning to feed back early results through these networks. In addition to in-country dissemination and impact, we focus on disseminating at international forums, both academic and policy-oriented, including presenting at key conferences such as the UK Forum for International Education and Training (UKFIET) and the Comparative and International Education Society (CIES).

Hindsight reflections

Young Lives is a long-running research programme with considerably more potential for institutional and individual researcher learning than shorter-term projects, but this naturally comes with its own challenges. Longitudinal data analysis relies upon developing ways of measuring change, but in education the issue is complicated by the shifting goals of the education system as children develop. For example, an achievement test administered at age 8 is no longer appropriate at age 15, so that understanding 'development' requires more than the simple measurement of change and is a constantly 'moving target'. The interdisciplinary nature of education as a field of application in social research offers a wide range of analytic techniques. Through the development of the education research programme at *Young Lives*, I have had to select methodological tools from psychometrics, economics and statistics to address emerging research questions in diverse contexts, emphasising to me the dynamic nature of the research process in a field such as education in developing countries. Moreover, analytic models and 'cutting-edge' developments in the social sciences emanating from Western contexts are not always illuminating elsewhere, so that the need to adapt and select methods appropriate to the research question and context may be considered even more pressing in the *Young Lives* study countries. Many examples of such learning come to mind. For example, the school survey in Vietnam included a number of questions to children on attitudes to schooling and friendship relations with peers. Adapting these items to context required careful attention to 'positive response bias' in that children in Vietnam are typically not disposed to say they 'don't like school' or are 'not friends' with others in the class, in a way that would not necessarily be the case in the UK, or, as we discovered, was also not the case in our sample in Ethiopia. While the value of keeping an open mind is clearly important for the researcher, my experience of education research has certainly reiterated this – the perceptions of policymakers and experts in the national capital were frequently different from our own and different again from what we found in the field. For example, while we anticipated considerable sensitivity around testing teachers, in practice teachers were most often supportive of our study and were typically keen to participate.

Bibliography

Boyden, J. and Dercon, S. (2012) *Child Development and Economic Development: Lessons and Future Challenges*. Oxford: Young Lives. www.younglives.org.uk/files/working-papers/boyden-and-dercon-child-development-and-economic-development

Young Lives (2012) *Changing Lives in a Changing World: Young Lives Children Growing Up*. Oxford: Young Lives. www.younglives.org.uk/files/books-and-book-chapterse/changing-lives-in-a-changing-world

Woodhead, M., Frost, M. and James, J. (2013) 'Does growth in private schooling contribute to education for all? Evidence from a longitudinal two-cohort study in Andhra Pradesh, India', *International Journal of Educational Development*, 33(1): 65–73. www.younglives.org.uk/files/journal-articles/woodhead-et-al_ijed-article_pre-publication_feb2012

SECTION 4
ENGAGING AUDIENCES AND DISSEMINATING FINDINGS: THE IMPACT OF RESEARCH

Introduction

It is easy to assume that dissemination is something researchers do once their study is finished, a coda to the 'real' work of research. The fieldwork is over, the data have been analysed, and now it's time to summarise your findings and communicate them to the wider world. In their different ways, the four chapters in this final section of the book challenge that simplistic characterisation. The authors explore the relationship between engagement, dissemination and impact and in so doing demonstrate the diverse ways in which research with children and young people can make a difference to policy, practice and to young people's lives.

In recent years social researchers of all kinds have found themselves under increasing pressure to demonstrate the impact of their research on the wider social and economic world beyond the research community. This shift in emphasis has not been universally welcomed; however, one positive result has been the opportunity to re-examine the relationship between research and audience. It has encouraged researchers to engage their audiences not only in dissemination, but also in the production of new knowledge, as has been discussed by several authors in the preceding sections of this book. The chapters in this final section offer more detailed examples of best practice in including research participants, and other key stakeholders, in the whole research process, with a particular focus on dissemination

In organising this section of the book, we have made a division based on some of the main *audiences* with whom researchers need to engage: the research community, policymakers, practitioners, and children and young people themselves. All empirical research seeks to influence academic debate and to contribute to the 'expert' discourse of the research community. However, perhaps most research about the experience of children and young people will also seek to have an impact, if only indirectly and to differing degrees, on public policy, and may seek to bring about some kind of change in professional practice, as well as improving the lives of young people themselves. Whilst thinking about the key audiences of research has been our starting point, there are obvious continuities and overlaps between these different constituencies. Moreover, common themes emerge in these four chapters which are perhaps more important than the specific focus of each individual chapter.

A major common theme is the importance of actively engaging audiences and stakeholders from an early stage and throughout the research process. Running alongside this is a shared sense that this engagement needs to be active and participatory, rather than passive or simply act as a receptacle for 'findings'. The four chapters between them examine research at both a national and international level, and cover the age range from early childhood to youth. Each chapter takes a specific research study, or series of linked studies, and weaves its discussion of dissemination, engagement and impact through a rich first-hand account of research practice.

The first chapter in the section, by Martin Robb, has as its primary focus academic dissemination – the sharing of findings with the research community. Here research is seen as contributing to, and seeking actively to shape, a continuing conversation about the issues with which it is concerned. The chapter takes as a case study a research project on the role of gender in work with boys, and provides examples of interrelated and overlapping conversations around achieving academic impact, influencing practitioners and engaging the young people who are the subject of the research. The chapter assesses the effectiveness and value of different ways of communicating research, from more traditional methods using the spoken and written word, through to newer approaches making use of mass media and the internet.

Chapter 16 by Sandy Ruxton explores some of the ways in which research with children and young people can have an impact on public policy. The author uses as an example his own work at European Union level, on research projects which he argues had a major impact on the direction of EU policy, ensuring that children and young people's interests and perspectives are taken into account in future policy development. However, Ruxton also points out some of the challenges for researchers hoping to influence public policy. Exploring the history of thinking about the relationship between research and policy, he concludes that the process is far from straightforward and is inevitably complex and 'messy'. Ruxton ends by offering suggestions for other researchers wanting to ensure that their work has an influence on policy processes and outcomes.

The next chapter, by Chris Pascal and Tony Bertram, explores the impact of research on practice, drawing on the authors' own substantial experience of participatory, practice-led research on early childhood. The authors conducted a professional development programme working with the research findings from *Children Crossing Borders*, a five-country study that examined the practices, values and expectations of pre-school practitioners, and the views and experiences of parents and children from 'immigrant' communities. Pascal and Bertram explore how research can lead to new ways of thinking about and relating to children, which in turn may lead to new pedagogies. They make the case for ensuring that research involving children's perspectives has an impact on children's worlds. This aim, the authors argue, calls for a paradigm shift in the values, actions and thinking of both researchers and practitioners.

This final section of the book ends, appropriately, with the voices of children and young people. Chapter 18, co-written by academic researcher Mary Kellett with Alex Mann and Joseph Liley, two 11-year-old researchers, explores the impact on children themselves of being involved in undertaking and then disseminating research. The inclusion of the boys' own report on their study means that children's voices are represented in a very direct way in this concluding chapter. The chapter discusses the outcomes of the process for the child researchers, both in terms of their developing ethical understanding and also the development of skills that are transferable to other areas of their lives. Drawing on this and other examples of child-led research, Kellett explores the potential but also the challenge of redefining whose knowledge counts in the research process.

Together, these four chapters demonstrate that disseminating the findings from research, in a way that will have an impact on the wider world, is a complex and many-layered process. Although it is important to pay attention to the methods of dissemination, this final section of the book underlines the paramount significance of engagement, providing concrete examples of what that might mean. The accounts of actual research discussed in these chapters provide clear illustrations of how research can contribute to changes in our understanding of children's and young people's experience, and can make a real difference, often in surprising and unexpected ways, to policy and practice, and to the lives of children and young people.

15 Disseminating Research: Shaping the Conversation

Martin Robb

Introduction: Dissemination as an ongoing process

Anyone undertaking research with children and young people will be keen to ensure that their findings are disseminated to as wide an audience as possible. But what do we mean by 'dissemination': what do you disseminate, how, and to whom? This chapter began life as an exploration of 'academic' dissemination – the process of communicating research findings to the wider research community. However, in writing the chapter it has been difficult to separate this kind of dissemination from the process of communicating with other audiences, such as practitioners and the young people who are the subject of research. The chapter is based around a case study in which I describe the dissemination strategies of a research project, exploring the role of gender in work with boys, in which I was engaged. Using this study as an example has reinforced the interconnections between academic, policy and practice dissemination, at the same time as emphasising the importance of viewing dissemination as an ongoing process.

There has been increasing emphasis from funding bodies on demonstrating research impact. Despite some concerns about the constraints this may place on social research (Fernández-Armesto 2009; Shepherd 2009), it can be argued that foregrounding impact encourages researchers to move away from seeing dissemination as an 'add-on' at the end of a study, or as a one-way process in which research findings are simply put 'out there' in the hope that they will have some kind of influence on policy, practice or wider public understanding. A focus on the impact of research at least encourages researchers to engage actively with the audiences they hope to influence, rather than viewing them as passive recipients of knowledge. Arguably, it also forces researchers to begin this process of engagement at an early stage, and to integrate communication with key stakeholders into the research process from the beginning, rather than bolting it on artificially at the end of a study.

This chapter will consider what it means to engage stakeholders in the process of dissemination, and how in doing so research with children and young people can maximise its potential impact, primarily on the academic conversation, but also on policy, practice and the children and young people who are the subjects of research. The image of dissemination as a conversation is a useful one, and it can be helpful to think of it as a process of contributing to a continuing discussion about the issues that are the focus of the research. More accurately, we might want to talk about a series of overlapping conversations, each with its own rules and conventions. Using more formal academic language, we could describe these conversations as *discourses*, associated with particular discourse communities and observing particular discursive rules (Potter and Wetherell 1987).

Discourses do not exist in completely separate boxes, sealed off from one another. It is tempting to see academic discourse (the ongoing conversation of researchers and educators) as a rarefied discussion played out in seminar rooms or in the pages of small-circulation journals, with no connection to wider public discussion. However, there are many channels through which expert discourse influences other kinds of discourse, including policy discourse and wider public debate. Admittedly this process can be slow, intermittent and fraught with potential for misunderstandings, but there is evidence that it does happen. One example is the impact of research on disability. A couple of decades ago, a small group of radical disability researchers, including colleagues at The Open University, used research findings to challenge the dominant medical model of physical and mental disability, which viewed disabled people in mostly negative terms, and pioneered new understandings of disability that emphasised agency and autonomy (see e.g. Swain et al. 2010). Over time, this new approach has found its way into policy and professional practice, and more recently into popular discourse, so that by the time of the 2012 Paralympic Games the perception of disabled people as active, autonomous and capable seemed to have become a new 'common sense', replacing those former pathologised ways of thinking.

How can researchers set about influencing both the expert discourse of academic research, and the policy, professional and public discourses with which it interacts? As already noted, specific discourses have their own conventions governing the ways in which valid contributions can be made to the ongoing conversation. There is also a range of ways in which those contributions can be made, with varying effectiveness. The remainder of this chapter will explore some of those dissemination methods, taking my current research project as an example. The next section introduces that study, before moving on to explore how the research team plans to disseminate its findings and engage key stake-holders in the process.

Researching gender and work with boys

New social research, including research with children and young people, does not take place in a vacuum or appear from nowhere. If researchers want their work to have validity and to be taken seriously by the community of researchers, they need to take account of the pre-existing conversation or discourse in their chosen field. New knowledge always builds on existing knowledge. That is why, when developing a research proposal or seeking funding, researchers need to demonstrate an awareness of previous work in the field and the ways in which the planned study builds on and extends what has already been written.

I am currently involved in a two-year research project, funded by the Economic and Social Research Council, on gender identities and practices in work with boys. Based in the Faculty of Health and Social Care at The Open University, the study is being undertaken in partnership with Action for Children, a national voluntary organisation. In order to understand the thinking behind the study, it will be necessary to tell something of the story of how the project came about. I hope this will also provide an illustration of the ways in which new research builds on previous research, and thus an example (in retro-spect) of how research contributes to a continuing conversation, prompting and facilitating further research and the production of new knowledge.

In the late 1990s I carried out a small-scale interview study with men working in day care centres for young children (Robb 2001). In the course of their inter-views, a number of the (mostly young) men described having had a particularly close relationship with their mothers, and they also talked about the importance in their lives of other female figures, such as grandmothers and aunts. It also emerged that a number of these male workers had been brought up by lone mothers. Given the way in which mothers', and particularly lone mothers' influ-ence on their sons has often been pathologised, this seemed to represent a new and refreshing insight. Could it be that the decision to work in a traditionally feminine occupation, and to espouse a more 'caring' masculinity, might be related to a strong maternal, or at least female, influence in a boy's upbringing?

From this project I moved on to a study of fatherhood and masculine identity (Robb 2004a, 2004b), interviewing men who identified themselves as 'involved' fathers of young children. Very few of these men regarded their fathers as a major influence on their own parenting and a number cited their *mothers* as having had the greater impact on the way they brought up their own children. Not long after this, I supervised a postgraduate research study on young fathers who were in contact with social services (Reeves 2008). It was striking that many of the young men interviewed described close relationships with their mothers or grandmothers, and there seemed to be a correlation with their determination to stay with their partners and work at being a 'good' father.

I decided to pursue this issue further, initially by looking more closely at boys' relationships with their mothers, a topic on which there seemed to be a distinct lack of research. I was able to undertake a small-scale study, carrying out secondary analysis of interviews with young men who had participated in the longitudinal *Inventing Adulthoods* study (see Chapter 13 by Henderson and Thomson in this volume). My analysis confirmed that mothers could be a key influence on boys' developing gender identities, and particularly on their attitudes to parenthood.

These findings appeared to contrast with an increasingly dominant public discourse focusing on boys' need for positive male role models. It is a truism that young men have become a key focus of public and political anxiety, and of policy and practice interventions, over the past decade. Concerns have encompassed boys' apparent educational under-achievement relative to that of girls; suicide and mental health problems; and concern about offending and anti-social behaviour (Featherstone et al. 2007; Robb 2007; Ruxton 2004). Boys have increasingly been defined in media debate and public policy as 'at risk' and as a 'risk' to others. A range of commentators has argued that the absence of fathers and the lack of male role models in the lives of many boys are key factors in their involvement in crime and in educational under-achievement (Dennis and Erdos 1992; Lammy 2011). Concern about a lack of male role models has also encompassed public services, and in particular primary education, where there appears to have been a real decline in the proportion of male teachers (Harnett and Lee 2003; Martino 2008). Recent years have also witnessed successive campaigns to increase men's representation in services where they have always been a minority, such as early years childcare (Cameron et al. 1999; Brannen et al. 2007).

It became apparent that a discourse focused on the importance of male role models had become the common currency of popular and policy discussion, consisting of a set of assumptions and rhetorical strategies that were accepted as 'common sense'. This discourse has been used to justify a range of interventions, including efforts to strengthen fathers' involvement with their children and to increase the engagement of adult male mentors with young men through a variety of programmes. This emphasis intensified during the outbreak of public anxiety that followed the disturbances in some English cities in August 2011. Although both young men and young women were involved in the riots, much of the political and media reaction focused on the anti-social behaviour of boys. Responses by both government and opposition politicians to the riots frequently diagnosed an apparent lack of male role models for young men as a key factor behind the disturbances (Mahadevan 2011; Lammy 2011).

Many of the assumptions about the need for strong male role models in boys' lives seemed to rest on very little research evidence (Hicks 2008). Thus this issue actually offered a striking example of the failure of social research to have an impact on policy, practice or public understanding. It also pointed to a lack of research that might either support or challenge the commonsense assumptions that dominated popular thinking. Although there had been some research on the effect of men's absence from primary school teaching, there seemed to have been little investigation of the issue in relation to other services used by boys and young men, such as youth work, youth justice or social care. With two colleagues, I identified a need for new research that would explore the extent to which the gender of the professional worker made a difference to the effectiveness of work with vulnerable boys in contact with welfare services. Taking this a step further, we were interested in exploring exactly how gender 'works' in relationships between boys and those caring for their welfare. Having established a partnership with Action for Children and obtained research funding, we planned to conduct interviews and focus group discussions with both young male service users and with adults who worked with them, in order to explore these issues.

This brief overview has shown how the current study developed as a result of reflection on earlier research, both my own and other people's, and thus repre sents an illustration of how previous research can influence new research. However, as well as building on the existing conversation about gender and work with boys, we also hope to shape that conversation ourselves. In the remainder of the chapter, I will explore our strategies for ensuring that the study achieves maximum impact.

Academic impact: Influencing the expert conversation

One of our key aims as a research team is to produce new knowledge about the part played by gender identities in work with boys. We want our research to have academic impact and to influence the thinking of other researchers working in similar fields. However, as noted earlier, it is difficult to separate academic dissemination from other kinds of impact. Thus, even the more academic methods of dissemination that we plan for this study will inevitably also involve policymakers and opinion formers, as well as the organisers and providers of services for young people.

For example, like many large research projects, we intend that our first and most high-profile dissemination activity will be a national conference. Conferences and seminars are often the first step in communicating new research, offering an early opportunity for researchers to present their findings and to receive feedback on their ideas. For those involved in large-scale or collaborative research, this may mean organising an event specifically to publicise that study, while for those undertaking individual or small-scale research, it is more likely to involve giving presentations at conferences organised by others. Some conferences are aimed mainly at practitioners, such as teachers or social workers, while others are primarily designed for academic researchers to share their work with each other. However, in practice the distinction between academic and professional conferences can become blurred, particularly in relation to research concerning children and young people. For example, for some years The Open University collaborated with a consortium of family and parenting organisations to organise the 'Family Futures' conference which attracted a wide-ranging audience, ranging from academics and politicians to parents and practitioners. As well as providing a first opportunity for researchers to share their work and to receive feedback on it, conferences also enable researchers to make connections with others doing similar work and thus to place their research in the context of the wider conversation around their field of interest.

Conferences and seminars inevitably reach a relatively small audience, so in order to influence wider debate there is a need to communicate research findings in written form. Like other research studies, our current project plans to produce a final report which can be launched at the conference and distributed to interested parties. However, the principal means for influencing debate amongst researchers remains the academic journal article. The peer-reviewed article is still the most highly valued form of publication for academic research, and this is the forum where researchers who want to influence the expert conversation on their topic will seek to publish. Of course, if research is aimed primarily at practitioners, then a professional or policy journal might be more appropriate. However, academic journals tend to have a higher status, if only because of the process through which all published articles must pass. Peer review means that a journal will only publish articles that have been critically reviewed by independent experts. Work that has been published in a peer-reviewed journal will have passed a 'quality' threshold and will therefore be taken more seriously by others working in the field. Publishing in a journal means that an article is likely to be cited in other articles and books, and thus become a known text in the field, with the capacity to influence debate. My own experience of communicating my research findings in journal articles has been that it provides a location for my work which is accessible to other researchers and to which I can direct people interested in the topic (Robb 2004a). It has also generated communication with other researchers working in the same fields, and has led indirectly to new research and opportunities for collaboration.

The mass media: Joining the popular conversation

So far, we have considered fairly traditional means of disseminating research, using the spoken or written word. However recent years have seen increasing opportunities, and increasing pressures, for researchers to reach a wider audience for their work via the mass media. Newspapers and magazines have always sought out expert views on issues of current concern, and this is now increasingly true of television and radio. Researchers might find themselves called on to speak about their findings in a news interview or phone-in programme on their local radio station, or to make a more substantial contribution to a radio or television programme related to their field of interest. Many academic institutions and professional organisations now offer media training for their staff, recognising that broadcasting presents an opportunity to reach a general audience beyond the academic and professional worlds, and potentially to influence a wider public conversation.

Media exposure can create the chance to shape popular thinking, particularly if the topic is newsworthy. However, engaging with the mass media also presents challenges and pitfalls. Researchers can find that they need to simplify their message in the interests of brevity or to appeal to a non-specialist audience. While broadcasters might have a genuine interest in a particular topic, they also have an interest in producing lively programmes, which tends to mean messages that can be summarised in a pithy headline. Many researchers will have had the experience of being asked to contribute to a programme, only to discover that their views were not straightforward or controversial enough to be of use. For example, I was approached about taking part in a radio discussion on fatherhood, though it soon became clear that the producer wanted to stage a debate between two polarised opinions, and my more tentative and cautious conclusions were not, in the end, what was wanted. On another occasion, however, I contributed to a local radio station programme on boys' relationships with their mothers, in which I was able to use my research findings to challenge some stereotypical assumptions.

To increase the chances of gaining media exposure, it is important to ensure that information about new research findings can be found online, together with contact details. Having a good web presence is invaluable in facilitating dissemination via the media, and the internet can itself provide new opportunities for creative and interactive research dissemination.

New media: A new kind of conversation?

If the mass media provide opportunities for researchers to communicate with a wide audience via broadcasting, then the phenomenal growth of the internet and social media in the last few years has enabled many researchers to become broad-casters themselves, without the need for the mediation of an established media outlet. The advent of the worldwide web makes it possible for a researcher to communicate directly with any individual on the planet with access to a com-puter and a telephone line. Although academic researchers have hardly been in the vanguard when it comes to exploiting this technology, the last decade has seen a slow growth in the numbers taking advantage of new media to share their ideas and to interact with others in their field.

The involvement of academic researchers in online communication has passed through a number of chronological stages. In the early days, the con-cern was mainly to establish a web presence, perhaps a page on the website of a university or research organisation, listing research interests and publica-tions. At this stage, the involvement of researchers in the internet was focused on making existing content available online, offering a new means of accessing what was already there. The next stage involved researchers starting to create new content specifically for the internet. The advent of blogging – writing regular 'weblogs' or online diaries – was a major part of this. An online tool that began as a forum for sharing personal experiences or expressing strident political opinions began to be used by academics and researchers, whether individually in groups, posting short pieces about their work, or reports on events such as conferences.

One of the difficulties with blogging is creating an audience for your postings. How, amidst the clamour of tens of thousands of voices online, do you get your-self noticed and direct 'traffic' to your site? As with more traditional media, it is important to make sure that what is written is clear, accessible and touches on topics of current interest, perhaps linking to something currently in the news. However, growing an online audience has been made easier by the advent of social media, such as Twitter and Facebook. Although researchers working on children's issues have been relatively slow to make use of these media, this is beginning to change and will surely continue to do so.

As with the mass media, the benefits of sharing research online are obvious. Researchers are able to reach a diverse, global audience in a direct and immediate way. That audience will inevitably be diverse: it might include key researchers and influential policymakers, as well as campaigners and practitioners, and members of the public with a general interest in the subject. There is also the opportunity for a degree of interactivity which is rare in traditional forms of research dissemination. Of course, the lack of a filter points to one of the key dangers of online dissemination. Since anyone can comment on a blog or follow you on Twitter, there is the potential for the views expressed to be extreme or even abusive, particularly if the area of research is sensitive or controversial. As with the mass media, but to an even greater degree, there are also the pitfalls of brevity and compression. Is it really possible to have a serious discussion about research findings in tweets of 140 characters?

The open and democratic nature of online discussion is also both a huge advantage and a potential drawback. Since there is no peer review process for blog posts, it means that online postings, however well-written, will never have the status of a journal article which has survived an arduous critical process. In the brave new world of online communication, there are no quality assurance processes, and one opinion is as valid as another. This can certainly make for a livelier and more immediately 'impactful' conversation, but it can also result in a bewildering cacophony of voices. At the same time, it is clear that the internet will continue to grow in importance as a medium for disseminating social research, and there is a danger that ignoring it will mean that the conversation becomes dominated by more strident and less critically informed voices.

My own experience of using the internet to share my research has reflected these benefits and challenges. Initially, I created a blog as a site where I could post updates on my work and link to articles, reports and news items. For example, I posted a report on the seminar on young masculinities which prompted the current study of gender and work with boys. I have also commented on media stories that are of relevance to my research interests and occasionally used the blog as a forum for some tentative early analysis of research data. Having a blog has given my research a 'home', a place where I can gather together my work and direct those who might be interested in it. Generating interest in the blog has been made much easier since joining Twitter, which has made it possible for me to 'follow', and be followed by, hundreds of people – researchers, practitioners and members of the public – with similar interests. Through Twitter, and as a result of my blog, I have made contact with other researchers whose work I was unaware of, as well as making my own research more widely known, in ways that would hardly have been possible relying on more traditional means of communication.

For the current research project on gender and work with boys, a website will be created which will act as a contact point and a repository for information about the study. We also plan to include a regular blog, and a linked Twitter feed, which will make it possible both to provide regular updates on the progress of the study, and to engage interested parties in a continuing conversation about its focus. Not only are the internet and social media immediate and accessible, they are also inclusive and participatory, helping to transform both the creation and the exchange of new knowledge. New media create the potential for a new kind of relationship between a research study and its public, and for a broader definition of the research community, as they dissolve some of the boundaries between researchers and their audiences.

Engaging young people in dissemination

Online communication also has the potential for developing a new kind of relationship between researchers and the participants in research, especially where the latter are children and young people, who tend to have a greater confidence and facility with new technology. As a research team, we are keen to ensure that our study has an impact on the young people who are its subjects. As with all practice-based research, we anticipate that the impact on young people will mostly be indirect, through the influence we hope to exert on public policy and on professional practice. However, we would also like to have a more direct impact on the boys who participate in our study and through them on other young men in contact with welfare services.

We plan to involve our research participants in dissemination in a number of ways. At the most basic level, we intend to produce a version of our final report that is tailored to young people, using language and examples that they will find relevant and accessible. In addition, we are planning a variety of more imaginative ways of reaching out to young people. These include working with young people involved in Action for Children projects to produce a short video film which will present the story of the research study in an engaging way. Having produced the video, we intend to make it available via websites such as Action for Children's own site for service users and The Open University website. We hope this will encourage other young people, particularly those in the groups we are studying, to engage with the film and to comment on it. To facilitate this kind of feedback, we plan to set up an online discussion forum which will enable young people to take part in an ongoing conversation about the topics covered in the research.

There is always the danger that this kind of participation will be tokenistic and superficial, but it also opens up the possibility of new kinds of knowledge creation and exchange. Young research participants cease to be merely the recipients of new knowledge about themselves, and to some extent become part of the research team, helping to define that knowledge and how it is communicated to a wider audience. They are drawn into the conversation and become active contributors to it.

Engaging with practitioners

As a research team, we hope that our research will have a direct impact on the professionals and volunteers who provide services to vulnerable young men. At the same time, some of those frontline workers are themselves participants in our study; just like the young service users, and in a similar fashion we are seeking to engage those workers in the process of disseminating our findings.

There are a number of ways in which researchers can increase the likelihood of their work having an impact on professional practice. Indirectly, there may be a kind of 'trickle-down' effect, whereby new theoretical understandings become part of the common sense of policy and practice and, over time, influence new initiatives and bring about improvements to services. More directly, researchers can ensure that practitioners are included in invitations to conferences and seminars, and that the study's findings are presented at events which attract a professional audience. Events of this kind can offer something of a challenge to researchers, inviting them to think creatively about ways of making their research both interesting and useful to busy frontline workers.

When it comes to written publication, researchers need to ensure that reports are written in ways that appeal to practitioners, and that the study's findings are published in places where practitioners will read them. For example, as well as writing academic articles and chapters about my research on men and childcare, I have also published articles in professional journals aimed at (for example) nurses and health visitors. This requires a very different approach from writing for an academic audience: these magazines are usually looking for short, appealing features, free of academic jargon and with direct relevance to everyday practice issues. Some studies also have the development of practice guidelines as one of the intended outcomes of their research. Indeed, many practice-based studies, especially when funded by government bodies, stipulate this form of impact activity, often in preference to more academic outputs.

As far as our current project is concerned, we are planning a number of ways of engaging directly with practitioners. Here again, our partnership with a national voluntary organisation, employing hundreds of professionals as well as recruiting many more voluntary workers, should help to facilitate a collaborative approach. As well as engaging key personnel from Action or Children in the whole range of our dissemination activities, from organising the national conference to writing the final report, we are also planning a number of activities targeted directly at workers. For example, we plan to set up another online forum, this time using the agency's existing staff network, both to communicate our findings and to invite discussion of their implications for practice. We are also committed to presenting our findings at the regular staff development events that the organisation holds at locations throughout the United Kingdom. This means that both the workers who have participated in the study, and others who might find the research relevant to their work, will have an opportunity to hear about it and take part in continuing discussions about its findings. Finally, we plan to involve Action for Children staff in developing some practical guidelines for workers arising out of the study's findings.

Engaging with practitioners in the dissemination of research is both a challenging and a creative process. There is an inevitable tension between academic discourse and the more practically-focused conversation of those dealing directly with the needs of vulnerable children and young people. Researchers can find it difficult to translate their more theoretical findings into everyday language and to identify the practical utility of academic insights. There is an understandable fear among researchers of diluting or misrepresenting the often complex and nuanced understanding arising from research, while practitioners often have a wariness of knowledge that does not arise directly from hands-on experience. However, bringing these two discourses into conversation with each other can be a productive process, from which both sides can benefit, and new kinds of knowledge emerge.

Conclusion

In this chapter we have discussed ways of ensuring that the dissemination of research findings is not simply an afterthought at the end of a project but an integral part of the research process from the outset. The chapter has also considered how a new emphasis on demonstrating the impact of research can prompt researchers to engage from an early stage with key stakeholders, such as professionals and the young people who are the focus of the research. We have seen how dissemination and engagement can be seen as contributing to a range of continuing conversations, and how these different discourses overlap and interact with each other. Finally, our discussion has demonstrated the part that can be played by contemporary methods, such as the internet and social media, in reaching different audiences and in engaging research participants in both the generation and the communication of new knowledge.

References

Brannen, J., Statham, J., Mooney, A. and Brockmann, M. (2007) *Coming to Care: The Work and Family Lives of Workers Caring for Vulnerable Children*. Bristol: The Policy Press.

Cameron, C., Moss, P. and Owen, C (1999) *Men in the Nursery*. London: Chapman.

Dennis, N. and Erdos, G. (1992) *Families without Fatherhood*. London: IEA Health and Welfare Unit.

Featherstone, B., Rivett, M. and Scourfield, J. (2007) *Working with Men in Health and Social Care*. London: Sage.

Fernández-Armesto, F. (2009) 'Poisonous impact', *Times Higher Education*, 3 November. www.timeshighereducation.co.uk/409403.article (accessed 14 October 2013).

Harnett, P. and Lee, J. (2003) 'Where have all the men gone? Have primary schools really been feminised?', *Journal of Educational Administration and History*, 35(2): 77–86.

Hicks, S. (2008) 'Gender role models ... who needs 'em'? *Qualitative Social Work*, 7(1): 43–59.

Lammy, D. (2011) *Out of the Ashes: Britain after the Riots*. London: Guardian Books.

Mahadevan, J. (2011) 'Riots blamed on absent fathers and poor school discipline', *Children & Young People Now*, 15 August. www.cypnow.co.uk/cyp/news/1049472/riots-blamed-absent-fathers-poor-school-discipline (accessed 14 October 2013).

Martino, W.J. (2008) 'Male teachers as role models: Addressing issues of masculinity, pedagogy and the re-masculinization of schooling', *Curriculum Inquiry*, 38(2): 189–223.

Potter, J. and Wetherell, M. (1987) *Discourse and Social Psychology: Beyond Attitudes and Behaviour*. London: Sage.

Reeves, J. (2008) *Inter-Professional Approaches to Young Fathers*. Keswick, UK: M&K Ltd.

Robb, M. (2001) 'Men working in childcare', in P. Foley, J. Roche and S. Tucker (eds), *Children in Society: Contemporary Theory, Policy and Practice*. Basingstoke: Palgrave/The Open University.

Robb, M. (2004a) 'Exploring fatherhood: Masculinity and intersubjectivity in the research process', *Journal of Social Work Practice*, 18(3): 395–406.

Robb, M. (2004b) 'Men talking about fatherhood: Discourse and identities', in M. Robb, S. Barrett, C. Komaromy and A. Rogers, *Communication, Relationships and Care: A Reader*. London: Routledge/The Open University.

Robb, M. (2007) 'Gender', in M.J. Kehily (ed.), *Youth: Perspectives, Identities and Practices*. London: Sage.

Ruxton, S. (ed.) (2004) *Gender Equality and Men: Learning from Practice*. Oxford: Oxfam GB.

Shepherd, J. (2009) 'Humanities research threatened by demands for "economic impact"', *The Guardian*, 13 October. www.guardian.co.uk/education/2009/oct/13/research-funding-economic-impact-humanities (accessed 14 October 2013).

Swain, J., French, S., Barnes, C. and Thomas, C. (2010) *Disabling Barriers – Enabling Environments*. London: Sage.

16 Achieving Policy Impact: Researching Children's Issues at EU Level

Sandy Ruxton

Introduction

This chapter examines the ways in which research on issues affecting children and young people can influence the processes and outcomes of policymaking. It uses specific examples from the author's experience to make points which are of wider interest and value for those exploring ways of using research in their own practice, or thinking about embarking on research with the aim of changing policy and practice in their field. The chapter draws upon examples of effective work to raise the profile of child policy at European Union level, from the mid-1990s – when 'children' were not mentioned in the EU Treaties – to the inclusion of explicit references in the Lisbon Treaty in 2007 and the development of EU action across a range of policy areas (including child poverty and well-being, child participation, and asylum and immigration).

A key factor in fostering the emergence of a child rights perspective at this level was the impact of two research reports commissioned from the author by Euronet (the European Children's Network),[1] which provided the basis for

---

[1]The European Children's Network was a coalition of networks and organisations campaigning at European level for the interests and rights of children between 1995 and 2009. Its activities included policy development, research and projects involving children and young people directly. The Network led successful campaigns for the inclusion of references to children's rights in the Charter of Fundamental Rights and the EU Constitutional Treaty; published influential reports on child poverty and social exclusion, and on discrimination against children; organised a participation project for children on the *Future of Europe*; contributed to relevant EU fora; and worked with successive EU Presidencies to promote children's rights.

sustained advocacy. The first, *A Children's Policy for 21st Century Europe*, was published in 1999 and set out for the first time a vision for the future of children's policy in the EU. The second was a revised and updated version which responded to the changing policy context, published in 2005 with the title *What About Us? Children's Rights in the European Union*.

This chapter begins by exploring how understanding of the relationship between research and policy has evolved. Having set out the European policy context for the reports, it describes how each was developed and used by campaigners to advocate for children's rights, and traces the progress of European policymaking over a decade. It concludes with an analysis of the creation, mediation and application of research knowledge in this case study, and highlights key issues in achieving impact with research.

Understanding the relationship between research and policy

In the early years of the social sciences, it was often assumed that the knowledge created through research would inevitably influence the development of policy. Policymakers would, it was argued, obviously take notice of research findings and make decisions about the direction of policy based on this transfer of knowledge. But over time it has become clear that this one-way 'linear' approach, whereby research is effectively packaged, disseminated to others and then straightforwardly used in various settings, is insufficient to describe how research affects the policy process and policy outcomes in practice. Moreover, the assumption that there is a clear divide between research and policymaking (and researchers and policymakers) is increasingly questioned.

Empirical investigations from the 1970s onwards of the extent to which policymakers were 'using' the findings of research highlighted a number of shortcomings to this linear model. One set of difficulties surrounds the concept of 'using' research, and what precisely might be meant by this. Another is that research is only one influence – and in many cases by no means the dominant one – alongside other factors that may have a bearing on policy development. Policymakers also draw upon personal experience and connections, and have to take into account pressures from a variety of sources, including the law, the media, constituents, campaign groups, donors, iconic cases, and so on. They have to deal too with the constraints of developing policy within increasingly complex organisations and departments, each with their own set of traditions, political interests, budgetary limitations and staff capacities – and often far from united in their overall purposes. In short, policymaking is often a messy and unpredictable process.

Having said this, studies that began to analyse the relationship between research and policy also suggested that research *was* having some impact on policy, although not necessarily an immediate and direct impact on decisions. Research findings were, however, valued by policymakers who were interested in what good quality research had to say. Research was also seen to provide new ideas and concepts, to offer new perspectives on policy dilemmas, and to provide an opportunity for policymakers to rethink their approaches (Weiss 2009).

From around the 1990s, various models have been hypothesised to explain *how* research has an effect on policy-making. These have tended to focus increasingly on the relationships developed between research producers and users, and the extent to which knowledge is embedded within organisations and systems. The framework used by the European Commission (Commission of the European Communities 2007) to study 'knowledge-based' policy and practice in education and training (adapted from Levin's approach, 2004) is helpful. This 'knowledge continuum' highlights three interdependent dimensions of knowledge-based policymaking: *knowledge creation* (the production of research-based knowledge); *knowledge mediation* (the brokerage of such knowledge in terms of making it accessible and facilitating its spread); and *knowledge application* (the utilisation of research and evidence by decision-makers).

Background and European Union context

To understand the motivation behind, and the impact of, my two research reports for Euronet,[2] it is important first to highlight the context within which they appeared (Ruxton 2001; Stalford 2012). At EU level the focus on children within policymaking had been non-existent since the establishment of the European Economic Community by the Treaty of Rome in 1957. This position remained the same up to the 1990s. There was a lack of legal 'competence' to address children's issues at that time,[3] and very few initiatives in relation to policy affecting children. Respect for the principle of subsidiarity meant that child welfare policy remained primarily the responsibility of individual Member States, even though it was becoming increasingly clear that aspects of Community policy (e.g. child safety issues in consumer policy) were having direct and indirect effects on children.

---

[2]These reports built upon my 1996 book *Children in Europe*, which had also helped to raise the profile of children's issues at EU level, and created momentum and support for the European Commission to propose that a larger project on the child dimension of EU policy should be undertaken.

[3]The only basis for addressing children's issues was set out in section 3.1 of the 1989 Communication from the Commission on family policies, which stated that there should be regular consultation at Community level on four principal themes, the first of which was 'the impact of Community policies on the family, *notably child protection*' (italics added).

Nevertheless, the political environment for the EU to take some (limited) action in relation to children became more favourable by the mid-1990s.[4] In 1995, Austria, Finland and Sweden joined the European Union – countries with a strong tradition of support for children and children's rights.

In 1996, public revulsion at a particularly horrendous child abuse case (the 'Dutroux' case) in Belgium, together with scepticism that the Belgian state could respond effectively, led to calls for the European institutions to take action. Pressure from European Parliament resolutions led to the inclusion of a reference to 'offences against children' in the EU's 1997 Amsterdam Treaty (European Communities 1997) and the setting up of two European Commission programmes to tackle violence against women and children, particularly in relation to issues with a transnational dimension.[5]

Using research to influence children's policy at EU level: *A Children's Policy for 21st Century Europe*

Reflecting these shifts in the political climate, in 1998 the European Commission proposed to fund a significant project on the child dimension of EU policy. This contract was won by Euronet, who then engaged me to carry out a study to define Euronet's vision for the future of children's policy in the EU.

In order to define this vision more clearly and identify practical steps to implement it, the report had four stated objectives: to audit EU legislation and policy and its impact on children within the EU; to set out the arguments for the development of a distinctive EU 'children's policy'; to identify a framework for, and the key components of, a comprehensive EU 'children's policy'; and to make recommendations for the development of EU legislation, policy and structures. The project was guided by an Experts Group, including prominent academics and policymakers from across the EU and the management committee of Euronet.

To launch this project and feed into the report a major conference was held in Belfast in May 1998, within the framework of the UK Presidency of the EU. It was attended by over 150 children, young people and adults from 11 EU Member States, and their recommendations for a 'Children's Agenda for Europe' were discussed and refined. To stimulate further debate, a series of three seminars was

---

[4]In 1991 the European Parliament published the 'Groner' report on the problems of children in the European Community, which was the first to call for the creation of a legal basis to enable a Community policy on children to be formulated. In 1992 a Community 'Recommendation on Childcare' was adopted to help parents reconcile their work and caring responsibilities, building on research by the European Commission's Network on Childcare and other Family Responsibilities.

[5]The most well known of these was the Daphne Programme which still exists today.

held in Madrid, Paris and Vienna during 1998, each bringing together non-governmental organisations (NGOs) and experts from 'clusters' of EU Member States to address key themes (e.g. children as consumers, children as citizens, child participation, child protection, and children and the European social model).

The report was largely based on a review of existing publicly available documents, particularly those produced by European institutions. Interviews were also conducted by myself, Euronet staff and national NGO members with key decision-makers within the EU, the primary objective being to explore the opportunities for, and obstacles to, the development of an EU child policy. A secondary purpose was to raise awareness about Euronet's project and issues in relation to children's rights more generally. Whilst most of the interviews ran fairly smoothly, it was evident that existing activity within the EU institutions was largely dependent on the commitment of isolated individuals, with no evidence of coherent attempts to 'join up' policy initiatives.

The report identified a range of interlinked weaknesses in EU policymaking at that time, which resulted in children's rights being ignored, overridden, or addressed incoherently at European level.[6] It argued that the development of a coherent EU children's policy was needed if children's rights and interests were to be taken into account fully. It therefore recommended practical next steps to develop existing programmes and initiatives, and measures to strengthen EU structures affecting children (including the setting up of a Children's Unit within the European Commission) and improve liaison between children's NGOs and the EU institutions. It concluded with a headline call for the insertion of a clear legal base in the EU Treaties so that the Community could contribute to the promotion and protection of children's rights, whilst respecting the principle of subsidiarity.[7]

The 80-page A5 report was initially available in English and French, together with a summary leaflet in all the (then) 11 Community languages. Subsequently the report was also translated into German and Spanish. This was obviously important in terms of reaching the largest audience possible and informing interested groups and organisations, especially at Member State level, about the report and its findings. A regular newsletter was also published and circulated to

---

[6]For example, children's interests were found to be a low political priority, even though increased attention was being accorded at national and local level to policymaking for children. There was a lack of overall policy direction and co-ordination between and within EU institutions. And although the EU had taken some action to benefit children (e.g. in relation to violence against children, consumer policy, education and youth employment), this was limited in scale and scope.

[7]That is, the principle that a policy issue ought to be addressed at the lowest possible tier of government, and EU intervention should only take place if local or national authorities cannot do so.

interested parties to keep them informed of the development of the project, to pass on up-to-date information about EU activities, and to begin the process of building more solid networks and partnerships for future action.

The final report was launched in January 1999 in the European Parliament at a seminar attended by MEPs, Commission officials and a wide range of civil society organisations, with a keynote presentation by the author. A further meeting and reception was held in the Parliament in November the same year in order to maintain momentum and build stronger links with parliamentarians, some of whom had by then formed a cross-party Children's Alliance. Throughout the year, Euronet and Save the Children staff also sought to promote the findings of the report in as many relevant fora as possible, including in meetings with MEPs and senior officials in the European Commission. As a result of this pressure, the European Commission initially committed to developing a Communication (i.e. a statement of policy) on children; however this was unfortunately dropped the next year.[8]

Instead, campaigners turned their attention during 2000 to negotiations over the content of the proposed 'Charter of Fundamental Rights' of the European Union, which introduces certain political, social and economic rights for EU citizens into EU law (European Union 2000). Drawing on the report, Euronet made a submission to the body elaborating the Charter, and published a special edition of its newsletter setting out the arguments for including children's rights in the text. Euronet received several positive replies from Convention members, and national member organisations supported the submission through letters and meetings with their country representatives on the Convention. These activities led to the inclusion of a specific children's rights article – Article 24 – in the Charter. Although the Article was a welcome step forward, the Charter did not at that stage have binding force.[9]

Work to promote the findings of Euronet's research then fed into debates around the Convention on the Future of Europe, intended to pave the way for reform of the EU. The Convention started at the beginning of 2002 and finished its work in

---

[8]In response to an oral question in the Parliament, Social Affairs Commissioner Vitorino announced on 15 November 1999 that the Commission would publish a Communication on children to mark the 10th anniversary of the UNCRC. However, progress unfortunately stalled. By July 2000 the President of the European Commission, Romano Prodi, had reneged on this commitment, stating in a letter to MEPs that 'competence for action concerning children remains with the Member States, given the lack of a clear legal basis in the Treaty for the Community to safeguard children's rights in terms that go beyond the existing framework'. It was several years before the debate about a possible Communication re-emerged on the political agenda.

[9]The wording of Article 24 was also weaker than that of the UNCRC, stating for example that children 'may' express their views freely in matters concerning them, rather than enshrining this as a right (as in the UNCRC, Article 12).

2003 with proposals for a constitutional treaty to the European Council.[10] As the Convention developed, Euronet was very active in pushing the key messages from the research. One-to-one meetings were held with various members of the Convention, including the Vice-President. Euronet worked closely with one of the Convention working groups (on Social Europe), and its cause was championed by Helle Thorning-Schmidt (then a Social Democrat MEP and now Danish Prime Minister) who inserted several references to children's rights into the group's final report. Within the framework of a pan-European campaign ('Children are European Citizens Too') funded by the European Commission,[11] Euronet also ran a series of national consultations (including one in Brussels where children were able to meet with individual Convention members) to promote the participation of young people in the discussions on the future of Europe.

Following these activities, in 2003 children's rights were, for the first time ever, recognised in the 'draft Treaty establishing a Constitution for Europe' arising from the Convention's work (European Convention 2003). The text of the Constitution included the protection of children's rights as part of the internal and external objectives of the European Union, meaning that children's rights would be mainstreamed into the EU's legislation and the policies and programmes for which the EU has competence.

This was not, however, the end of the story, as this campaigning success was almost derailed by larger political forces. EU Treaties can only be modified with the consent of all of the Member States within an Intergovernmental Conference (IGC). Following protracted negotiations the 'Treaty establishing a Constitution for Europe' was signed in October 2004. It then had to be ratified by all Member States, but was heavily rejected by the public in referenda in France and the Netherlands in May 2005. For a second time, child rights campaigners feared all their hard work would be undermined by this debacle, and that the newly-inserted references to children's rights in the draft Constitution would simply be lost.

What About Us? Children's Rights in the European Union

This was a frustrating period for Euronet, as clearly children's rights issues were a minor part of the 'big-picture' political negotiations between Member States

---

[10]Valéry Giscard d'Estaing was appointed as Chairman of the Convention. The Convention was composed of 105 members representing the governments and national parliaments of the Member States and candidate countries, the European Parliament and the European Commission. Observers representing the European Economic and Social Committee, the Committee of the Regions, the social partners and the European Ombudsman were also involved.
[11]Part of the 'Prince Programme' organised by the European Commission's Secretariat General, Public Debate on the Future of Europe Unit, Task Force on the Future of the Union.

about the EU's future shape. How then to ensure that the gains that had been made in relation to children's rights during the process of the debates around the draft Constitution could be protected?

One aspect of the strategy was to make sure that the arguments that had been effective so far were still heard – and by new audiences. This was made more important by the fact that European Parliament elections had taken place in June 2004, with a large number of members being elected for the first time (including from the 10 Central and Eastern European countries that had acceded to the Union the same year). A new team of Commissioners also took up office in November 2004. Building the understanding of, and relationships with, these new arrivals was a vital task.

It was also important to demonstrate that addressing children's rights was becoming an everyday aspect of activity at European level. Indeed, in recent years, alongside the pressure that Euronet and others had mounted for a legal base for children, there were signs of EU action in relation to (among other issues) child protection, child poverty and social exclusion, asylum and migration, and discrimination against children. An Intergovernmental Group ('L'Europe de l'Enfance'), attended by Ministers with responsibility for children's policy and high-level officials, had been meeting twice yearly since 2000 to exchange best practices. The Charter of Fundamental Rights was also increasingly regarded within the EU institutions as endorsing action in relation to children's rights, even if it did not amount to the comprehensive legal base sought by Euronet. Building on the political momentum provided by the above initiatives, the European Commission began work in 2005 on a 'Communication on Children', intended to provide a comprehensive policy statement on the protection of children.

In order to both reflect and influence these important developments, in 2006 an expanded report was published by Euronet (Ruxton 2005), building on the earlier report. Whilst some of the basic analysis of the 1999 report remained in the later edition, the changing context set out above necessitated a comprehensive rewrite. Whereas the earlier report had elaborated at some length the arguments for a specific 'children's policy', the new report mentioned the importance of this but did not dwell upon it. Instead it sought to show in more detail what was happening across a range of EU issues that affected children, either directly or indirectly, and to make policy recommendations in each of these areas. New sections were added on asylum and migration, residential care and adoption, and family separation. 'Core' recommendations (e.g. in relation to inserting a legal base in the Treaties, developing an EU children's rights policy, and providing leadership on children's rights) were also revised to make them realistic and appropriate for the current EU context. Overall, although large gaps remained in the information base, there was far more data publicly available on children in the EU and a far greater number of references were included as a result. The presentation was more professional too, with a colour cover and black and white photographs inside.

The later report, at least double the size of the earlier one, drew upon material from a range of sources. These included: the outcomes from three regional seminars in Poland, the Czech Republic and Slovenia in 2005 with children's NGOs from Central and Eastern Europe (organised by Euronet and funded by the European Commission); results from previous Euronet consultations with children on social exclusion and discrimination, and conferences organised with children; specific input from NGOs at Member State level, and European NGOs; and a literature search of reports and papers published by Euronet, other NGOs, international organisations, and EU institutions.

Based on the methodology that had been effective in the earlier report, interviews were undertaken with key officials within the European Commission and European Parliament to explore particular policy areas. Given that Euronet's name and campaigns for children's rights were by this stage much better known within the EU institutions, this time it proved possible to engage, via well-connected intermediaries, high-level policymakers within the European Commission.

A meeting was also held in Brussels in June 2005 to discuss the interim findings with other key stakeholders. A consultation process was undertaken with Euronet members during July–August, and comments obtained from academic and policy experts both on specific sections and on the report as a whole. The final report was launched in London in November 2005 to coincide with a 'L'Europe de l'Enfance' meeting of government representatives during the UK Presidency of the EU.

The report was a key influence on the development of the Commission's Communication (Commission for the European Communities 2006), which was eventually published in July 2006 – indeed it was almost too successful in influencing the content of the Communication. When Euronet sent the draft text of the report to the Commission official responsible for leading on the development of the Communication, as he had requested, he simply reproduced large sections of it word-for-word in the draft Communication! Flattering though this was, it gave the impression that the Commission had been wholly 'captured' by NGOs; fortunately it was soon recognised that this would make it problematic for Member States to support the Communication and the text of the draft Communication was significantly amended. Nevertheless the traces of Euronet's work were still very visible in the final document, which provided an important statement of the Commission's commitment to addressing children's rights – a strong justification for the added value of EU action.

After the reports: Children's rights inserted into the EU treaties

Discussion had also been continuing during 2005–6 on the draft Constitution, which still contained the references to children's rights that would provide an effective legal base for action in this field. Following the defeat of the Constitution in the referenda and a 'period of reflection', Member States agreed in 2007 to abandon the Constitution and to amend the existing treaties, which would remain in force. They also agreed a detailed mandate for a new intergovernmental conference to negotiate a new treaty. These negotiations eventually became the Lisbon Treaty, which was adopted in 2007 and eventually ratified by all Member States in 2009,[12] after clearing various hurdles at national level.

Fortunately for child rights campaigners, the insertion of children's rights in the new Treaty was far from being the most contentious element, and the text of the earlier rejected Constitution remained largely intact. Promoting children's rights was therefore included among the Union's objectives for the first time (Article 3), providing a sound basis for the EU to implement concrete measures to ensure that the 'best interests of the child' are considered in all relevant policy areas. This Article does not create new powers for the EU, however it enables actions to be taken which specifically target children as a group, and allows for the commitment of budgetary funds for this purpose.[13]

The inclusion of child rights references in the Treaty represented a huge milestone in Euronet's campaign, even if it occurred many years later than campaigners had hoped. The evidence is very strong that the arguments set out in both Euronet reports, together with the sustained relationship building and advocacy that took place at national and European levels by children's NGOs, were critical factors in this success.[14]

---

[12] As part of the negotiations, the Czech Republic, Poland and the UK were granted an opt-out from the EU's Charter of Fundamental Rights, which became binding on Member States in relation to EU legislation as a result of the Lisbon Treaty.

[13] Among other changes relevant to children's rights introduced by the Lisbon Treaty, the EU will accede to the European Convention on Human Rights and is able to accede to international Treaties and Conventions, including the UNCRC and its Optional Protocols.

[14] The Treaty's references to children's rights were significant, however further lobbying has been undertaken by children's NGOs since to ensure that the references are used as a basis for practical action. In 2011 the European Commission published an 'EU Agenda for the Rights of the Child', building on the 2006 Communication. Whilst the Agenda set out some important steps, campaigners have argued that it fails to provide a vision for how the UNCRC can be effectively implemented across EU policies in a consistent way. Nevertheless the Agenda has been accompanied by more specific legislation and initiatives to address issues such as child poverty and well-being, child care, asylum and migration, and children in the courts. Whilst this approach is often seen as piecemeal and lacking in coherence across directorates, there is little doubt that the EU institutions are more active in relation to children's rights than they have ever been.

Achieving impact with research

This section uses the framework of knowledge creation, mediation and application outlined earlier to explore a range of recurring themes and issues in conducting research, to look at how these played out in the Euronet research reports, and to assess the implications for those seeking to use research to influence policy.

Knowledge creation

Understanding the context within which research is produced is essential. The research undertaken for Euronet paid considerable attention to the legal, political and social background. For instance, the almost universal ratification of the United Nations Convention on the Rights of the Child worldwide (including by all EU Member States) provided a clear framework of legal standards and a strong political impetus for action at EU level. EU enlargement focused attention on child poverty and social exclusion as well as the treatment of children in institutions in the accession countries. Demographic change, and in particular the ageing population, changes in family structure and falling birth rates, prompted debate about implications for children and children's services. We made sure to address these (and other) 'big-picture' issues in the reports produced.

If research is to influence policy, then the task is considerably easier if the chosen issue is a strong one which can be easily understood and communicated. The Euronet reports described in this chapter were able to demonstrate how children's interests were often ignored, and their voices unheard in policymaking at EU level.[15] The fact that the EU was having a direct and indirect impact on children's lives (as the report showed in detail in subsequent sections), while children and children's organisations had little or no influence over this process, drew attention to an important weakness of the existing legislative and policy machinery. The Euronet reports set out clearly the arguments showing that the status quo was insufficient and what needed to be done to remedy this.

The justification for Euronet's research was therefore clear cut. It gave substance and credibility to advocacy efforts, provided new information and arguments to support the case for change, and demonstrated how the issues concerned could be addressed by the EU institutions. It also positioned the Euronet

---

[15]The Introduction to the 2005 report argued that: 'they [children] cannot vote, they have little or no access to the media, and limited access to the courts. Nor are they members of powerful lobbying groups. Without access to these processes that are integral to the exercise of democratic rights, children and their opinions remain hidden from view and they are, in consequence, denied effective recognition as citizens' (Ruxton 2005: 13).

network as experts on the issues involved to whom policymakers would turn when they needed help and advice. These are of course not the only reasons for undertaking research. It could, for instance, be done to show that there is a need for funding or intervention on a particular issue, or to support or discredit a specific method or practice, or to highlight incompetence or corruption in government, business, or elsewhere that affects the public interest (Work Group for Community Health and Development 2013).[16] But whatever the aims of undertaking research of this kind it is important at an early stage to be explicit about the reasons why it is being done.

In my experience the development of research for advocacy purposes of the kind described here is often very much based on what outcome researchers (and campaigners, if they are working with them) want to achieve in policy terms. With the Euronet research, those involved were convinced that the ultimate aims should be to insert a clear legal base for action on children's rights in the EU Treaties, to develop an EU children's rights policy, and to ensure greater leadership and co-ordination on children's rights within the EU institutions. Achieving these aims then depended on putting together strong and coherent arguments, and being able to distil the report into a set of clear and simple key messages that could be communicated to policymakers, the media and others. This provided the core of numerous briefings for decision-makers and submissions to various bodies over the period of the campaign.

It is often argued, with some justification, that it is very difficult to summarise complex research in a set of simple propositions, and it is acknowledged that the richness of some research may be undermined by distilling the findings too far. However, if researchers are interested in promoting their work to achieve some kind of change in policy or practice, they will find it useful to ask themselves what the top three key messages from their research would be, were they to meet with a high-level policymaker – even for a short time. It is important that researchers are able to describe their research and their findings in straightforward language, to identify what changes they would like to see, and what they therefore want the policymaker to do.

The presentation of the actual research is also important and researchers need to identify different ways to communicate their work. This should be in various formats, such as briefings and fact sheets, case studies, consultation responses, letters to policymakers, press releases, magazine articles, radio or TV interviews, and speeches. Obviously the choice of format will depend on the purpose and focus of the research. For the Euronet reports, a clear report structure was essential so that readers could assimilate the gist of the argument and

---

[16]See Chapter 31 of the online *Community Tool Box* (Work Group for Community Health and Development 2013).

recommendations quickly in the Executive Summary and the Introduction, but also find more detail on specific issues when they needed it. Language is critical; this is especially the case for European work where many, if not most, readers will not be native speakers and may struggle with complex English. Attention to images is also time well spent. For the cover of the earlier *Children in Europe* book (Ruxton 1996), we reproduced an eye-catching Picasso painting of a child playing with a toy truck. Many readers mentioned how arresting this image was, and how they were drawn to the text because of it.[17]

Knowledge mediation

Effective knowledge mediation is built upon understanding the audience(s) for the research, including their backgrounds and the assumptions informing their views. There is a tendency for researchers and campaigners to focus their communication efforts on elected representatives and to ignore the crucial role that civil servants play. In this case study, the main targets were policymakers *and* officials who would make decisions about the future direction of policy. Some of them also had power to grant funding through EU programme initiatives. In some cases it will be appropriate to include these groups in the design phase of research projects (e.g. on the advisory board), so that engagement with research users begins at an early stage.

In focusing primarily on these two groups (and on developing the understanding, capacity, and activity of a third: children's NGOs), it is clear that the audiences for Euronet's research were quite narrowly focused. Whilst ideally it would have been possible to mobilise public opinion behind a campaign on children's rights at EU level, this always seemed a very distant and long-term possibility. And whilst there was occasional media interest, particularly at European level, this remained the exception rather than the rule.

It is important too to think about what kinds of evidence policymakers and officials are liable to respond positively to. Wherever possible Euronet used robust quantitative data and evidence of the effectiveness of programmes and interventions; however the lack of attention to children's issues in general meant that there was a limited amount of such material available. And whilst it is sometimes suggested that policymakers ascribe more weight to quantitative data, qualitative studies can shed more light on how childhood is 'lived' in practice.

Often policymakers are swayed by economic arguments, especially in times of austerity when finances are tight. Perhaps surprisingly, not very much analysis of

---

[17]Note that this did cause an extra layer of difficulties for the publisher, given the need to obtain (and pay for) the right to reproduce the image from the Picasso museum in Paris.

this issue was done for the Euronet reports; in retrospect, failure to assess clearly the costs and benefits of addressing children's rights was a weakness of this research.

The research also drew upon interviews undertaken with staff in EU institutions, with parliamentarians at European (and to a lesser extent national) levels, and with other key stakeholders. Most of the interviews were semi-structured, and in many cases were conducted on a confidential basis to allow respondents to speak openly.[18] These discussions were nevertheless extremely helpful in ensuring that the arguments and recommendations were realistic and targeted to the intended audiences.

Policymakers are often responsive to powerful testimony from someone affected by an issue. Whilst it is particularly important to them if it affects one or more of their constituents directly, children are not voters; nevertheless, some of the consultation events set up by Euronet where children met policymakers appear to have been influential. In the research reports, we tried to ensure that children's voices were represented as well, although sometimes it was hard to integrate the rather disparate conclusions from consultations with children into the closely argued texts.

A central component of knowledge mediation is the relationships that are developed between research producers and research users. As described earlier in the chapter, from the mid-1990s Euronet developed strong relationships with key policymakers in the European Commission and Parliament, and in many cases these relationships were sustained over a decade or more. A range of methods was employed to reach the target audiences, including briefings and submissions, letters and emails, presentations at seminars and conferences, and individual meetings. These interactions helped to raise awareness of the issues involved within the EU institutions, and to unlock much needed funding to sustain campaigns.

Of the approaches outlined in the previous paragraph, individual meetings are often the most effective mechanism for relationship building. Through MEPs and other personal contacts, Euronet had good access to policymakers at a high level. Whilst most of these meetings were very successful, they were not always straightforward. On one occasion, for example, a Euronet staff member and I went to meet the Director General of the Social Affairs Directorate. He greeted us cordially with 'Would you like to make your presentation now?', when we had not come expecting to give a presentation but to ask him a set of pre-prepared

---

[18]In some cases interviews were 'on the record', and it was possible to include telling quotes from them in the reports. See e.g. A Danish MP told his interviewer that 'when the big elephants fight, the little delicate things are overlooked. ... It is not very prestigious for a strong powerful Prime Minister to return back home and tell his citizens he succeeded in negotiating a bill on children's policy' (Ruxton 1999: 13).

questions! There are various ways of making effective use of such opportunities and avoiding a debacle of this kind. Firstly, it is important to be very clear about the objectives and agenda of such meetings, and as far as possible to make sure that these are understood and shared by both sides beforehand. Researchers should also find out as much as possible about the person they are going to meet and examine their track record beforehand. Ideally, a researcher should come away from a meeting having established their credibility, got over their key points, and demonstrated the value to the policymaker of a continuing relationship.

Another important step in relationship building is for researchers to identify sympathetic 'champions' and nurture their involvement and support for the campaign. As mentioned earlier, one such example for Euronet was Helle Thorning-Schmidt, who as an MEP played a critical role in ensuring the insertion of references to children's rights in the EU Treaties.[19] The development of wider policy networks is also key. Through its member organisations (including most notably Save the Children, Defence for Children International, and the NSPCC), Euronet itself brought together representatives of children's NGOs from a wide range of countries and sectors to campaign for the objectives set out in the reports. Although the extent to which Euronet was able to make the links between the European and national levels is debatable, some members were able to generate advocacy activity within their own countries; this both drew upon and supported the campaign at European level. By the time of the second Euronet report, strong links had been established with various other players (e.g. UN agencies) who supported Euronet's objectives, even though they were not actually members.

The establishment by the European Commission in 2006 of a 'European Forum for the Rights of the Child' also fostered a more regular dialogue between officials, campaigners and researchers Even though in the early years of its existence, the Forum struggled to define an appropriate role for itself, it did come to act as a significant arena for exchanging ideas and knowledge. Within the European Parliament, the emergence of an informal Children's Rights Alliance, bringing together MEPs from different political groups and countries, was important in co-ordinating parliamentary support for Euronet's campaign. There were therefore various types of formal and informal policy networks that developed from the 1990s onwards at European level, which provided fora for discussing and shaping responses to the new ideas emerging from Euronet's research (and from elsewhere).

---

[19]Another was the then Labour MEP Lyndon Harrison (now Baron Harrison), who regularly raised children's issues in the European Parliament and arranged several meetings between Labour MEPs, researchers and campaigners.

Knowledge application

If research is not taken up and used by policymakers, it is often assumed that this is because of a failure to communicate findings effectively. Whilst this may well be an issue, often too little attention is focused by researchers on the priorities and agendas of policymakers. In practice, the openness of policymakers to new ideas is episodic, and linked to factors such as changes of administration, scandals, crises and failures. Research therefore needs to capitalise on any windows of opportunity that arise (Newman et al. 2013). For instance, when political parties are drawing up election manifestos, they are often more open to new ideas and thinking – and this can be especially true of parties in opposition. Tracking the twists and turns of the legislative process, and attempting to intervene at appropriate moments, is also essential. In particular, it is important to identify and exploit potential policy 'hooks'; in the case of the Euronet research, debates over the Charter of Fundamental Rights and the European Constitution provided just such opportunities.

It is relevant to return here to the question of what is meant by 'using' research. Research evidence is frequently cited in policy debates, however it is often exploited to back up pre-existing political positions rather than to truly inform. Whilst it is almost impossible to ensure that research is not misrepresented by policymakers and others, this threat reinforces the need for researchers to clarify their key messages and highlight any caveats which should be attached to their findings.

Although the relationships that develop within networks of collaborating research producers and users are significant (Best et al. 2008), such linkages, although necessary, are not sufficient on their own for research to have an impact. More recently, increasing focus has also been accorded by academic commentators to the ways that knowledge becomes embedded within organisations, and interwoven with their priorities, cultures and contexts (Nutley et al. 2010) – and to the fact that this is a key factor in whether research is used.

It is beyond the scope of the individual researcher to ensure the conditions exist for their research to become 'embedded' as this usually depends on wide-scale intervention over a considerable period of time. Nevertheless, it is useful to be aware of whether such conditions exist, and what kinds of initiatives may foster a receptive climate.

So what is the evidence that children's rights have become embedded in EU institutions and systems over the period under discussion in this chapter? There is still only a very small number of officials in the EU institutions who can be said to have an understanding of child rights approaches. Nevertheless, it no longer seems particularly controversial to suggest, at least within certain parts of the Commission, that policymakers should take children's rights into consideration when developing policy and programmes at EU level. Indeed, children's issues have to some extent taken their place alongside other equalities strands with a much longer history of EU action, such as gender or disability. Moreover, there is some activity in relation to children across a range of themes, from child poverty and well-being, to education and training, childcare, violence against children, asylum and migration, and consumer issues. Little of this was happening in the mid-1990s, and it seems reasonable to suggest that the research reports we have undertaken, and all the associated campaigning by Euronet, have been a key factor in this transition.

Having said this, 'embedding' an issue or approach within an institutional setting implies more than that there should be some relevant activity. So far, a systematic attempt to train and build the capacity of staff to address children's rights has been lacking within the EU institutions, although some training has been provided by UNICEF and Save the Children. And whilst there is now a Children's Unit in the Justice directorate of the Commission, which has also played a role in training, the Unit remains small – and understaffed for the range of responsibilities and tasks that they are now engaged in. There is also a lack of coherence across directorates on this issue, and co-ordination mechanisms are still relatively weak (Stalford 2012). There are therefore still significant challenges to address before children's rights can be said to be truly 'embedded' in the EU institutions.

Conclusion

For around two decades, there has been a growing movement to encourage decision-makers at all levels to take increased account of research findings. This push probably achieved its most significant support in the early endorsement by the UK government under New Labour of 'evidence-based policy'. Simply put, the message was that decision-makers should pay attention to the evidence produced by researchers, and that doing so would lead to improvements in policy development and positive outcomes in practice.

However this assumption turned out to be overly optimistic, tending to under-emphasize the 'messiness' of the policy process and put 'research' on too much of a pedestal. Research is often presumed to always represent an advance on what has gone before, whereas researchers are fallible – and what is more, their findings are frequently contested (Weiss 2009). It is perhaps unsurprising that the less ambitious term 'evidence-*informed* policy' has been preferred in recent years.

What then are the key lessons from this case study for those embarking on research projects if they are keen to influence policy? First, there is a need to develop a sophisticated understanding of how research percolates into policy-making and how to exploit the opportunities that present themselves. Second, researchers should think about the channels of communication, and how their key messages can best be brought to the attention of the relevant decision-makers and policy communities. This may be through a researcher's own initiative, but it can also be in conjunction with other effective communicators, such as NGO campaigners. Third, it is essential to be realistic about what is feasible. Researchers should not expect direct and immediate consequences to flow from their research findings. Rather, they need to be aware of the diverse ways in which research can over time become embedded in the thinking and practice of policymakers and the culture of the organisations that they inhabit, and work to make this happen.

References

Best, A., Terpstra, J.L. and Moor, G. (2008) 'Windows on our world: Conceptual and organisational models for knowledge to action', paper presented to the NORFACE seminar 'Improving the Use of Evidence in the Policy Process', Oslo, October.

Commission of the European Communities (1989) 'Communication from the Commission on family policies', Brussels, 8 August 1989, COM(89) 363 final.

Commission of the European Communities (2006) 'Communication from the Commission: Towards an EU strategy on the rights of the child', Brussels, 4 July 2006, COM (2006) 367 final, http://eur-lex.europa.eu/LexUriServ/LexUriServ.do?uri=COM:2006:0367:FIN:EN:PDF (accessed 24 March 2013).

Commission of the European Communities (2007) 'Towards more knowledge-based policy and practice in education and training', Commission Staff Working Document, Brussels, 28 August 2007, SEC(2007) 1098.

Commission of the European Communities (2011) 'An EU Agenda for the rights of the child, communication from the Commission to the European Parliament, the Council, the European Economic and Social Committee and the Committee of the Regions', Brussels, COM (2011) 60 final, 15 February 2011, http://eurlex.europa.eu/LexUriServ/LexUriServ.do?uri=COM:2011:0060:FIN:EN:PDF (accessed 24 March 2013).

European Communities (1997) *Treaty of Amsterdam Amending the Treaty on European Union, the Treaties Establishing the European Communities and Certain Related Acts.* Luxembourg: Office for Official Publications of the European Communities, www.europarl.europa.eu/topics/treaty/pdf/amst-en.pdf (accessed 24 March 2013).

European Convention (2003) 'Draft Treaty establishing a Constitution for Europe, CONV 850/03, Brussels, 18 July 2003, http://european-convention. eu.int/docs/treaty/cv00850.en03.pdf (accessed 24 March 2013).

European Union (2000) 'Charter of fundamental rights of the European Union', 7 December 2000, *Official Journal of the European Communities*, 18 December 2000 (OJ C 364/01), http://eur-lex.europa.eu/LexUriServ/LexUriServ.do?uri= OJ:C:2010:083:0389:0403:en:PDF (accessed 24 March 2013).

Levin, B. (2004) 'Making research matter more', *Education Policy Analysis Archives*, 12(56).

Newman, K., Capillo, A., Famurewa, A., Nath, C. and Siyanbola, W. (2013) *What is the Evidence on Evidence-informed Policy?* Oxford: International Network for the Availability of Scientific Publications (INASP), www.inasp.info/uploads/ filer_public/2013/04/22/what_is_the_evidence_on_eipm.pdf (accessed 24 March 2013).

Nutley, S., Morton, S., Jung, T. and Boaz, A. (2010) 'Evidence and policy in six European countries: Diverse approaches and common challenges', *Evidence & Policy*, 6(2): 131–44, www.ingentaconnect.com/content/tpp/ ep/2010/00000006/00000002/art00001;jsessionid=7aidof7r6bl0k.alice (accessed 24 March 2013).

Ruxton, S. (1996) *Children in Europe*. London: NCH Action for Children.

Ruxton, S. (1999) *A Children's Policy for 21st Century Europe: First Steps*. Brussels: Euronet, www.crin.org/docs/RuxtonReort_FirstSteps.pdf (accessed 24 March 2013).

Ruxton, S. (2001) 'Towards a children's policy for the European Union?', in P. Foley, J. Roche and S. Tucker (eds), *Children in Society: Contemporary Theory, Policy and Practice*. Basingstoke: Palgrave Macmillan/The Open University.

Ruxton, S. (2005) *What About Us? Children's Rights in the European Union: Next Steps*. Brussels: Euronet, www.crin.org/docs/Ruxton%20Report_WhatAbout Us.pdf (accessed 24 March 2013).

Stalford, H. (2012) *Children and the European Union: Rights, Welfare and Accountability*. Oxford and Portland, OR: Hart Publishing.

Weiss, C. (2009) 'Foreword', in F. Carden, *Knowledge to Policy: Making the Most of Development Research*. New Delhi: Sage.

Work Group for Community Health and Development (2013) *Community Tool Box*, University of Kansas, http://ctb.ku.edu/en/tablecontents/index.aspx

17 Transformative Dialogues: The Impact of Participatory Research on Practice

Chris Pascal and Tony Bertram

Introduction

The discipline and practice of participatory, practice-led research (Eisenberg et al. 2006; Reason and Bradbury 2008; McNiff 2010), though challenging, has grown rapidly in recent years, and it is now widely accepted as making an important and serious contribution to the knowledge base of early childhood. Over many years, our work in the Centre for Research in Early Childhood (CREC) in Birmingham, England, has embraced, exemplified and contributed to the development of practitioner researchers, action researchers and practice-based researchers (Pascal 1993, 2003; Koshy and Pascal 2011; Bertram and Pascal 2012a, 2012b). Another parallel challenge with which we have been engaged is to authentically, practically and ethically acknowledge the young child as an active partner in our research practices. Since the UN Convention on the Rights of the Child was ratified by the UK Government in 1991, the child's right to have a voice, and to have his/her opinions heard, has led to many providers and practitioners in the field of early childhood to seek ways to involve children's opinions and perspectives in the evaluation and development of practice. Many researchers in early childhood have been sensitised to the challenge of inclusive research, in which our youngest children are viewed as subjects rather than objects in a research process that is set in the context of a democratic encounter (Learning and Teaching Scotland 2006). CREC has a strong commitment to including the voices of children as an integral part of all its research and development work.

We operate through an ethos of empowerment of all participants, and aim for participatory research practice which has at its heart an active involvement in promoting the rights of children as citizens with voice and power. A further issue in achieving this goal has been ensuring that young children's voices are not just listened to but that practice responds, authentically, genuinely and actively to what they have to say. It is this concern that is the subject of this chapter.

We have made visible our continuing struggle to operate authentically within a participatory paradigm (Bertram and Pascal 2012b) in the belief that early childhood research should and could be more democratic, participatory and empowering, and should also be deeply ethical, political and transformational in its orientation (Pascal and Bertram 2009). This means ensuring that shifts in practice flow as a clear part of the research process. The influences on us, in our journey as early childhood researchers, have been deep and profound, ranging from the inspirational children and parents with whom we have collaborated, and dialogues with radical foresighted policymakers and politicians, and those who were not, to risk-taking and risk-averse university tutors and students, and, of course, to the many courageous theorists and scholars whose texts and ideas have both challenged and spurred us on to think differently and creatively about the complexity of the 'real world' (Robson 2011) of multi-professional practice with families and young children. Key partners in this journey have been the courageous practitioner researchers on whom we have depended to open up their practice to new knowledge, alternative perspectives and transformative actions. It is this critical element of transformative research which is often over-looked but is vital if research is really to make a difference to shift practice and transform lives.

This chapter explores the struggles and challenges we, as researchers, have faced in achieving a power shift to enable participatory research, and in particu-lar, research which listens attentively to young children's perspectives, in order to impact directly and clearly on practice. It will draw upon the work of a series of research and development projects we have undertaken over the last 15 years in which we have tried to work alongside children, to explore, document and improve the realities of their life in early childhood settings. These projects include the *Baby Effective Early Learning (BEEL)* project (Bertram and Pascal 2006), the *Accounting Early for Life Long Learning (AcE)* project (Bertram et al. 2010) and especially, the *Children Crossing Borders (CCB)* project (Bertram and Pascal 2007) and its subsequent application, the *Opening Windows (OW)* project (Bertram and Pascal 2008). Through the work of these projects we will explain how we have attempted to provide space for multiple voices in the research pro-cess and use this dialogue to change practice. We will share our learning about how to create a climate in early childhood settings which can better listen to the voices of children in the production of knowledge and understanding and in the generation of new practice. From this experience, methodological and epistemo-logical lessons for researchers and practitioners will be identified and troubled further: we are still learning.

We are well-embedded in the theory and practice of practitioner- and practice-based research, as we set out later in this chapter, and have worked hard to explore and develop a participatory paradigm in the research and develop-ment process. However, more recently we have come to understand that our worldview needs to be modified in response to our own felt inadequacies and the troubling paradoxes we face in attempting to live out our participatory and transformative vision in our research practice. We are conscious of the need to respond to a continued and sometimes reasonable professional critique of the robustness of our participatory methods as a means to change practice. This has led us to accept that praxis (reflection and action) in itself is not enough and that in order to authentically realise a transformative participatory paradigm in our work we need to develop a worldview in which reflection (phronesis) and action (praxis), done in conjunction with others, needs to be immersed within a much more astute awareness about power (politics) and a sharpened focus on values (ethics) in all of our thinking and actions (Pascal and Bertram 2012) if it is to realise its ultimate aim of social and practice transformation. We see this mix of phronesis, praxis, ethics and power as at the heart of what we increas-ingly recognise as a 'praxcological' worldview in modern early childhood research. We believe this paradigm is helping us to shift our research work into what we hope will be a more profound and intensely participatory, and thus more authentically democratic, phase in which participants are empowered to generate knowledge which generates change. In this development we should acknowledge our important collaboration with our Portuguese colleagues, João and Júlia Formosinho (2012) and their team at the research centre of the Childhood Association in Braga (Oliveira-Formosinho and Barros Araújo 2004, 2006; Oliveira-Formosinho 2009).

Children's voice and practice change

Progress in listening better to children's voices and achieving more democratic practice continues, and there has been further action to embed children's right to participate in the development of Children's Services. However, the deeper changes in values and attitudes required to realise this commitment for all chil-dren in all early childhood settings are much harder to make a reality. In many settings these hard fought for rights of children are not yet evident in practice and there is often little evidence of practitioner research with children impacting on practice in any deep or significant way. Many children are not listened to in their daily lives, whether at home or in schools, and the development of their capacity to participate effectively as citizens in shaping their lives is thus restricted. This situation particularly characterises the reality of our youngest children, who can remain 'silenced' and often excluded from the decisions which shape their lives with the rationale that they are 'too young' to express their rights and voice and that we, as adults, have to act on their behalf. We have also found that in 'crossing the border' from home to school, children from migrant, travelling, asylum-seeking and refugee families across a range of diverse communities and backgrounds are even less likely to be heard and have even less impact on practice in early childhood settings (Bertram and Pascal 2006, 2008).

It is our view that, if all our children are to enjoy the rights enshrined in the UNCRC, then research and practice needs to fundamentally reshape its paradigm to become more inclusive, participatory and action focused. Our own work, and that of other researchers and practitioners in the field, has documented the challenges to making this paradigm shift happen (Woodhead 1999; Lloyd-Smith and Tarr 2000; Lewis and Lindlay 2000; Clark and Moss 2001; Formosinho and Araújo 2004, 2006; Formosinho and Formosinho 2012; Dahlberg et al. 2006; Lancaster 2006). Perhaps in response to this body of work which promotes children's perspectives, we can also trace a growing recognition in the early years sector of the importance of listening to young children's perspectives. The impact of such research as the Mosaic approach (see Chapter 12) reflects an embedding of the view of young children as citizens with rights and voice in our services, with the underpinning notion, well expressed by Lloyd-Smith and Tarr (2000), that 'reality experienced by children and young people in educational settings cannot be fully comprehended by inference and assumption'. At the heart of this view is that the actual experiences perceived by the child cannot be inferred by others and so practitioners and researchers must include their voices as they speak, and not as we infer or interpret their point of view. It is our belief that our task as researchers is to meet this challenge and open our eyes, ears and minds to these voices; to become expert and active listeners to children and to recognise the many ways in which children skilfully communicate their realities to us (Malaguzzi 1998).

Why impact on practice is important

Going beyond listening to children and encouraging their participation in decision-making and practice development is important for many reasons. Educationalists emphasise the importance of participation in empowering children as learners, enabling them to make choices, express their ideas and opinions and develop a positive sense of self (Roberts 2002; Bruce 2005). Other writers foreground the benefits of their participation to society as a whole and for development of citizenship. As Miller (1997: 6) points out, children who learn to participate in their early years are more likely to become, 'more capable and involved citizens … with respect for the principles and practice of democratic life'. Although we might subscribe to this view, we should also be cautious as it looks at children as future adults and therefore frames them in terms of what they are not (yet). However, for us, this perspective has validity only if we see children as active citizens in the here and now, already participating in a democratic life in which they have full rights and responsibilities that they are practising continually in their daily interactions with the world, engaging in what Biesta, Lawy and Kelly (2009) call 'learning democracy'. Hallett and Prout (2003) and Dahlberg, Moss and Pence (2006) allude to this view in the ethical and philosophical stance they adopt which acknowledges children as actors and stakeholders in their own lives, challenging the traditional view of children as empty vessels and vulnerable beings who are incapable of acting with agency and on their own behalf. They see children as powerful, competent individuals who are well able to express preferences and make informed choices to shape their world and transform it.

In our view as researchers in early childhood, giving status to children's voices in our research work acknowledges children's right for their views and experiences to be taken seriously as we consider practice responses. We feel that listening well to children can make a difference to our understanding of their priorities, interests and concerns, and how children feel about themselves and their lives. We have found that listening can challenge assumptions, raise expectations and provide unexpected insights into how practice might be better shaped.

These ideas about childhood, children's rights, democratic participation and voice have profoundly affected our research and development work and led us to adopt an ethical code which states that children are to be supported as active participants in any research and development process and that their voices should always form a central and equally considered part of any evidence base which concerns them. It also acknowledges that we are 'answerable' (Bakhtin 1981) for the way these voices are documented and represented in our research outputs and for their impact on practice.

Methodological consequences

We have struggled over the last 15 years to rise to the challenge of living out this philosophical, ethical and transformative perspective in all our research work. As we suggested earlier, the *Effective Early Learning* programme (Dupree et al. 2001; Bertram and Pascal 2006), the *Accounting Early for Life Long Learning* programme (Bertram et al. 2009, 2010) and especially the *Children Crossing Borders* research project (Bertram and Pascal 2007) and the *Opening Windows* programme (Bertram and Pascal 2008) all attempt to adopt an inclusive and participatory stance with young children in order to generate knowledge which can transform practice. The challenge in each of these projects was to develop an equalising research ethic, which redistributes power amongst all participants, actively challenges entrenched, inequitable practices and relationships and supports the 'silenced' and 'domesticated' to 'name their world' and so 'shape their world' (Freire 1972).

This work has been particularly challenging in a recent research project, *Children Crossing Borders (CCB)*. This was a major international project that aimed to examine the practices, values and expectations of pre-school practitioners, and the aspirations, expectations and views of parents and children from 'immigrant' communities, in multi-ethnic cities in five countries (France, Germany, Italy, UK and the USA). The focus was on the children of those families whose presence in the host country was new, whose status was vulnerable, and who faced the difficulties of overcoming cultural, linguistic, and sometimes racial and religious differences, between their home and host culture. It is these immigrants who continue to be the subject of intense political and social debate in the UK and other EU countries, as well as in the US, and whose voices are most rarely heard. There is perhaps no social issue more challenging for the countries of the European Union than immigration, confronting them with increasing diversity. It is a key political issue that connects domestic to international policies, that is closely linked with urban poverty and related social problems, and that reflects core concerns about what it means to be a nation, a people and a union. The treatment of immigrants has become even more salient in the post-9/11 climate, with heightened anxieties about national security and rising xenophobia. The economic downturn may only exacerbate this. For most young children of parents who have come from other countries and cultures, early childhood education and care (ECEC) services are the first context in which they come face to face with differences between the culture of home and the public culture of their new country. For parents who have recently come to a new country, enrolling their child in an early childhood programme also brings the cultural values of their home and adopted country into contact and, often, conflict. For countries with high rates of immigration, ECEC programmes are key sites for enacting national goals for social inclusion and the creation of new citizens. This adds a further dimension to our dialogue about the impact of research, which in this sense extends the responsibility of research to generate new understandings and knowledge which have the capacity to transform political discourse and practice at a local, national and international level. It is perhaps here that some of the biggest challenges lie if we are to realise our transformative intent. We are researching in a context in which the perceived threats of mass immigration and the consequent perceived loss of traditional values and cultures in British communities is highly emotive. This places early childhood research, which is attempting to change current realities, in a potentially perilous place, through which researchers need courage, ethics and deep social integrity to navigate. However, we would argue that this is exactly where we should be if impact is what we are striving for.

In this climate, the *CCB* project aimed to give voice to those who are usually silent and sought to generate evidence which would encourage open interaction, dialogue and responsive action between and about children, parents and practitioners in our richly diverse communities. In the English team, we worked hard to ensure children's voices were also included in the dialogues. There is a critical shortage of studies on the experiences of children of immigrants in ECEC services and on what immigrants from different cultures want from these services and we aimed to address this omission.

The *CCB* project adopted the innovative, anthropological methodologies of Tobin's study *Preschool in Three Cultures* (Tobin et al. 1989) which suggested that pre-schools are looked to as key sites for preserving and reflecting cultural beliefs and practices about early childhood education and care. The core data collection method in the *CCB* project was the use of Tobin's video cued, multi-vocal stimulus method to encourage reflection and discussion amongst parents, practitioners and children in facilitated focus groups based on video material. These dialogues form the major part of the project data. We made videotapes of typical days for 3- and 4 year olds in ECEC settings in each of the five countries, and then used these videotapes, not primarily as data, but as tools to stimulate a multi-vocal, inter-cultural dialogue. The videotapes were used as a cue to draw out, in focus groups, the beliefs and concerns of children, parents and community leaders from immigrant communities, of teachers and administrators who work in settings that serve the children of newly arrived immigrants, and of ECEC experts and policymakers. By showing the same set of videotapes to these participants in each of the five nations, we hoped to highlight similarities and differences in how each nation approaches the promises and challenges of bringing immigrants into the fabric of society in order to provoke a dialogue about how countries' ECEC services might effectively respond to this dynamic.

In the English team we took a lead on exploring the potential of the method to capture young children's voices as an equitable and symmetrical part of the dialogue we were encouraging between parents and practitioners. This work has had a powerful impact on our thinking and actions as researchers on the project and generated a good deal of interest, demonstrating even more firmly the importance and potential of including children in all our research work. It was this work that led us to realise more sharply the challenges in the next phase of this project, where, once the voices of children and parents had been expressed and documented, we attempted to ensure that practice (and policy) responded actively and respectfully to what they had to say.

From research into practice: the *Opening Windows* programme

This second phase of work is still underway, and we are continually learning from practitioners and participating children and parents about how to embed more equitable, constructive dialogues in our early childhood services. Our analysis of the first phase of work had shown us that:

- There was a strong demand for more open dialogues from parents, practitioners and children in all communities in which we worked. We witnessed almost an awakening in the awareness of participants to their right to have and express their voice and to the mutual benefits of listening to each other and sharing aspirations, motivations and ambitions for themselves and the services they used. What Freire (1972) called a process of 'conscientization' had occurred. This is evidence of impact in itself.
- There was a clear awareness by parents, practitioners and children of the inequity in the relationships in the preschools and a desire to challenge this through more dialogue and training. We documented many stories of racism, stereotyping and inequitable treatment in parents and children's lives, and practitioners were both aware of and uneasy about how their services might perpetuate such practices. In many cases, practitioners felt more 'helpless' in changing these realities than did the parents and children. Optimistically, we found an openness to change in all quarters.
- An interesting finding was that parents in the study did not generally want their child to be taught in their home language but in the language of the majority community. However, parents did want someone to be able to talk to them, preferably in their home language, who understood their culture and that they had something useful to say and could make a contribution to their child's education. This illustrates that sometimes we make assumptions about desired practices which evidence challenges.

These findings, which are derived from our analysis of the views expressed in the focus group dialogues, challenged us to develop a strategy for opening and deepening equitable and respectful dialogues in ECEC settings. These messages have been taken into the next phase of work which involves the creation of a Professional Development programme, called *Opening Windows* (Bertram and Pascal 2008), which flows from and into the *Children Crossing Borders* research. This programme offers training materials and activities that aim to change practice by encouraging more open interaction and equitable dialogues between the children, parents, practitioners and researchers in our richly diverse communities. The idea of 'opening windows' comes from a quote by Mahatma Ghandi (1945):

I do not want my house to be walled in on all sides, and my windows to be closed. Instead, I want the cultures of all lands to be blown about my house as freely as possible. But I refuse to be blown off my feet by any.

We, and the community of practitioners that worked with us in this project, were inspired by the idea of opening our early childhood institutions and practices to feel and breathe the diversity of cultures and world views that prevail in twenty-first-century communities, and how this openness to difference and diversity might actually strengthen community cohesion and identity for all. This is the intention of the participatory paradigm which we are hoping to embed in early childhood research and practice. It is also interesting that a further stimulus for this professional development work came from our research funders, who, as a condition of our funding, required us to develop documented interventions in practice using the research findings to evidence the impact of this work. Sticks and carrots can both be useful in ensuring research makes a meaningful contribution to social development.

Our impact work was also deeply inspired by Freire's dialogic and reflexive action in a 'pedagogy of the oppressed' (1972) where he promotes the challenge of working with those who are 'domesticated' or 'silenced' with the clear aim of 'liberation'. His work of course was with adults but we have applied these radical ideas to our work as researchers and practitioners with children. The first step in this process of liberation is 'consciousness raising' and the development of self-hood in the oppressed (practitioners and children) with the intention of helping them to name their world and to begin to shape it, that is, it is an empowerment approach. From this flows the co-construction of 'generative themes' for dialogue which are meaningful to participants and are generated by the participants themselves. This work is realised through the creation of 'cultural circles' or 'encounters' in which symmetrical and reflexive dialogues are stimulated and supported in a variety of ways between 'oppressors' and 'oppressed', or the silencers and the silenced: in this case, it is researchers/practitioners and children. The capacity of young children to adopt and participate actively in such encounters has been shown in the popularity of 'circle time' which has become a predominant activity in early childhood settings. The key difference is that we are aiming to create cultural circles in which children are given the floor to initiate and generate their own ideas and where dialogues are symmetrical in terms of power distribution.

In this project we have trained researchers and practitioners to use a variety of exploratory (research) techniques/approaches which encourage the voices, dialogues and narratives of children to be listened to, given status and acted upon. This model of symmetrical dialogue was initially modelled by the research team, but increasingly practitioners and parents have been encouraged and empowered to take over this role and embed it into their daily ways of working and being with children. The development process has been fully documented, and participants were encouraged to keep journals, so that the impact of the project intervention could be fully evaluated.

A journal extract from a participating practitioner which illustrates the impact of the research on thinking and practice in one setting is offered below:

It seems to me that even the challenge of the title needs to be addressed in a creative way to ensure movement and integrity in how we really engage with others to make a difference in the lifelong learning opportunities we provide for our children. As I read the quote from *Opening Windows*, one displayed and regularly quoted at our nursery school and Children's Centre, I started to see that my role as Head Teacher/Head of Centre, was to restore the house, to reconstruct the house for today's purpose and then to open the windows and doors to let the community cultures and breeze in. In fact this is what I have been doing since I started, not as a linear project but simultaneously planting, nurturing, growing ideas and possibilities with staff, parents, children and the local community.

After the *Open Windows* programme with CREC I was compelled to continue as the principles of *Open Windows* seemed to sit so comfortably with my own core values. I am so very much aware of the trouble and hot spots of the dialogue around equality and diversity and *Open Windows* almost gave me permission to be transparent and open to share my values with others in a positive and constructive way.

Out of the Open Windows programme has come:

Home visits, nursery practitioners revisited the reasoning and consequence of this tradition after talking with parents at *Open Windows* dialogue – changed to Initial Contact Meeting to be held at nursery or as a home visit if requested – all families chose to come to nursery … emphasis was put on the learning with parents and family so far and how this was transferred and then shared between key worker and family … practitioners said 'children settled quicker this year than before'.

Code of Conduct was developed and shared three expectations for all – to be kind and friendly, to be safe and take care and to be sensible and helpful. This underpins the new behaviour policy and is a shared starting point to continue a dialogue with children, families and practitioners.

OW principles and success criteria to be shared with staff – summer term inset – and be the foundations of our equalities and diversity policy due to be reviewed in the summer term.

The importance of truly implementing symmetrical dialogues as continuous setting practise – opportunities planned into School Improvement Planning.

Community Art Project – the first meeting with parents was around a set of photographs of the centre from the adults' view and the child's view. I noticed that we had a lot of railings and in my 'open house' (nursery) there were lots of bars. This did not seem right. I decided to make this space into an art gallery as if we were in Paris or London. After talking this through with an artist who was working in the centre, we decided to continue the open dialogues through this project based around 'naming our world'.

A key finding from the *Opening Windows* intervention was that practitioners and parents needed to develop new confidence, competences and commitment before symmetrical dialogues could begin. The process of redistributing power was harder than we had anticipated. This difficulty was expressed in many ways, with many practitioners and parents resisting the opportunities to allow children to 'name their world' and shape their dialogue with it (Freire 1972). Many showed a reluctance to 'take the lid off' the existing status quo, fearing that they would not be able to control or handle what followed. We have found that this resistance or 'internalised oppression' (Freire 1972) has to be acknowledged and worked through respectfully and compassionately.

Our experimentation and innovations in this project have led to a programme with the express aim of developing strategies and practices which support democratic, equalising and participative encounters within early childhood services for researchers, practitioners, parents and children. This has meant initial work to enhance the skills of participants, both researchers and practitioners, in understanding diversity, values clarification, supporting open dialogues, handling conflict and developing active listening approaches. Once this preparatory work has been completed we introduce a menu of strategies to create and sustain democratic encounters with children from babyhood onwards, including:

- Video Stimulated Dialogue
- Cultural Circles
- Critical Incident Analysis
- Story Telling and Naming Your World
- Wishing Trees
- Listening Posts
- Map Making
- Guided Tours
- Focused Observations
- Photography and Film Making.

We continue to experiment and add to this menu and are exploring the joys of technology, which provides us with an increasing number of tools and strategies for documenting and stimulating more expressive narratives and voices, and to which young children adapt with skills and enthusiasms that are hard to match.

Emerging methodological and epistemological lessons

Through the research and development programmes set out in this chapter we have tried to show how we have experimented with a variety of strategies to stimulate children's voices and to document them accurately and authentically, and to use this knowledge to transform practice. We have found that research can have strong lessons for practice but translating these into professionally focused change programmes to ensure impact takes time and involves an intense period of follow-up collaboration, innovation, documentation and development within 'real-world' settings. Our experience has shown that to achieve impact requires an extended commitment to the process, deep attachment within the context where change or impact is desired and a firmly held belief in equitable, distributed, social action. Impact has to be learned, earned and focused on as a major element in any research project, rather than just aspired to with responsibility passed on to others. We have found that the impact phase of our research has needed as much, if not more, transformational and connected leadership as the research phase, yet this can often be missing when research is planned and executed.

A key message is that we are still innovating and learning as this work progresses and as we learn more about the diversity of children's lives in England. Young children need to be given a variety of forums and means to express themselves, and practitioner researchers need to listen with all their senses to what is being communicated and then to reflect deeply about what this expression means and use this understanding to transform their practice. Issues that have arisen as we have explored the creation of symmetrical and transformative dialogues include:

- **The need to reflect more on the environmental contexts for listening.** Children need listening spaces, places, time and resources if they are to be able to express themselves as themselves. Younger children, particularly, need time and attentive adults who are really tuned in to their mode of expression.
- **How to more effectively support and vary the interpersonal and intrapersonal nature of the dialogic process.** We have found that practitioner researchers need to explore and develop a set of socio-emotional competencies and capacities and also to develop a critical self-awareness of their own values and beliefs and an understanding of how these shape their behaviours and responses to others.
- **The courage required to redistribute the power so that children have a sense of their strength and rights.** Adopting a transformational position to practice can be perilous, as practitioners need to be willing to suspend taken-for-granted assumptions, challenge and unlock existing practices and take some risks with new ways of being and knowing which are more equitable, respectful and empowering for all involved.
- **How to suspend the impulse to direct and control what is voiced and how it is expressed.** Redistributing power and control in a democratic community of learners, which includes children and parents, means that the unpredictable and the uncertain have to be welcomed and worked with. This does not mean an abdication of control or power, rather that power is shared and dynamic and works for the collective rather than for the individual. This creates a new and potentially exciting democratic imperative in our early childhood settings.

- **How to stimulate, document and interpret what is voiced in an authentic, respectful and accurate way.** We need to explore, innovate and experiment with new technologies and new communication possibilities as we encourage more expressive encounters in our early childhood settings. Non-orthodox methodologies, particularly creative expressive techniques such as storytelling, drama, mime, music, dance and visual imaging offer profoundly different opportunities for new kinds of dialogue and interpretations of meanings which we can and should now explore.
- **How to ensure the training approach and programme design is ethically, politically and contextually aware (locally, nationally and internationally).** Our reflections have made us realise that old models of professional development which are transmissive, directed and externally led may be redundant in the new world of open access and self-generated learning. However, as new professional learning possibilities emerge we need to be extremely careful that they don't further distance, exclude or disempower the less powerful. Keeping ethics and power (strong praxeological intent) at the forefront of our considerations is crucial as we move forward to realise transformation and impact.

Concluding comments

Our work has shown us that children are able to express their opinion in ways that are very perceptive and that give a real insight into how their lives are and what meaning they are making of them. These insights provide a profoundly challenging alternative dimension to our knowledge and understanding of ECEC and what shapes the lives of young children. The challenge to researchers is how to ensure these perspectives have an impact on children's worlds. It is clear that supporting and catching children's voices is complex, challenging and multi-layered, involving a profound paradigm shift in the values, actions and thinking of researchers and practitioners. We are reminded of Woodhead's (1999) perceptive comments from over a decade ago:

> Morally, it seems to me that as teachers, students and researchers, we have a responsibility to be attuned to how the tasks of childhood are perceived, felt and understood by those children, their parents and other carers who have to solve the problems of living and growing up, in circumstances that may be vastly different from those that shape our own personal and academic priorities. (1999: 20)

> The question is about the status we accord the child through the methodologies we adopt and the conclusions we draw; and about whether we allow children the space to alter our agenda of presuppositions. (1999: 18)

Taking this demanding agenda forward with integrity to ensure children's voices really do have impact on practice is challenging and we should acknowledge that the participatory research conducted to date, including that done by ourselves, has only been partially successful in this respect. In our own work this critique has caused us to look at projects in which we have been involved, such as the *Effective Early Learning (EEL)* programme, the *Accounting Early for Life Long Learning (AcE)* programme and the *Children Crossing Borders (CCB)* project and to ask some deeper, reflective and critical questions about how authentically democratic and participatory we have been in this work and how transformative its impact has really been for those involved. We acknowledge that we still have work to do to realise authentic and genuinely participative and transformative research practice. Our work is entering a further phase of reflection and action (Pascal and Bertram 2012) in which we are attempting to explore more expressive and more unorthodox methodologies to give better voice to children in order to change practice and improve children's lives.

Bibliography

Bahktin, M. (1981) *The Dialogic Imagination: Four Essays*, ed. M. Holquist, trans. C. Emerson and M. Holquist. Austin: University of Texas Press.

Bertram, T. and Pascal, C. (2006) *Baby Effective Early Learning (BEEL): A Handbook for Evaluating, Assuring and Improving Quality in Settings for Birth to Three-Year-Olds*. Birmingham: Amber Publications.

Bertram T. and Pascal C. (2007) 'Children crossing borders: Enhancing the inclusion of children in pre-school settings', *Childcare in Europe*, May.

Bertram, T. and Pascal, C. (2008) *Opening Windows: A Handbook for Enhancing Equity and Diversity in Early Childhood Settings*. Birmingham: Amber Publications.

Bertram T., Pascal, C. and Saunders, M. (2010) *The Accounting Early for Life Long Learning Programme*. Birmingham: Amber Publications.

Bertram, T. and Pascal, C. (2012a) 'Editorial', *European Early Childhood Education Research Journal*, 20(1): 1–2

Bertram, T. and Pascal, C. (2012b) 'Praxis, ethics and power: Developing praxeology as a participatory paradigm for early childhood research', *European Early Childhood Education Research Journal*, 20(4): 477–92.

Bertram, T., Pascal, C. and Saunders, M. (2009) *Accounting Early for Life Long Learning Programme*. Birmingham: Amber Publications.

Biesta, G.J.J., Lawy, R. and Kelly N. (2009) 'Understanding young people's citizenship learning in everyday life: The role of contexts, relationships and dispositions', *Education Citizenship and Social Justice*, 4(1): 5–24.

Bruce, T. (2005) *Early Childhood Education*. London: Hodder and Stoughton.

Clark, A. and Moss, P. (2001) *Listening to Children: The Mosaic Approach.* London: National Children's Bureau and Joseph Rowntree Foundation.

Dahlberg, G., Moss, P. and Pence, A. (2007) *Beyond Quality in Early Childhood Education and Care: Postmodern Perspectives,* 2nd edition. London: Falmer Press.

Dupree, E., Bertram, T. and Pascal, C. (2001) 'Listening to Children's perspectives of their early childhood settings', paper presented at the 11th European Early Childhood Education Research Association Conference, Alkmaar, The Netherlands, 1 September.

Eisenberg, E.M., Baglia, J. and Pynes, J.E. (2006) 'Transforming emergency medicine through narrative: Qualitative action research at a community hospital', *Health Communication,* 19: 197–208.

Formosinho, J. and Araújo, S.B. (2004) 'Children's perspectives about pedagogical interactions', *European Early Childhood Education Research Journal,* 12(1): 103–14.

Formosinho, J. and Araújo, S.B. (2006) 'Listening to children as a way to reconstruct knowledge about children: some methodological implications', *European Early Childhood Education Research Journal,* 14(1): 21–31.

Formosinho, J. and Formosinho, J.O. (2012) 'Towards a social science of the social: the contribution of praxeological research', *European Early Childhood Education Research Journal,* 20(4): 591–606.

Freire, P. (1972) *Pedagogy of the Oppressed.* London: Penguin Books.

Hallett, C. and Prout, A. (eds) (2003) *Hearing the Voices of Children: Social Policy for a New Century.* London and New York: Routledge Falmer.

Koshy, V. and Pascal, C. (2011) 'Nurturing the young shoots of talent: Using action research for exploration and theory building', *European Early Childhood Education Research Journal,* 19(4): 433–50.

Lancaster, P. (2006) *RAMPS: A Framework for Listening to Children.* London: Daycare Trust.

Learning and Teaching Scotland (2006) 'Listening to children: Towards a shared understanding for early years education in Scotland', *Perspectives 2: A Series of Occasional papers on Early Years Education.* Glasgow: Teaching & Learning Scotland.

Lewis, A. and Lindsay. G. (eds) (2000) *Researching Children's Perspectives.* Buckingham: Open University Press.

Lloyd-Smith, M. and Tarr, J. (2000) 'Researching children's perspectives: A sociological perspective', in A. Lewis and G. Lindsay (eds) *Researching Children's Perspectives.* Buckingham: Open University Press.

Mahatma Ghandi (1945) *Teachings of Mahatma Gandhi,* ed. Jag Parvesh. Chander: DJVU.

Malaguzzi, L. (1998) *The Hundred Languages of Children.* New York: Ablex Publishing.

McNiff, J. (2010) *Action Research for Professional Development*. Dorset: September Books.

Miller, J. (1997) *Never Too Young*. London: National Early Years Network.

Oliveira-Formosinho, J., and Araújo, S.B. (2004) 'Children's perspectivies about pedagogical interactions', *European Early childhood Education Research Journal*, 12(1): 103–14.

Oliveira-Formosinho, J., and Araújo, S.B. (2006) 'Listening to children as a way to reconstruct knowledge about children: some methodological implications', *European Early Childhood Education Research Journal*, 14(1): 21–31.

Oliveira-Formosinho, J. (2009) 'Togetherness and play under the same roof: Children's perceptions about families', *European Early Childhood Education Research*, 17(2): 233–48.

Pascal, C. (1993) 'Capturing the quality of education provision for young children: A story of developing professionals and developing methodology', *European Early Childhood Education Research Journal*, 1(1): 69–80.

Pascal, C. (2003) 'Effective early learning: An act of practical theory', *European Early Childhood Education Research Journal*, 11(2): 7–28.

Pascal, C. and Bertram, A. (2009) 'Listening to young citizens: The struggle to make real a participatory paradigm in research with young children', *European Early Childhood Education Research Journal*, 17(2): 249–62 .

Pascal, C. and Bertram, A. (2012) 'Praxis, ethics and power: Developing praxeology as a participatory paradigm for early childhood research', *European Early Childhood Education Research Journal*, 20(4): 477–92.

Reason P. and Bradbury H. (eds) (2008) *Sage Handbook of Action Research: Participative Inquiry and Practice*, 2nd edition. London: Sage Publications.

Roberts, R. (2002) *Self Esteem and Early Learning*. London: Paul Chapman Educational Publishers.

Robson, C. (2011) *Real World Research*, 3rd edition. London: John Wiley and Son.

Tobin, J.J., Wu, D.Y.H. and Davidson, D.H. (1989) *Preschool in Three Cultures, Japan, China, and the United States*. New Haven, CT: Yale University Press.

UN Convention on the Rights of the Child (1991) see Articles 12 and 13 of the UNCRC, on line at www.unicef.org/crch/files/Rights_overview.pdf

Woodhead, M. (1999) 'Towards a global paradigm for research into early childhood education', *European Early Childhood Education Research Journal*, 7(1): 5–22.

18 Engaging Children and Young People in Research

Alex Mann, Joseph Liley and
Mary Kellett

Introduction

It feels fitting to conclude this Reader with the voices of children and young
people. In the first chapter we considered images of childhood and influences
on research. Here, we close that circle with a focus on research *by* children and
young people. The concept of child-led research has gained credence in the last
decade, in response to changing perspectives on their status in society, recognition of their role as consumers and increased attention to children and young
people's rights. The notion of children designing and leading their own
research opens up new protagonist frontiers. Child-to-child enquiry generates
different data from adult-to-child enquiry. Children and young people observe
with different eyes, ask different questions and communicate in fundamentally
different ways. They are party to the subcultures of childhood and youth which
give them unique 'insider' perspectives, devoid of adult–child power relations,
critical to our understanding of their worlds. The sum of these parts makes a
valuable contribution to the impact of research and the diversity of its
dissemination.

This chapter describes some of the processes and challenges of child-led
research as exemplified in one model (Kellett 2005). In particular, it considers the
impact of children and young people's research outputs. Discourse is woven
around a specific example of original research by the first authors, aged 11. This
serves as an illustration of impact, engagement and dissemination, anchored in
the reality of children's lived experiences.

Processes of child-led research

A barrier to children as researchers is not their lack of adult status but their absence of research skills. Many, perhaps most, adults would not be able to undertake research without some training. Comprehensive tuition and quality support are, therefore, central tenets in the empowerment of children as researchers. Extensive pilot work (Kellett 2003, 2004) informed the design of an accessible research training programme for children, delivered through the Children's Research Centre (http://childrens-research-centre.open.ac.uk). The training is differentiated on age and ability and content is distilled using interactive games and activities. The first authors were part of a group of pupils from an English Middle school who engaged with this training process during 2011–12. The training programme is divided into four parts:

1 Research design

     i What is research?
    ii The relationship between research and truth
   iii Different kinds of research
    iv Research ethics
     v Learning from other people's research

2 Data collection

     i Observation techniques (participant observation and systematic observation in real and suspended time)
    ii Interview techniques (structured, semi-structured, unstructured, focus groups, questionnaires)
   iii Experiment (controlling variables, determining validity)

3 Data analysis

     i Coding and analysis from qualitative data
    ii Measurement, scaling, graphical representation, coding and analysis from quantitative data

4 Research dissemination

     i Clarity and structure of research report writing
    ii Identifying and targeting appropriate audiences
   iii Alternative dissemination techniques (e.g. video diary, drama, posters, song, story narrative)
    iv Presentation skills.

The overarching aim of the training is that children internalise the three core elements of a good research process: that it should be sceptical, systematic and ethical (Robson 2011), to enable them to identify areas of interest for their own investigations. A core mission of the CRC is that children lead their own research from conception to dissemination. The topics they choose to investigate are entirely self-generated and are not influenced or prompted by adults. Teaching aids such as the 'Think prompt sheet' (Figure 18.1) are used to assist this process of the self-identification of an area of interest or concern for them to investigate.

Outcomes for development of children's ethical understanding

Child researchers, like all other researchers, must conform to rigorous ethical standards when undertaking their own research. A strong emphasis is placed on ethics during the training programme including discussions, debates and acting out of ethical dilemmas through role play. The CRC teaching content covers: informed consent; confidentiality and anonymity; absence of deception; safe storage of data; avoidance of harm and disclosure of abuse. In the research study featured in this chapter, Alex and Joseph reflected deeply on the ethical issues of researching what children worry about. They brainstormed the topic with their peers first, to get a sense of what areas of concern were surfacing and whether or not children would experience any distress reflecting on matters that caused them worry or anxiety. The sensitive nature of some issues such as bullying and bereavement that emerged from this brainstorming steered them towards voluntary, anonymous questionnaires as a data collection tool. They also sought advice from their form teacher and headteacher and obtained informed consent from teachers and participants to administer the anonymous questionnaire during school time. An explanation of what the research was about was included at the beginning of the questionnaire and the voluntary nature of participation was made explicit.

There are still many unresolved ethical issues relating to child-led research. What is the balance of ethical responsibility between the young researchers and the adult supporters? Should ethical standards be policed by adults or by children or a combination of both? And how is this best facilitated – ethics committees in the schools where child-led research is happening or by universities or by an independent body or all of these? In this current phase of activity, the CRC, which itself undergoes ethical clearance from its institution's ethics committee, assures the ethics of the children's research following initial ethical scrutiny by peer young researchers. If any ethical issues do arise, these are almost invariably sorted out at peer level. An example is a discussion that took place where two 12-year-old researchers wanted to investigate a possible correlation between height and speed of running.

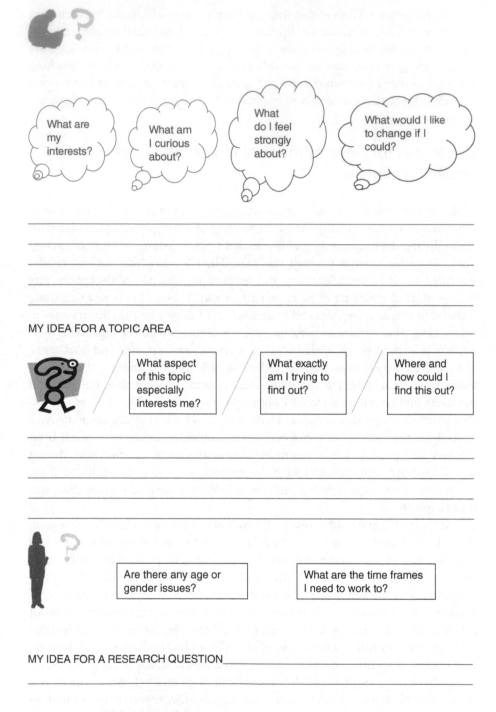

Figure 18.1 Think prompt sheet

Their peers readily advised them against a research design where classmates would be measured and timed against a 100-metre run during a Physical Education lesson, pointing out the potential distress this could cause in terms of loss of self-esteem, embarrassment and possible humiliation. As the concept of child-led research evolves, ethical committees for child-led research are mushrooming in schools and youth organisations tasked with monitoring ethical issues arising from research by children and young people. Sets of guidelines are beginning to materialise on the global stage for research with and by children such as The International Charter and Guidelines for Ethical Research Involving Children (Powell et al. 2011).

The impact of research by children and young people

Arguably, the biggest impact of research by children is the contribution it makes to our knowledge and understanding of childhood and children's worlds (Alderson 2012). Inevitably, children's research is small-scale. They are busy individuals engaged in full-time education and have a host of life apprenticeship activities to juggle alongside increasingly demanding homework schedules and exam pressures. Thus, children's research is often an exploratory snapshot of a particular subject or issue. But when several children produce similar 'research snapshots' around a theme it can build into a powerful montage and generate sufficient evidence to prompt larger investigations.

Child-led research is not expected to mimic adult research either in its methodology or dissemination, or to supplant adult research about childhood. One would not want to spawn a model that only valued research *by* children and young people and ignored the validity of adult research *about* children or adult–child participatory research. Nor would one want to promote a model of child-led research that was elitist and accessible only to the articulate middle-class youth. Equally undesirable is a hierarchical structure where one form of childhood research is valued more highly than another. There is room for all of these perspectives and each can speak to and inform others in a transactional dialogue of complementary bodies of knowledge. One of the strengths of child-friendly participatory methods is their orientation to an authentic perspective. Dissemination of child-led research is just as likely to feature song, drama, photo diaries and video documentaries as the more traditional adult-style research reports, although many children do choose to adopt a formal reporting genre such as the one featured here.

To illustrate the discursive points made so far, the next part of this chapter features an original research study by the first authors, 11-year-old boy researchers.

Children's worries: A small-scale investigation of the views of 12- and 13-year-old children, by Alex Mann and Joseph Liley, aged 11

Introduction

As two Year 7 students at a middle school in Bedfordshire who had been trained in research techniques, we were very interested to research what children worry about. We chose this topic because we wanted to help adults better understand the issues that worry children of our age. We felt that as young researchers we might get different results than if adults were to undertake this research.

We had read some interesting work about children's worries which had been researched by children and had looked at the issue online.

We also wanted to learn how worried children could best be helped with their problems and then pass the information on to adults.

The issues we wanted to cover were:

- What do children in Year 7 and Year 8 worry about?
- How does it affect them?
- What are the issues Year 7 and Year 8 children most worry about?
- What helps them with their issues, who helps and how effective is it?

We also wanted to find out whether worries changed across the age groups we were looking at and whether boys and girls worried about different things.

Methodology

We decided to collect our data by using questionnaires so that we could get as much information as we could.

We used a list of possible worries from which respondents could select which applied to them as this would make it easier to analyse. We used a 5-point scale to measure how much each issue affects them as this provides a good range of responses. We also had more open questions to find out who helped the children and how effective it was and included a section on 'What else could be done'. All were put on a single table to make it easier to record responses. We also needed to know their year and gender so we gave them boxes to tick ...

We chose to do the research with our year group [Year 7] and the one above [Year 8] as we could easily access them. We had to get permission from our headteacher and our form teacher to undertake this research.

We also interviewed our school counsellor because she would know a lot about children's worries ... This guided us in our selection of possible worries to put in our questionnaire.

We chose two classes in our school and we gave out questionnaires explaining that participation was voluntary. We were in the room and so was the teacher but children filled them in privately in their own workspace. We got 33 questionnaires back.

(Continued)

(Continued)

Ethics

We told the children what our research was about and made the questionnaires anonymous so they would feel able to tell the truth and so that it would be more accurate. We spoke to our class teacher and to the head teacher who gave us permission to do this as part of a Personal and Social Education (PSE) lesson but we still asked the children for their consent and explained about it being voluntary. We told the two classes that their responses would be dealt with confidentially.

Results

The 33 questionnaires were split between boys and girls and year as shown in the table below.

	Girls	*Boys*	*Year Total*
Year 7	10	7	17
Year 8	8	8	16
Gender Total	18	15	33

We used Excel to put all the results of the survey together and make it easier to put together charts and tables to analyse them.

To make the analysis of the open questions easier, we grouped similar answers together to make categories.

For questions where children had to choose a number on a 5-point scale we mainly looked at the average.

The answers to the question 'How often do you get worried?' are shown in the figure below.

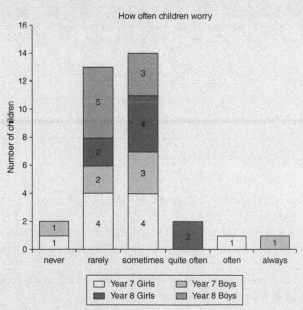

Figure 18.2 How often children worry

(Continued)

(Continued)

- A majority of the children are either worried 'rarely' or 'sometimes'.
- Of the people that worry more than 'sometimes' 3 out of 4 were girls.
- Year 7 are spread out over the whole range whereas Year 8 are only between 'rarely' and 'quite often'.
- There doesn't seem to be much difference between boys and girls.

When a comparison is made by gender we found the following:

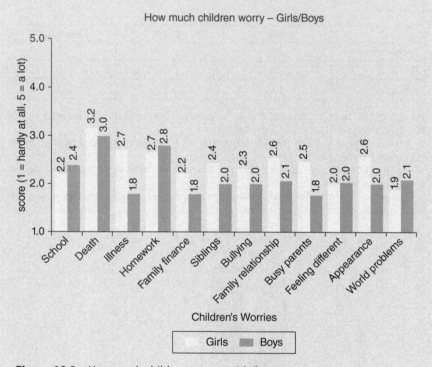

Figure 18.3 How much children worry – girls/boys

- What affects children most is a loved one dying, with a score of 3.2 for the girls and 3 for the boys.
- Homework also worries both boys and girls (2.8 and 2.7 respectively).
- Worrying about appearance, busy parents and illness are all prominent worries for mainly girls.
- Family finance, world problems and feeling different are not worried about as much as other issues by neither boys nor girls.

(Continued)

(Continued)

When we looked at differences between the two age groups we found the following:

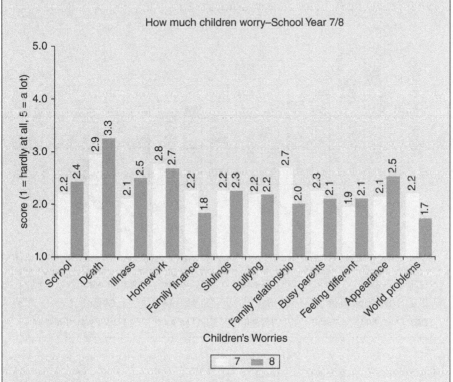

Figure 18.4 How much children worry – School Year 7/8

- Year 7 are more affected by family relationships (2.7), world problems (2.2) and family finance (2.2) than Year 8 (2.0/1.7/1.8).
- Year 8 tend to worry more about death and illness (3.3/2.5 compared to 2.9/2.1 for Year 7) and appearance (2.5 compared to 2.1 for Year 7).

When we looked at how much children worry by age groups and gender together we found that illness, appearance and busy parents are mainly a worry for girls regardless of their year group. For homework and death Year 7 girls and Year 8 boys are the most worried.

(Continued)

(Continued)

We also looked at who was helping children with their worries and found the following:

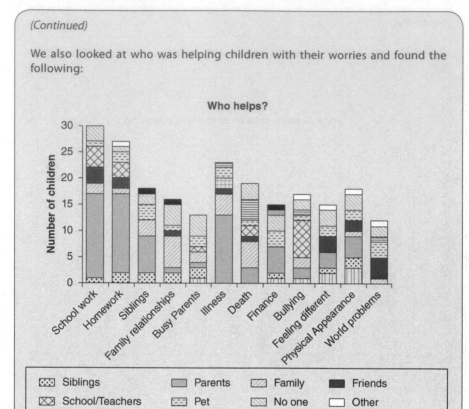

Figure 18.5 Who helps?

- This graph shows that parents help a lot especially with school work, homework, illness and siblings.
- For feeling different and physical appearance, children tend to help themselves.
- Parents, friends, family and siblings help with every worry.
- For bullying it is the school/teachers who are helping the most.

We also tried to find out what else could help children with their worries. Very few children answered this question and when they did, a lot answered 'nothing', 'don't know/not sure'. ...

Below are the summary tables of what else could help for three sources of worries (Homework, Illness and Bullying) as examples.

(Continued)

(Continued)

Homework	Answers
Less homework	4
No homework	2
Concentration	1
They learn the new methods	1
Do it earlier because it gets me stressed when I do it late	1
Get rid of it	1
Help	1
I try more to understand	1
Nothing	6
Not sure	1
No answer	14

Illness	Answers
Better medicine	1
Calpol	1
People leave me alone when I feel worse	1
Rest more	1
That I notice it's easy	1
Don't know	1
Not sure	2
Nothing	5
No answer	20

Bullying	Answers
Stopped quicker	1
I tell someone	1
Not have bullies	1
Don't know	1
Not sure	1
No/nothing	5
No answer	23

(Continued)

(Continued)

Discussion

From the results of our questionnaire, it looks like nearly all children worry sometimes but a few worry a lot. Their main worries are about school (Homework and School work) as well as death of a loved one. There are no big gender differences, although it looks like girls worry more about appearance, busy parents and illness than boys. The big differences between the year groups were that Year 7 seem to be more affected by family relationships, world problems (2.2) and family finance while Year 8 worry more about death, illness and appearance (2.5 compared to 2.1 for Year 7). Most of the children are getting the help they need to deal with the issues and this comes mainly from family and friends.

We think it would be useful to share these research findings with teachers and parents so that they might be better able to understand and support us with our worries. It is possible that if we had involved older or younger children we might have had different results.

Quite a lot of children did not answer all the questions (especially the open questions), which limits the interpretation of the results. Some of the answers were difficult to understand (e.g. people [had] written names of friends/family or pet rather than their status).

We should have encouraged the children to fill in all the questions (maybe by offering them a **sweet** if they completed all the questions) and also to explain that they should write status/relationship with people/pets they mentioned in their answers.

For each category of children (Year 8 boys, Year 8 girls, Year 7 boys, Year 7 girls) we only had between 7 and 10 questionnaires. This makes it difficult to know if what each group have said is representative of that age group and gender. It would have been good to do the survey with more classes of Year 7 and Year 8 in the school to get more questionnaires for each category and be more sure of our findings. Perhaps that could be our next research.

Conclusion

We feel that our main finding is that children do have some worries and that they vary from child to child. There are some differences related to gender and age. It also shows that children are helped in dealing with these worries and that such help can always be improved. We have also learnt a lot about the issues associated with collecting data and if we had the same opportunity we could improve our research and take it further. The research experience has given us a real understanding of just how much is involved in planning, carrying out, and reporting research. I am delighted that our research is being used – it makes the hard work even more worthwhile.

Impact and outcomes from children's research

As mentioned earlier, most children's research is small-scale and bounded in a local context. Alex and Joseph's research generated valuable knowledge for the school they attended and, through wider dissemination, raised awareness about what some 11-year-olds worry about. A first step in their research was to brainstorm within their peer group, in the absence of adult prompts and influences, the main issues that children of this age worry about. The list of categories they formulated may well have looked very different if it had been compiled with, or by, adults. So, their investigation had its origins in the authentic experiences of 11- and 12-year-olds (Year 7 and Year 8 in English schools), and was explored without adult–child power relations, thus succeeding in lessening adult filters and adult mediation and getting closer to the reality of children's lived experiences in that particular context. In Alex's own words:

> My hope is that this research helps those who feel alone to find a way to know they are never truly on their own. Being 11 or 12 years old does not stop you from understanding the way the world works.

There are some examples of impact at policy and practice levels. Shannon Davidson, aged 10, carried out some research about what it is like for children living with Graves disease, a chronic thyroid disorder (see Davidson 2008). Among Shannon's findings was a strong consensus that children wanted to have access to a support group or, if a physical group was not possible then at least a web-based virtual support group. A theme of loneliness and social isolation emerged from Shannon's data, not least because Graves diseases is a rare condition and sufferers are spread thinly across the UK. Some of the participants in Shannon's research were linked to Great Ormond Street Hospital so she shared her research findings with members of the Hospital management board who took it very seriously. She was invited to discuss with them how they could help establish better support for children with Graves disease, and for sick children more generally, who suffer similar social isolation. This resulted in a regular page of the Great Ormand Street newsletter being allocated to the Graves group of children and an invitation to Shannon to be the child editor.

Investing in Children is a not-for-profit organisation that encourages societal change and improved investment in children. The Patient and Public Involvement Trust commissioned them to find out what young people thought about hospitals in County Durham. Part of that research was a study led by young people (Cole et al. 2009). The young people's investigation explored the potential benefits of a young person's liaison officer acting in an intermediary role within the health service. Their research asked 'How effective are young people's health liaison officers and why are they needed in our local NHS trust?' Findings from their research confirmed a need for a young people's health liaison officer in County Durham. They were able to make a series of recommendations for how such a role would work optimally. Cole et al. (2009) put together a research report from their findings and presented it to the Trust Board for Children's Hospital Services in County Durham. It was received very favourably and since then the young people have been meeting regularly with the Trust Board.

We know from numerous sources (see e.g. Clark and Akerman 2006) that, as a group, girls currently outperform boys in the primary years. Professionals in any service area will always strive to eliminate personal bias in their practice whether this is triggered by race, culture, gender, sexual persuasion or any other factor. Many practitioners are not aware of subconscious biases seeping into their practice. Helen Dandridge, aged 10, conducted some research into whether girls and boys were treated differently by teachers at their school (Dandridge 2008). After comprehensive training in the research process, Helen and her co-researchers began their investigation by searching the internet for any opinions being expressed by children on this subject. On websites such as the BBC *Newsround* (a children's topical news programme) they found some strong views being expressed that boys and girls are treated differently in school, so they decided to find out what the situation was in their own school. There were no significant gender differences in pupil numbers in the classes. They collected three complementary sets of data: a self-designed questionnaire for 9–11-year-olds in their school, lesson observations and an analysis of the gender differences on the school's Golden Time Chart (Golden Time was a free choice activity period on Friday afternoons which was prized by pupils but could be withdrawn by teachers for bad behaviour). Questionnaire results showed that 80 per cent of 11-year-olds thought that girls were chosen over boys to help with special jobs in the classroom and 63 per cent thought that teachers treated boys and girls differently as a response to their behaviour. When Helen and Nihal analysed the Golden Chart Time sheet they found a similar picture of many more boys being denied Golden Time than girls. Their report concluded that boys and girls were treated differently at their school although they did not think this was any deliberate act on the part of teachers. However, they did comment that the teachers were nearly all female and wondered whether this had any impact on the gender interaction.

They presented their research to teachers and governors to raise awareness and succeeded in getting gender issues onto the school management action plan.

One example of youth-led research which had a substantial impact on policy and practice is an investigation commissioned by the *Diana Award* in collaboration with CRC (Tarapdar et al. 2011) into young people's experiences of cyberbullying and how these experiences differed with age (the comparative cohorts were aged 12–13 years and 14–15 years). From across nine regions of the UK, 1,512 young people participated in this study. The findings from this study highlighted shocking levels of cyberbullying hitherto underestimated by adult research. Worrying levels of cyberbullying in the home environment surfaced with increased intensity and sophistication for the older age group. Results revealed that most parents lacked awareness and the internet skills to protect their children. A critical finding was the ineffectiveness and lack of youth engagement with internet provider cyber safeguards. The young people's research made several recommendations to government and to internet providers. Their research hit 71 media outlets and was actively responded to by Virgin, Google and Carphone Warehouse. But not every instance of child-led research is going to have this kind of policy impact. Managing child researchers' outcome expectations is one of the responsibilities of the adults who support them. However, a universal outcome from engagement with research appears to be the impact on individual self-development. Apart from the generation of new knowledge, an important impact is the effect that child-led research has on the children themselves. Lansdown (2002) discusses a range of benefits that children link with increased participation, such as acquiring new skills, building self-esteem and contributing to making the world a better place.

How does engagement in research affect the self-development of young researchers?

Evaluation data collected from the young researchers, their parents and teachers (Kellett 2004) identify 10 principal benefits:

1 raised self-esteem and sense of worth
2 Increased confidence
3 development of transferable study skills: organisation, management, analysis and evaluation
4 sharpening of critical thinking skills
5 heightened ethical awareness
6 enhanced problem-solving ability
7 more effective communication
8 development of independent learning
9 increased participation in other aspects affecting their childhoods
10 contribution to knowledge being valued.

There appears to be a real development in self-esteem and sense of worth. This stems from children's realisation that they are being listened to. Their research voice has an evidence base which makes them feel it is being taken seriously and has more chance of being acted upon:

> I felt really important. (12-year-old girl)

> It's made her realise that other people value her and what she thinks. I think for R that's particularly important. I know that everyone wants to be valued, for R it was particularly important. I think she realises that other people do value what she thinks. (parent of child researcher)

> (Kellett 2006: 13)

Perhaps the most notable impact on the young researchers is the increase in their confidence. This starts to grow when children discover they have interesting findings to share and are generating new knowledge. Disseminating their research hones their presentation and communication skills which adds further to their growing levels of confidence:

> I even presented my research at an international conference, which was a brilliant opportunity. I can't believe I did it or that I'm talking to you here today because I didn't used to be very confident – I'd get nervous even doing a two minute talk in class. (11-year-old researcher presenting to a group of prominent youth advocates)

> (RCP 2013)

> Like now when we have to talk in front of others in class, before I might have not put myself first, but now I just say I'll go first. I don't mind. (10-year-old girl)

> (Kellet 2006: 13)

> I think it has helped me as I have got more confidence. I know about and think about new things. (11-year-old boy)

> (Kellett 2006: 14)

Undertaking his own research transformed the self-esteem of a 17-year-old boy with dyspraxia who had spent the majority of his school life on the verge of exclusion due to perceived behavioural difficulties. Whatever his behavioural troubles, the one thing Deano felt passionate about was poverty in Africa (see Bentley and Gamble 2005). So he researched the views and understandings of his peers about the ever-escalating debt and interest trap that contributed to the poverty crisis in that continent. When he got to his feet at a national conference to present his findings he began with a preamble in which he talked of how doing the research had given him a sense of worth and confidence – and kept him in school. He spoke of how he had never imagined he could achieve so much learning as he had done through the research training, his internet searches on African debt and his pulling together and analysing of the data. In the audience was a representative of an NGO who offered him voluntary experience in Africa which boosted his life chances and career prospects.

Are research skills transferable in young people's lives?

One of the impacts of the research process on young people is that the core skills of being sceptical, systematic and ethical help them in all aspects of their lives. When interviewed, a 12-year-old boy talked about this – confirmed in the remarks from his parent:

> Learning about research has opened my mind a lot more. If I see on TV or in the news-paper 'studies show that …' I always think about the research behind it and I don't necessarily believe it all. I question it – that was a key thing in the training – being scep-tical. (12-year-old boy)

> (RCP, 2013)

> The research, the process – has transferred into his school work. I think it definitely has. His approach to school work is different. Whereas in the past he would have done his homework as quickly as possible so that he could have then played on his game, or gone outside, whereas he now definitely takes more time thinking through the layout of things and I think that's from the research, the process before doing the research study where they learned the methodology. I think bits of that have definitely come out through his school work. (parent)

> (Kellett 2006: 14)

For many young people, engagement in research sharpens their critical thinking skills and they take this forward into other aspects of their lives. A 12-year-old researcher spoke about how he used his interview skills to ask probing questions of exhibitors at an IT exhibition he attended and that he would not have had the knowledge or confidence to do this before he had carried out his own research. Parents also note transferable skills in their children:

> It gave her understanding. I can see that. When she looks at an article she can see the weaknesses. She has learnt what it is to do something systematically. She knows. She can apply that understanding to other things that she reads. She can think systemati-cally. (parent)

> Research is allowing them to practise true empathy, of actually thinking about what other people are feeling and thinking about what the impact is on them. They won't ever get that apart from hard life knocks I suppose. You build up the ability to empathise. The research teaches that to begin with. You go out and you've got to think about people, their thoughts and not just on your thoughts. (parent)

We know how it feels to talk unrehearsed and answer questions from the floor, and she (daughter) handled it so well. She was answering questions. It was great. (parent)

I think it's helped them with clarity of speech. It's skills they wouldn't get until later in life. Thinking through processes, planning and the various sorts of skills they've gained. (parent)

(Kellett 2006: 14–15)

Valuing children's knowledge generation

As child-led research begins to become more common, there is a notable shift in the willingness of adults to receive and connect with the findings children and young people are generating. This is evident in invitations that are flowing *to* children to disseminate rather than children having to constantly push to get their voices heard or having to speak through mediated adult voices. This in turn adds to children's appreciation of the importance of their insider perspectives:

Everyone has their own point of view. Children have their own point of view and it's different to adults, because your point of view changes as you get older. When you're a teenager you have a different point of view. When you're a child you have a different point of view. (11-year-old boy)

It's important to see things through children's eyes. Children see things differently to adults. I think if an adult had done this research he wouldn't have got the same responses. They wouldn't have asked the same questions. (10-year-old boy)

(Kellett 2006: 16)

Conclusion

In exploring issues relating to research with children and young people, the final section of this book has focused on impact, engagement and dissemination. It is pertinent to end with messages from child researchers and to consider how we might take these forward in our own lives and practice settings. We have all been children once but this does not mean we understand what it is to be a child in contemporary society. The mechanics of growing up, of negotiating transitions and rites of passage may bear some similarities to our own childhoods but the contexts are different. The present generation of children are growing up in an era where the certainties of tradition are being challenged and knowledge is contested. In embracing uncertainty we demonstrate a willingness to grapple with different perspectives and discourses – and take responsibility for them. The impact of insider perspectives from children and young people, as voiced through their own research, is integral to that process and will enrich collective outcomes and understandings into the next generation and beyond.

References

Alderson, P. (2012) 'Rights-respecting research: A commentary on "the right to be properly researched: research with children in a messy, real world"', *Children's Geographies*, 10(2): 233–9.

Bentley, D. and Gamble, L. (2005) 'Young people's awareness of poverty in Africa', available at: www.open.ac.uk/researchprojects/childrens-research-centre/research-children-young-people/aged-13-15 (accessed 17 October 2013).

Clark, C. and Akerman, R. (2006) *Social Inclusion and Reading: An Exploration*. London: National Literacy Trust.

Cole, L., Davies, R., Fenwick, M., Hailes, R., Maddison, A., Miller, L. and Stobbart, A. (2009) 'How effective are young people's health liaison officers and why are they needed in our local NHS trust?', available at: www.open.ac.uk/researchprojects/childrens-research-centre/files/crc-pr/file/ecms/web-content/cole.pdf (accessed 17 October 2013).

Dandridge, H. (2008) 'Are girls and boys treated differently in school?', available at: www.open.ac.uk/researchprojects/childrens-research-centre/research-children-young-people/aged-9-10 (accessed 17 October 2013).

Davidson, S. (2008), 'What children think about having a thyroid disorder', . www.open.ac.uk/researchprojects/childrens-research-centre/research-children-young-people/aged-9-10 (accessed 17 July 2013)

Kellett, M. (2003) 'Empowering Year 5 pupils as active researchers', paper presented at the annual conference of the British Education Research Association, Herriot Watt University, September 2003.

Kellett, M. (2004) 'Developing critical thinking skills in 10–12-year-olds through their active engagement in research', *Teaching Thinking Skills*, 14: 32–40.

Kellett, M. (2005) *How to Develop Children as Researchers: A Step-by-Step Guide to Teaching the Research Process*. London: Sage.

Kellett, M. (2006) 'Pupils as active researchers: Using engagement with research process to enhance creativity and thinking skills in 10–12-year-olds', British Educational Research Association Annual Conference 6–9 September, University of Warwick, UK.

Lansdown, G. (2002) *Promoting Children's Participation in Democratic Decision-Making*. Florence: Innocenti Research Centre, UNICEF.

Powell, M.A., Graham, A., Taylor, N.J., Newell, S. and Fitzgerald, R. (2011) 'Building capacity for ethical research with children and young people: An international research project to examine the ethical issues and challenges in undertaking research with and for children in different majority and minority world contexts', report prepared for the Childwatch International Research Network, Oslo, Norway.

Robson, C. (2011) *Real World Research*, 3rd edition. Oxford: Blackwell.

Royal College of Practitioners (2013) 'Young People as Tomorrow's Citizens' Conference, Royal College of Practitioners: London, 21 March.

Tarapdar, S., Kellett, M. and young people (2011) *Young People's Voices on Cyberbullying: What Can Age Comparisons Tell Us?* London: The Diana Award.

Index

what is research?

Why do we do research involving young people

What is the diff between doing research: <u>with</u>, <u>by</u>, about young people?

what are the potential impacts research can have?

We live in a world that bases knowledge off from ~~biological~~/science perspective.

"systematic Pursuit of knowledge" Research done through <u>empirical Inquiry</u> - observation, gather info from populations in order to discover facts through/ of populations to be able to help, with improving policies, practises and making it a 'better world' for everyone in it. It falls away from "common sense" views such as religious/political

Investigating the world by using observation, experiment Research: psychological + social measurement.

Range from psych, social research, natural science

Research is when observing, experiments, it using methodologies such as explicit procedures. other people must be able to evaluate if the methods that has been used ~~it not~~ or findings that been found were found based on preconceptions, preferences and beliefs of the researcher

---

with (p.41) - Child work in progress if fail to bring into account of YP perspective - which is the people being investigated.

Research is encouraged to be done by the children themselves, with little or no adult involvement. (PAR)

YP - recognized as the experts in their own life.

Range from ~~adult~~ = primary reader to child actively researcher participant. /Influencing the design, outcome

What is the history of the development of research ethics? What are x3 ethical Issues to consider when doing research with yaupeop?
Describe some of the tension involved in these ethical issues.

Beginning of 1947 "Nuremburg Code" emerged and stressed the importance of doing research with respect to subjects involved in the research and how important consent and and informed participant were.
The start of research ethics. Unfortunately, the view of the child as not yet adult resulted in them not being able to consent, informed or voice.
Research ethics has through history changed based on the moral panics/ existing in the societies at the time.
Ethics developed from the medical research when populations suff were born with
Ethics being influenced by and modified when pertain from 0 – 10 existing ethical concerns, ethics has changed from me and modified with time. In order to protect nd help populations that may have been left out from esearch, and treated bady as they have been experiment n +++
Consent, Competence, Rights to privacy+ Confidentiality (p. 94)

What are some factors that influence a researchers social position?
Why is it important for researchers to think about their positionality in their research? What does it mean for a research to be an insider/outsider? Can a researcher be both inside + outsider?

p. 47
p. 23-24

What is a theory and why is theory important when doing research with young people? Discuss x2 theoretical frameworks + how they approach the study of young people?